WILLMAKER®

by Attorneys

BARBARA KATE REPA
STEPHEN ELIAS
RALPH WARNER

NOLO PRESS · BERKELEY

Your Responsibility When Using Self-Help Law Books & Software

We've done our best to give you useful and accurate information in this software manual. But laws and procedures change frequently and are subject to differing interpretations. If you want legal advice backed by a guarantee, see a lawyer. If you use this software, it's your responsibility to make sure that the facts and general advice contained in it apply to your situation.

Keeping Up-to-Date

To keep its books and software up-to-date, Nolo Press issues new printings and new editions periodically. New printings reflect minor legal changes and technical corrections. New editions contain major legal changes, major text additions or major reorganizations. To find out if a later printing or edition of any Nolo book is available, call Nolo Press at (510) 549-1976 or check the catalog in the *Nolo News,* our quarterly newspaper.

To stay current, follow the Update service in the *Nolo News.* You can get the paper free by sending us the registration card included in your WillMaker package. In another effort to help you use Nolo's latest materials, we offer a 25% discount off the purchase of any new Nolo book if you turn in any earlier printing or edition. (See the "Recycle Offer" in the back of the book.)

This manual was last revised in: **September 1993.**

FIFTH EDITION (5.0)
First Printing   September 1993

Book design   Jackie Mancuso
Cover design   Toni Ihara
Illustrations   Mari Stein
Index   Sayre Van Young
Printing   Delta Lithographics

Nolo books are available at special discounts for bulk purchases for sales promotions, premiums and fundraising. For details contact: Special Sales Director, Nolo Press, 950 Parker Street, Berkeley, CA 94710.

ISBN   Windows 0-87337-233-6   DOS Windows 0-87337-204-2
Library of Congress Card Catalog No. 84-63151
© Copyright 1985, 1986, 1988, 1990 and 1993 by Nolo Press

Acknowledgments

WillMaker originated as a joint effort by Nolo Press and Legisoft to bring self-help law into the computer age. In 1992, Nolo and Legisoft parted ways, and Legisoft is no longer involved with this product. However, Nolo acknowledges the important and original contributions of Legisoft's Jeff Scargle and Bob Bergstrom.

In addition, we extend heartfelt thanks to the following folks.

For programming: Michael Sexton, Gloria Sadowski, Mick Radtke, Inventure—and to Albin Renauer, who coordinated their efforts.

For their copious document-checking: Patti Gima and Fred Horch.

For researching: Katherine Jaramillo.

For proofreading and proofreading again: Ely Newman.

And a special thanks to the patient souls in Technical Support—Adam Stanhope, Xavier George and Ben Graboske.

About Nolo Press

The leading publisher of self-help law books and software since 1971

Nolo Press was founded in 1971 to show people how to do their own routine legal tasks and avoid costly lawyer fees. Early on, bar associations thundered against self-help law, claiming that lawyers were essential to help with even simple legal procedures. But Nolo persisted, sure that informed people armed with top-quality self-help information did not have to depend on lawyers. Over the years, more than three million customers have proven us right. Today, Nolo publishes over 70 self-help law books, audio tapes, videos and software packages—and is more committed than ever to making the law accessible.

About the Authors

Barbara Kate Repa, a Nolo author and editor, is president of the Bay Area Funeral Society and public member on the California Board of Funeral Directors and Embalmers. An advocate for the elderly, she maintains a small but tasteful shrine to Claude Pepper in her San Francisco home.

Stephen Elias practiced law in California, New York and Vermont until publishing his first Nolo book in 1982. Since then, he has written and edited more than 25 Nolo products. His hobbies include reading just about any type of book, playing tennis and taking long walks around the Sonoma County town where he lives.

Ralph Warner, who began his legal career as a legal aid attorney, is co-founder and publisher of Nolo Press. Since launching Nolo—and the self-help law movement—in 1971, Ralph has written, edited and vetted innumerable books and projects for Nolo Press. He lives bravely in Berkeley, in a house perched atop the Hayward Fault.

About the Illustrator

Mari Stein is a freelance illustrator and writer who has illustrated many books for Nolo Press. She now enjoys the life of a writer/illustrator/yoga teacher/spinner and shepherdess on Enchanted Rabbit Mountain, an 175-acre ranch on the summit of the Greensprings in Ashland, Oregon.

WillMaker License

This is a software license agreement between Nolo Press and you as purchaser, for the use of the WillMaker program and accompanying manual. By using this program and manual, you indicate that you accept all terms of this agreement. If you do not agree to all the terms and conditions of this agreement, do not use the WillMaker program or manual, but return both to Nolo Press for a full refund.

Grant of License

In consideration of payment of the license fee, which is part of the price you paid for WillMaker, Nolo Press as licensor grants to you the right to use the enclosed program to produce wills for yourself and your immediate family, subject to the terms and restrictions set forth in this license agreement.

Copy, Use and Transfer Restrictions

The WillMaker manual and the program and its documentation are copyrighted. You may not give, sell or otherwise distribute copies of the program to third parties, except as provided in the U.S. Copyright Act. Under this license agreement, you may not use the program to prepare wills for commercial or nonprofit purposes, or use the program to prepare wills for people outside your immediate family.

Commercial Use of This Product

For information regarding commercial licensing of this product, including use by educational institutions and nonprofit organizations, call Nolo Press at (510) 549-1976.

Disclaimer of Warranty and Limited Warranty

This program and accompanying manual are sold "AS IS," without any implied or express warranty as to their performance or to the results that may be obtained by using the program.

As to the original purchaser only, Nolo Press warrants that the magnetic disk on which the program is recorded shall be free from defects in material and workmanship in normal use and service. If a defect in this disk occurs, the disk may be returned to Nolo Press. We will replace the disk free of charge. In the event of a defect, your exclusive remedy is expressly limited to replacement of the disk as described above.

Your Responsibilities for Your Documents

Although best efforts were devoted to making this material useful, accurate and up-to-date, please be aware that state laws and procedures change and may be interpreted differently. Also, we have no control over whether you carefully follow our instructions or properly understand the information in the WillMaker disk or manual.

Of necessity, therefore, Nolo Press does not make any guarantees about the use to which the software or manual are put, or the results of that use.

Any documents you make using WillMaker are yours and it is your responsibility to be sure they reflect your intentions. Have your WillMaker documents reviewed by an attorney in your state who specializes in wills and estate planning if you want a legal opinion about the effect of the documents or their legal interpretation.

Term

The license is in effect until terminated. You may terminate it at any time by destroying the program together with all copies and modifications in any form.

Entire Agreement

By using the WillMaker program, you agree that this license is the complete and exclusive statement of the agreement between you and Nolo Press regarding WillMaker.

WILLMAKER®

5

**WINDOWS
USERS' GUIDE**

Users' Guide

Part 1. Introduction

Part 2. Installation and Startup

Part 3. Getting Acquainted With WillMaker

Part 4. Using WillMaker to Create Documents

Part 5. Problems Running WillMaker

Part 1. Introduction

A. Welcome to WillMaker 5

WillMaker 5 for Windows is a computer program that helps you create three kinds of documents: a will, healthcare directions in case of a terminal illness or permanent coma (also known as a "living will"), and a document setting out your final arrangements. These three documents provide necessary legal instructions for family, friends and others in case of your death or permanent incapacitation.

With WillMaker, you and the members of your immediate family can create these three legal documents for yourselves. Although WillMaker gives you the option of making all three documents, you do not have to create all three. You can easily create just the documents you want—each kind of document serves a different purpose and is valid by itself.

The following table describes what each kind of document is used for and provides references to the legal section of this manual (which follows this Users' Guide) for more information:

Documents In Your WillMaker Portfolio		
DOCUMENT	**WHAT IT CAN DO**	**LEGAL MANUAL REFERENCE**
Will	• Leave property to family, friends and organizations • Name a guardian to care for your minor children • Arrange for management of property you leave to minors • Cancel debts others owe you • Specify how debts and taxes you owe are to be paid • Name alternate beneficiaries • Designate a personal representative or executor	Chapters 1 through 12
Healthcare Directives	• Instruct healthcare providers as to what life-prolonging treatments you want if you are: — close to death from a terminal condition, or — in a permanent coma • Name a trusted person to see that your wishes are carried out	Chapter 13
Final Arrangements	• Describe any organ or body donations you have made • State your preferences about body burial or cremation • Specify any ceremonies you want held • Name a trusted person to see that your wishes are carried out	Chapter 14

Using WillMaker you can produce these documents in an evening or two at your computer, but we encourage you relax and take your time. Remember, WillMaker doesn't charge by the hour. These are important decisions you are making. Be sure to consult this manual and the on-line help that accompanies every screen if you have any questions about the law, or how to use this program. You can stop an interview at any time and pick up again where you left off.

1. What You're About to Do

Here's a brief description of how WillMaker 5 for Windows helps you make these important decisions and produce these necessary documents.

After you install the program and start it up, you'll receive a brief orientation to how to use the computer program. Then you'll be asked to enter your name. This creates your first WillMaker portfolio—the computer file that stores your three documents.

▶ **If You've Written a Will With a Previous Version of WillMaker**
▶
▶ If you have used WillMaker 4.0 for DOS and want to update a will, take the time
▶ now to read Part 4, Section A5 on how to convert your WillMaker 4.0 data file to
▶ work with WillMaker 5 for Windows. Also see Section 2, below.
▶

Once your portfolio is created, you come to a screen which allows you to work on any of the three documents that make up your portfolio.

Making your documents with WillMaker is much like being interviewed. Each document has its own interview. You can start or stop an interview any time you like, go back to prior questions, or switch between interviews at any time. In each case, when you return to a document interview, you pick up exactly where you left off.

When an interview is complete, your answers are combined with the appropriate legal language to create the appropriate document. You can then display this document on the screen and print it. You can also revisit any part of any interview to revise or review your answers.

Other members of your immediate family can make their own WillMaker portfolios and produce their own documents. However, remember that the WillMaker license restricts the use of this product to you and members of your immediate family.

2. What's New in WillMaker 5 for Windows

Users of WillMaker 4.0 for DOS or Macintosh or earlier versions will notice the following changes and enhancements in WillMaker 5 for Windows.

• You can make up to 100 specific bequests in your will.

• You can name a property guardian to manage your children's property until they become adults, whether or not their property came through your will.

- You can use WillMaker to produce healthcare directions (a living will and proxy appointment) and a document setting out your final arrangements.

- You can refer to more extensive on-screen legal help.

- You can make up to nine WillMaker portfolios so that members of your immediate family can easily create their own documents from your copy of WillMaker.

- You can choose and change the page margins, line spacing, font and font size of your printed documents.

- You can use a mouse.

3. About this Manual

The manual is divided into two main parts.

The first part, the Users' Guide, explains how to use the WillMaker computer program.

The second part, the Legal Manual, contains legal information. It explains:

- how to write your will and plan your estate

- the different purposes and effects of your will, healthcare directions and final arrangements document

- the peculiarities of your state's laws, and

- when you should consult a lawyer.

Ideally, you should read and understand the Legal Manual before you begin using the WillMaker computer program.

If you have questions while running WillMaker, remember that you can press F1 to see help for the screen that you are working on. If help doesn't answer your question, refer to the Users' Guide or the Legal Manual.

If you have a problem operating WillMaker that neither on-screen help nor the Users' Guide can solve, take a short break from the keyboard and read Part 5, Problems Running WillMaker

If the problem continues, you can call Nolo Technical Support.

This manual provides instructions on menus to select, buttons to click and keys to press. To make these instructions easier to follow, we use the following typeface conventions:

- KEYS that you are supposed to press are in ALL CAPS.

- Key combinations are written ALT+F, which means "hold down the ALT key while pressing the F key."

- A key combination written ALT+F,X means "hold down the ALT key while pressing the F key, then let up both keys and press the X key."

- Names of **menus** and **buttons** are in **bold** type, with the **Hot key** underlined.

B. System Requirements

To run WillMaker you need:

- an IBM PC or compatible with at least 2 MB of RAM (Random Access Memory), a hard disk with at least 2.3 MB free space.

- a printer (to print out your final documents)

- Microsoft Windows 3.1 or later

- one floppy disk drive (for installation).

C. WillMaker 5 for Windows Package Contents

Your WillMaker 5 for Windows package should contain:

- one 3 1/2" installation disk

- a WillMaker manual

- a registration card, and

- envelopes in which to store your documents.

Be sure to send in your registration card as soon as possible so that we can inform you of changes or upgrades to the program. In return, we'll send you a free two-year subscription to the *Nolo News*, our quarterly newspaper that features timely, plain-English articles on estate planning and other areas of law of interest to consumers.

Part 2. Installation and Startup

A. Installing WillMaker 5 for Windows

You will need approximately 2.3 MB of free space on your hard disk to install WillMaker 5 for Windows and its accompanying help files.

1. Start your computer and start Microsoft Windows.

2. Insert the WillMaker Install disk into a disk drive.

3. Choose **Run** from the **File** menu of the Windows Program Manager or File Manager.

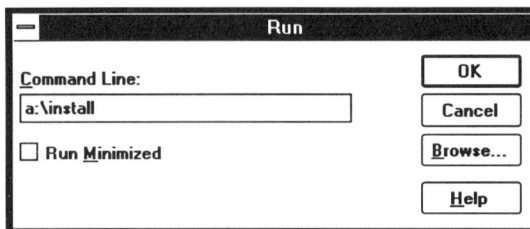

4. Type a:\install if your disk is in drive A, or b:\install if the disk is in drive B.

5. Click **OK** or press ENTER.

6. Follow the instructions that appear on the screen.

7. When the installation is finished, you will have a WillMaker Program Group on your desktop with the WillMaker application and a Read Me file.

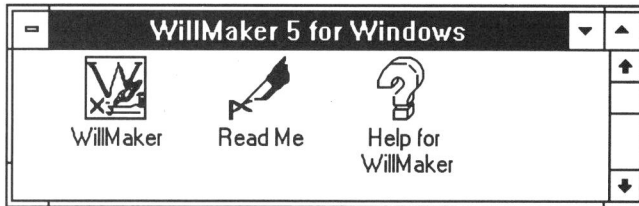

8. Double-click the Read Me icon and read its contents.

9. Double-click the WillMaker icon to start WillMaker 5 for Windows.

▶ **Read the Read Me file**
▶
▶ When the installation is complete, a new "WillMaker 5 for Windows" Program
▶ Group will appear on your Windows desktop. Double-click on the **Read Me** icon
▶ (important information that didn't make it into this manual.)
▶ (The README.WRI file is a *Windows Write* file. If you have removed Windows
▶ Write from your hard disk, you will not be able to read this file. See Part 5, of the
▶ Users' Guide for what to do if this is the case.)
▶

▶ **What Gets Installed on Your Hard Disk**
▶
▶ For you techie types, here's a list of the files that get installed on your hard disk
▶ when you install WillMaker 5 for Windows:
▶
▶ **wmw.exe**   the WillMaker application
▶ **wmwrsc.dll**   "resource" file that contains much of the WillMaker screen and
▶   document information
▶ **wmw.hlp**   the "readme" file
▶ **readme.wri**   the WillMaker Windows help file
▶ **xvt320tx.dll** resources used by the program
▶ **xvt320wi.dll** more resources used by the program

B. Starting WillMaker

Once you've installed WillMaker on your hard disk, you're ready to start the program. You can start the program from within Windows or from the DOS command line if Windows is not running.

1. From Windows

Preferred Method

1. Start Microsoft Windows 3.1 if is it is not already running.

2. Find the WillMaker Program Group and open it.

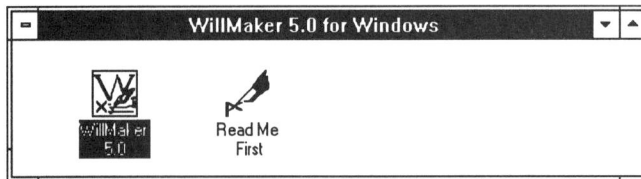

3. Double-click the WillMaker icon.

   The program will start and you should see the opening screen. If the opening screen doesn't appear, consult Part 5 of the Users' Guide. If the opening screen appears, skip to Part 3 to get acquainted with WillMaker, and then to Part 4 when you're ready to start making documents.

Alternate Method

If you can't find the WillMaker Program Group, as described above, start WillMaker this way:

1. Start Microsoft Windows if is it is not already running.

2. Choose **Run** from the Program Manager's **File** menu.

3. Type

C:\WM5WIN\WMW

Note If you didn't install WillMaker in the WM5WIN directory, type the name of the directory you named instead of WM5WIN.

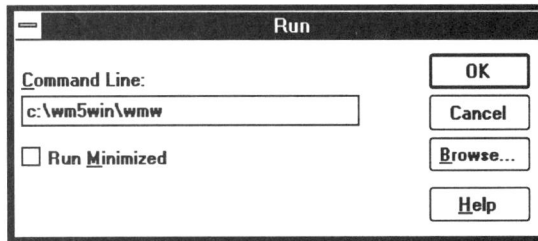

```
┌─────────────────────────────────────────────────────┐
│ ─                          Run                        │
├─────────────────────────────────────────────────────┤
│                                        ┌──────────┐   │
│  Command Line:                         │    OK    │   │
│  ┌─────────────────────────────────┐   └──────────┘   │
│  │ c:\wm5win\wmw                   │   ┌──────────┐   │
│  └─────────────────────────────────┘   │  Cancel  │   │
│                                         └──────────┘   │
│  ☐ Run Minimized                       ┌──────────┐   │
│                                         │ Browse...│   │
│                                         └──────────┘   │
│                                         ┌──────────┐   │
│                                         │   Help   │   │
│                                         └──────────┘   │
└─────────────────────────────────────────────────────┘
```

4. Click **OK** or press ENTER.

The program will start and you should see the opening screen. If the opening screen doesn't appear, consult Part 5 of the Users' Guide. If the opening screen appears, skip to Part 3 to get aquatinted with WillMaker, and then to Part 4 when you're ready to start making documents.

2. From the DOS Command Line

If Windows is not running, you can also start WillMaker 5 for Windows directly from the DOS command line by following these directions:

1. Start the computer and wait for C:> prompt to appear.

2. Change to the directory where you installed WillMaker 5 for Windows. If you used the "Easy Install" procedure, the directory is named "WM5WIN" so you would type:

CD\WM5WIN

and press ENTER.

3. Once you are in the WillMaker Windows directory, type:

WIN WMW

and press ENTER.

This will first launch Windows and then start WillMaker for Windows. You should see the opening screen. If the opening screen doesn't appear, consult Part 5 of the Users' Guide. If the opening screen appears, skip to Part 3 to get acquainted with WillMaker, and then to Part 4 when you're ready to start making documents.

Part 3. Getting Acquainted With WillMaker

A. Using On-Line Help

The WillMaker program and manual provide explanations of practical and legal aspects of each issue raised in the WillMaker interviews. You can get most of this information with a press of a key, using WillMaker's on-screen help.

WillMaker 5 for Windows uses the standard Windows Help system to give you extensive on-screen assistance every step of the way. Here's a summary of what's in the WillMaker help system and how to use it.

1. How to View Help

To view help for any particular screen:

- Press F1 or pull down the **Help** menu and choose **Help for this screen**.

There you'll find information that will help you with the specific task you are performing at that moment, such as entering your children's names or deciding how to leave property to minors.

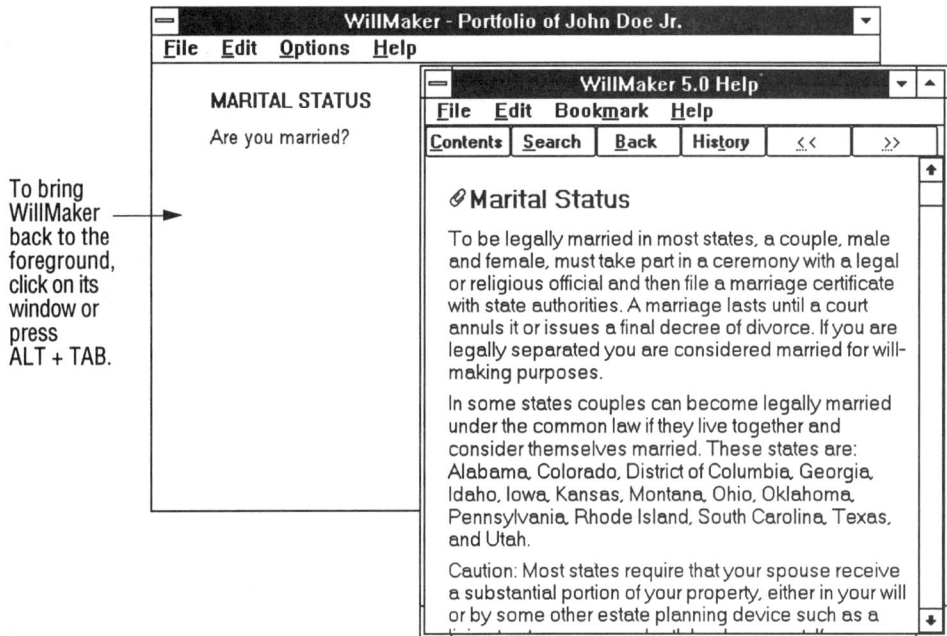

To bring
WillMaker
back to the
foreground,
click on its
window or
press
ALT + TAB.

To bring the main program window back to the front, click on the main WillMaker window or hold down the ALT key and simultaneously press the TAB key (ALT+TAB).

▶ **Help on Help Available**

▶ If you have never used help on a Windows program before, you may want to
▶ choose **How to Use Help** from the **Help** menu. This switches you over to the
▶ Microsoft Windows "Help on Help" file. To get back to WillMaker help, click the
▶ **Back** button repeatedly until the title bar of the help window reads "WillMaker 5
▶ Help."

2. Using the Help Window

The WillMaker Windows help screen has many useful features.

WillMaker help works like help on all other Windows programs. The
illustrations on the next several pages describe how to use the various buttons
and menus on the help window.

System button
Double-click here to close the
help window.

Minimize & Maximize buttons
Shrink the help window down to an icon or
zoom it to fill the screen.

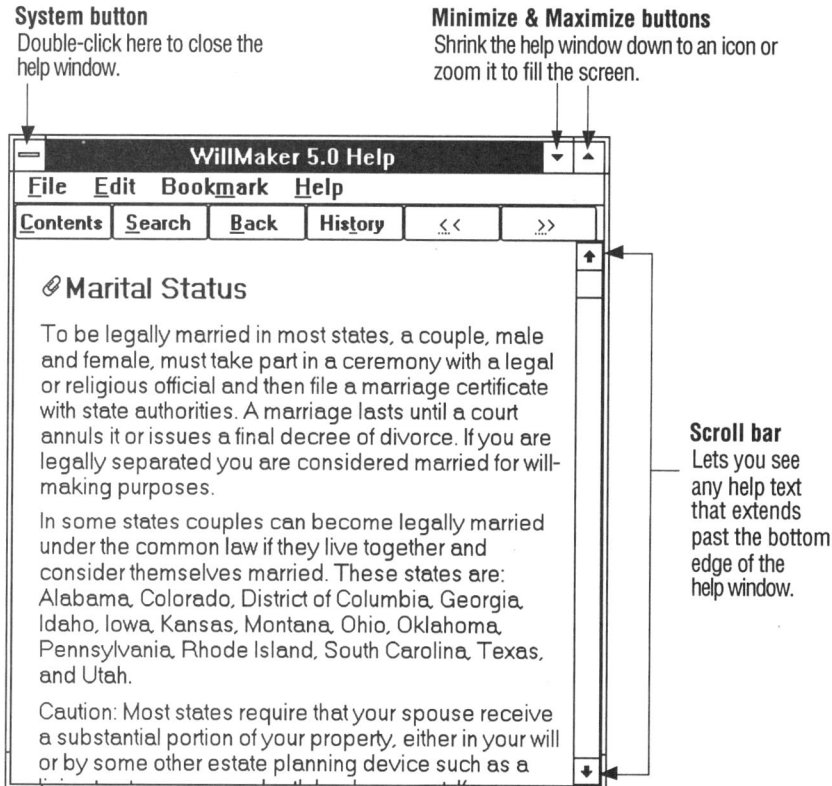

Scroll bar
Lets you see
any help text
that extends
past the bottom
edge of the
help window.

To close the Help window at any time, double-click the "system button"
(or "close box") in the top left corner, or press ALT+F4 while the help window
is the front-most window.

Menus in the Help Window

Windows Help has many helpful standard features which WillMaker users may
find useful. You can print any help topic, copy and paste it into your word

processing program, make "bookmarks" for relevant topics for easy later reference, and annotate topics with your own notes. See the illustration for more about these various features.

Edit menu
Lets you add your own annotations to this help topic, or copy the text of the help into a word-processing document.

File menu
Lets you print the current help topic, exit Windows help, or open a different Windows Help file.

Bookmark menu
Lets you add the current help topic to the Bookmark menu for easy later reference.

Help menu
Gives you information on how to use the Windows help system.

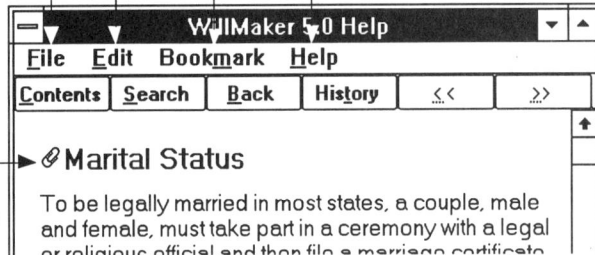

Paper clip
Indicates that you have attached an annotation to this help topic, using the Edit menu. Click on the paper clip to see your annotation.

WillMaker 5.0 Help

File   Edit   Bookmark   Help

| Contents | Search | Back | History | << | >> |

Marital Status

To be legally married in most states, a couple, male and female, must take part in a ceremony with a legal or religious official and then file a marriage certificate

Buttons in the Help Window

Buttons in the help window let you view a table of contents for WillMaker help, search help topics by keyword and go back to topics you've previously read.

WINDOWS USERS' GUIDE

```
┌─────────────────────────────────────────────────────────┐
│ ─        WillMaker 5.0 Help                        ▼  ▲  │
├─────────────────────────────────────────────────────────┤
│  File   Edit   Bookmark   Help                            │
├──────────┬────────┬───────┬─────────┬────────┬───────────┤
│ Contents │ Search │ Back  │ History │   < <  │    > >     │
└──────────┴────────┴───────┴─────────┴────────┴───────────┘
```

Contents button
Takes you to the table
of contents for the entire
help system.

Search button
Lets you search for
topics by keyword.

Back button
Steps you back through
the topics you have
most recently viewed.

Browse buttons
Let you page through a series of
help topics if two or more topics
are linked together.

History button
Shows a list of the last 40 help
topics you have seen since you
first opened help.

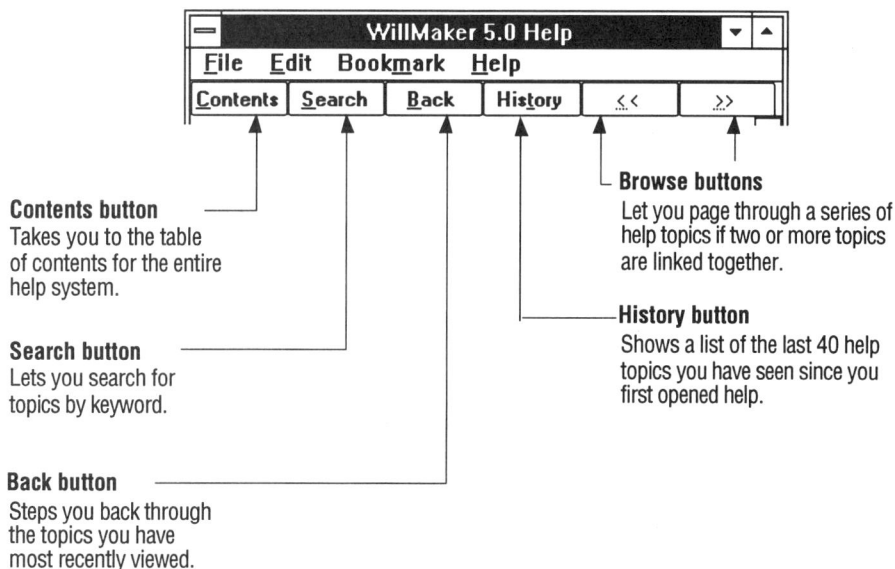

3. Other Available Help

If you pull down the **Help** menu within the WillMaker application, you will
see a variety of other help options available. Choosing **Help Contents** gives
you access to the entire help system.

▶
▶ ## This Manual
▶
▶ If you prefer to do your reading from a book rather than a computer screen, most
▶ of the information in the on-line help is also available in this manual. Note that
▶ the first half of this manual is the computer users' guide, and the second half is
▶ the legal manual. The legal manual explains the legal and practical issues so that
▶ you can assess the legal consequences of the decisions you are asked to make in
▶ the course of your interviews.

B. A Tour of a Typical WillMaker Screen

The WillMaker 5 window operates much like those found in other Windows applications you may be familiar with. This section describes how to use the various elements you'll see in the WillMaker window.

1. The Title Bar and Menus

System button
Double-click here to close the WillMaker application. Click once to see the System menu. (See text for description of the System menu.)

Title Bar

Minimize button
Click here to minimize the WillMaker application into an icon. To restore the WillMaker application to its full size, double-click on the icon that appears on your Windows desktop.

Menu Bar
WillMaker menus can be accessed by clicking on them or by holding down the ALT key and typing the underlined letter.

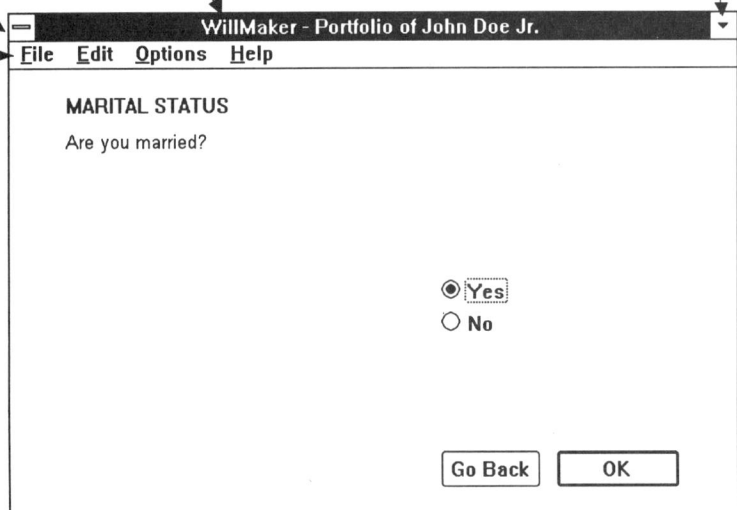

WillMaker - Portfolio of John Doe Jr.

File   Edit   Options   Help

MARITAL STATUS

Are you married?

◉ Yes
○ No

Go Back   OK

System Button

In the top left corner of the WillMaker window is a **system button** or "close box." Double-clicking on this box will exit the program and save any changes you have made. Clicking once on this box drops down the system menu which allows you to Minimize or Move the window using the keyboard.

Tip   To open the system menu with just the keyboard, press ALT+SPACEBAR. To close this or any menu again, press and release the ALT key.

Minimize Button

At the top right corner of the screen is the **minimize button**. Clicking once on this button shrinks the screen into an icon but keeps the program running. You can use this to hide WillMaker while you use other Windows applications. To restore it to full size, double-click on the iconized WillMaker application and continue where you left off.

Title Bar

In the **title bar** of the WillMaker window is the name "WillMaker," followed by the name of the current portfolio you are working on (for example, Portfolio of John Doe Jr.). Click, hold and drag the title bar to move the WillMaker window to a different part of the screen.

Menus

Below the title bar are the WillMaker **menus**. You select a menu by clicking on it, or by holding down the ALT key while pressing the underlined letter. For example, to select the **File** menu, press ALT+F. To close the **File** menu again, either choose a command from the file menu, or press the ALT key once again.

Once the menu is dropped down, you can choose any menu item or command in the menu by clicking it, or by pressing the underlined letter (the "hot key"). You can also move through menus by using the UP and DOWN ARROWS, or switch between menus by using the LEFT and RIGHT ARROWS.

Again, pressing the ALT key (without pressing any other keys) closes all menus.

2. Go Back, OK and Continue Buttons

The main portion of the WillMaker screen contains information, buttons, text fields (where you enter requested information), an **OK** or **Continue** button, and, on most screens, a **Go Back** button.

- The **Go Back** button always takes you back one screen.

- The **Continue** or **OK** buttons always take you forward to the next screen.

```
┌─────────────────────────────────────────────────────┐
│ ▄                   WillMaker                      ▼ │
├─────────────────────────────────────────────────────┤
│ File   Edit   Options   Help                        │
│                                                      │
│   ENTER PORTFOLIO NAME                               │
│   Enter the name of the person who will be using this portfolio: │
│                                                      │
│   ┌─────────────────────────────────┐               │
│   │John Doe Jr.                     │               │
│   └─────────────────────────────────┘               │
│                                                      │
│   A file for this portfolio will be created on your hard disk in the WillMaker │
│   directory. The file will have the first name you type here plus a three │
│   letter '.ww5' extension. Example: John Doe will be saved as 'john.ww5'. │
│                                                      │
│   If there is already a file by that name on your hard disk, the file will have │
│   a 1, 2 or 3 etc, after the last character of the file name. │
│                                                      │
│                                                      │
│                           ┌──────────┐ ┌──────────┐ │
│                           │ Go Back  │ │    OK    │ │
│                           └──────────┘ └──────────┘ │
└─────────────────────────────────────────────────────┘
```

The "Default" button
The default button is always the button with a slightly heavier outline. Pressing ENTER is always equivalent to clicking the default button.

Also notice that one of these buttons will always have a slightly darker black outline. This black outline indicates the **default** button. Pressing the ENTER key is always equivalent to clicking the default button.

To change which button is the default button, press the TAB key until the heavier outline moves to the button you want to use. For example, to make the **Go Back** button the default button, press the TAB key until the **Go Back** button has a heavy outline around it. At this point, you can press ENTER to activate this button. When you change the default button in this way, the change is not saved. When you return to this screen the default button will once again be the **OK** or **Continue button**.

C. Basic WillMaker Operations

1. Moving from Screen to Screen

Some screens, including a number at the beginning of the program, do not request any input from you. But these screens give you important information. Read the screen and advance to the next screen by clicking on the **Continue** button or pressing the ENTER key.

On other screens, you must answer a question or enter some words before you can proceed to the next screen. If the answer is what you intend, click the **OK** button and you will proceed to the next screen.

2. Going Back to the Previous Screen

Frequently, you may want to refer to information on a previous screen, or to change a previous answer. To do this, click on the **Go Back** button, which will take you back one screen in the program.

Each screen you back through will display your previous answer—with the answers on most screens appearing in context. You can back up this way at any point in the main sequence of screens in WillMaker.

If you're not using a mouse, press the TAB key repeatedly to move to the **Go Back** button (a black outline appears around the button), then press ENTER.

If you have just entered or changed data on a screen or changed your answer to a multiple choice question, you will get the following warning if you try to go back:

```
┌──────────────────────────────────────────────────┐
│ ─ │                 WillMaker                      │
├──────────────────────────────────────────────────┤
│                                                    │
│   ┌─┐   Any changes or additions you have  ┌──────┐│
│   │?│   made on this screen will be        │  OK  ││
│   └─┘   ignored if you Go Back now.        └──────┘│
│                                                    │
│         Are you sure you want to Go Back?          │
│                                            ┌──────┐│
│                                            │Cancel││
│                                            └──────┘│
│                                                    │
└──────────────────────────────────────────────────┘
```

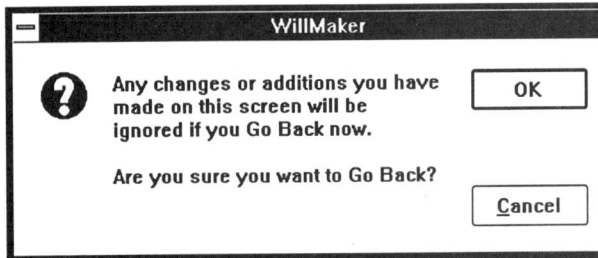

If you click **OK** (or press ENTER) your answer will not be saved, and you will go back to the previous screen. If you click Cancel (or press ESC) you will remain at the screen you were at in the program.

Once you're back at the main screen, you can save your changes by clicking **OK** to move one screen forward. At that point, your changes are added to your data file and will not be erased if you click **Go Back**.

Going Back from the Review Screen

After you have finished an entire WillMaker interview, you will come to a Review screen, which lets you jump back to the various parts of your interview, so that you can review or change your answers. (See Part 4, Section C for more information on the Review feature.)

3. Saving Your Work

There are two ways to save your work with WillMaker: automatically and manually.

The easiest way is to turn on the **Autosave** feature, found in the **Options** menu (ALT+O, A). When Autosave is on, your work is saved at every opportunity. Saving takes only a second, so you may not even notice it happening.

A check mark appears near the **Autosave** command in the **Options** menu to show that it is on. If there is no check mark, Autosave is off.

If you don't want your work automatically saved, leave Autosave off and manually save your work using the **Save** command in the **File** menu (ALT+F, S). The only reason to use this method is that if you make some major unintended change to your file, you could exit the program without saving, and then reopen your previously saved file.

Note If Autosave is on, the **Save** command in the **File** menu will never be available, because there is never anything more to save.

4. Exiting the Program

There are three different ways to exit WillMaker.

- Double-click the system button in the top left corner of the WillMaker window.

- Select **Exit** from the **File** menu (ALT+F, X)

  or

- Press ALT+F4.

When you quit, the program asks you if you want to save your work, or, if the Autosave feature is on, your work will be saved automatically. See Section 3, above, for more on the Autosave feature.

▶ **To Temporarily Minimize the WillMaker Window**

If you want to temporarily get the WillMaker window off your screen, but do not want to quit the program, click the minimize button (it looks like a down arrow) in the top right corner of the screen. This does not exit the program, but turns WillMaker into an icon on at the bottom of your screen. To restore the WillMaker window to full size, click the WillMaker icon at the bottom of your screen.

D. WillMaker Menus

WillMaker 5 for Windows has four menus: File, Edit and Options and Help. Here's a summary of what's in each of them.

Note Some of this information may not make sense until you have become more familiar with the program. You may want to skip this for now and return to it as needed. You can also get a description of what each menu item does by selecting the menu item with the arrow keys, and then pressing F1.

1. File Menu

File	
New	
Open...	Ctrl+O
Convert...	
Save	Ctrl+S
Print Options...	
Print Setup...	
Exit	Ctrl+Q

New

This command allows you to create a new WillMaker portfolio, by displaying the screen where you enter the portfolio name.

Open... (Ctrl+O)

This command takes you directly to the screen that lists the WillMaker portfolios you have made. See Part 4, Section A.3, Creating Additional Portfolios.

Convert

This command converts data files created with versions 4.0 and 5 of WillMaker for DOS and Macintosh, so they can be used in this program.

Save (Ctrl+S)

This command preserves your data and allows you to continue with the program.

Print Options

This command lets you change the font and type size of your documents before you print them out.

Print Setup...

This command lets you change your printer selection, using the standard Windows Print Setup dialog.

Exit (Alt+F4 or Ctrl+Q)

This command saves your data and exits the WillMaker application.

2. Edit Menu

Edit	
Undo	Ctrl+Z
Cut	Ctrl+X
Copy	Ctrl+C
Paste	Ctrl+V
Delete	Del
Select All	Ctrl+A

The **Edit** menu is similar to a word processing menu for cutting and pasting your answers to questions.

Undo (Ctrl+Z)

This command undoes the last typing or editing you did, provided you haven't left the screen on which the changes were made.

Cut (Ctrl+X)

This command removes the selected text from your document and places it on the clipboard.

Copy (Ctrl+C)

This command makes a copy of the selected text and stores that copy on the clipboard, but does not cut it from the document.

Paste (Ctrl+V)

This command adds text that you have previously cut or copied into the selected text or where the cursor is blinking.

Delete (Del)

This command clears the selection without putting it on the clipboard. That is, the selected text will not be saved.

Select All (Ctrl+A)

This command selects all of the text in the currently active text field.

3. Options Menu

Options
Skip Info Screens
Autosave
Switch to Other Document...
Erase Document and Start Over

Skip Info Screens

Some screens that appear in the WillMaker program explain a particular aspect of making a document but do not ask you to respond to a question or provide information. You can turn these information screens off by highlighting **Skip**

Info Screens on the **Options** menu. A check mark will then appear next to **Skip Info Screens**. You will then be presented only with screens that require you to respond or enter data.

> Because the information screens provide valuable guidance, you should skip them only if you have used the program before and are thoroughly familiar with all of the relevant legal issues.

Autosave

This command automatically saves your changes each time you complete a section of the program. Each "section" of the program is about 3 to 6 screens of related information. If this feature is on, a check mark appears near it. If it is off, the program saves only when you exit or when you choose **Save** from the **File** menu.

Switch to Another Document

This command lets you change between your will, healthcare directions and final arrangements document at any time by displaying the document menu screen.

Erase Document and Start Over

This command lets you erase the current document you are working on in your portfolio, without erasing the other documents in your portfolio.

4. Help Menu

Help	
How to **U**se Help	
Help **C**ontents	
Keyboard Shortcuts	Ctrl+K
Help for this Screen	F1
About Nolo **P**ress	
Nolo Press Catalog	
About **W**illMaker 5.0...	

How to Use Help

This command opens Microsoft's on-line help containing information on how to use the Windows help system.

Help Contents

This command gives you access to the entire help system, except for the help for the current screen.

Keyboard Shortcuts (Ctrl+K)

This command brings up a help screen listing all the keyboard commands for people who do not use a mouse or who prefer to use the keyboard.

Help for this Screen (F1)

This command displays useful information about the legal consequences of making decisions called for on a particular screen. Help is available for each screen in the WillMaker program by pressing F1 or choosing this menu item.

About Nolo Press

This tells you a little about the people who made this product, and why we do what we do.

Nolo Press Catalog

The Nolo Press Catalog is an on-line listing of Nolo's 80 publications on do-it-yourself law. You'll find up-to-date information on prices and current editions of books, software, videos, and tapes on business, consumer and family law.

About WillMaker 5

This command gives you version and copyright information, as well as information about available Windows memory.

Part 4. Using WillMaker to Create Documents

A. Creating and Using WillMaker Portfolios

Once you've started the program and gone through the first few introductory screens, you will be asked to create your first "portfolio." A portfolio is what WillMaker calls the file that contains the set of three documents that the program produces.

You create your portfolio by entering your name when you get to the screen shown here:

```
┌─────────────────────────────────────────────────────────────┐
│ ▬                        WillMaker                        ▼  │
├─────────────────────────────────────────────────────────────┤
│  File   Edit   Options   Help                                │
│                                                              │
│     ENTER PORTFOLIO NAME                                     │
│                                                              │
│     Enter the name of the person who will be using this portfolio: │
│                                                              │
│   ▶ ┌──────────────────────────────────────────┐            │
│     │ John Doe Jr.                             │            │
│     └──────────────────────────────────────────┘            │
│                                                              │
│     A file for this portfolio will be created on your hard disk in the WillMaker │
│     directory. The file will have the first name you type here plus a three │
│     letter '.ww5' extension. Example: John Doe will be saved as 'john.ww5'. │
│                                                              │
│     If there is already a file by that name on your hard disk, the file will have │
│     a 1, 2 or 3 etc, after the last character of the file name. │
│                                                              │
│                                                              │
│                                  ┌──────────┐ ┌──────────┐   │
│                                  │ Go Back  ├─│ ▶  OK    │   │
│                                  └──────────┘ └──────────┘   │
│                                                              │
└─────────────────────────────────────────────────────────────┘
```

Enter your name here. This becomes the name of your portfolio.

Click the OK button or press ENTER to confirm your answer.

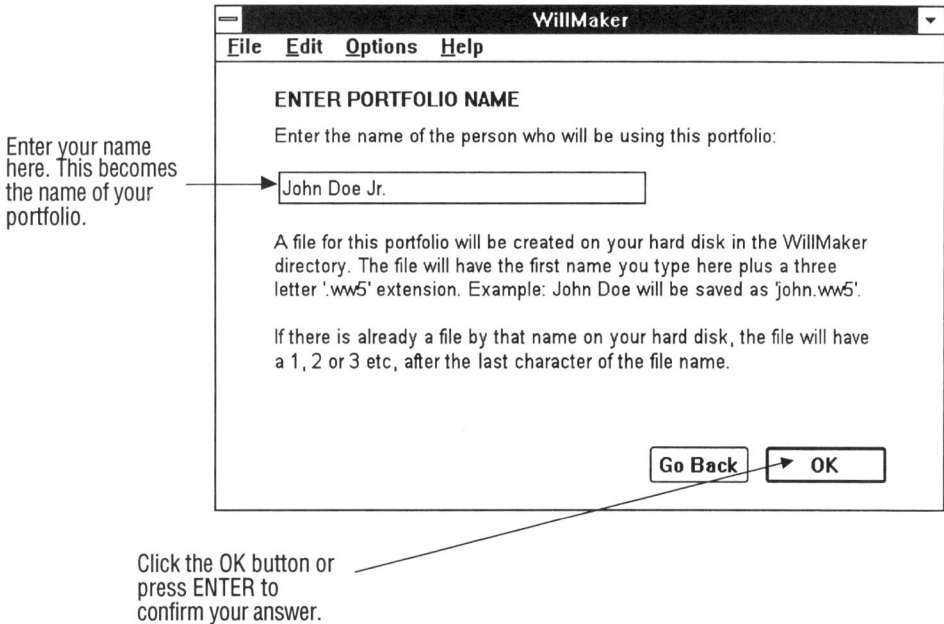

Once you enter your name and click **OK**, WillMaker creates a file on your hard disk in the directory where the WillMaker program is located. (If you used the "Easy Install" options, this will be the WM5WIN directory.) The name of the file is the first eight letters of your first name, plus the three-character extension ".WW5".

If you need to create more than one portfolio, or to convert files created with other versions of WillMaker, see sections 3-5, below.

---

1. Documents in Your Portfolio

Once you have created your WillMaker portfolio, you will see a list of documents in your portfolio:

- your Will,
- your Healthcare Directions, and
- your Final Arrangements document.

The name of the currently opened portfolio is always
displayed in the title bar of the WillMaker Window.

Your portfolio is stored
on your hard disk in the
WillMaker Windows
directory with your first
name and a ".ww5"
extension.

WillMaker - Portfolio of John Doe Jr.

File   Edit   Options   Help

DOCUMENTS IN YOUR PORTFOLIO

Portfolio Name: John Doe Jr.
Portfolio File Name: john.ww5

Your portfolio consists of three documents.
Select the document you wish to work on and then click "OK".

DOCUMENT	STATUS:
⊙ **Your Will**	Ready to Print
○ **Your Healthcare Directions**	Partially Complete
○ **Your Final Arrangements**	Not Started

To work on a document in
this portfolio click one of
these buttons, then click OK.

To switch to another
portfolio click this button.

Open Other Portfolio   **OK**

Each time you return to your documents list, WillMaker
displays the status of the documents in your portfolio.

To work on a document, click on its name, then click **OK** or press ENTER. This will begin the interview for that document.

The will interview asks you about yourself, your family, your spouse (if any) and about what property you want to go to whom. If you give property to minors, you're asked who should take care of their property until they are old enough to manage it themselves. If you have children, it asks who you want to be their guardian while they are minors. You're also given a chance to forgive debts that people may owe to you, and to appoint a person (an executor) to make sure your property is distributed according to the wishes expressed in your will.

The healthcare directions interview asks you to set out specific instructions about the types of medical care you want should you be diagnosed as having a terminal condition or being in a permanent coma. Individual life-sustaining procedures are listed on the screen and the help (F1) describes each one. You are allowed to pick and choose which life-sustaining procedures you'd like, or simply indicate you'd like all or none of the life-sustaining procedures administered. You can also name a representative who can supervise your directions to your healthcare providers based on the document you produce with WillMaker.

The final arrangements portion of WillMaker interviews you regarding your preferences and arrangements surrounding your burial or cremation and accompanying ceremonies, as well as any arrangements you may have made regarding organ donation.

2. Switching between Documents in Your Portfolio

To return to the "Documents in Your Portfolio" screen at any time, choose **Switch to Other Document** from the **Options** menu (ALT+O,D). You can switch to a different document even if you haven't finished working on a document. When you reenter a document that you've already started, you pick up right where you left off.

Your Document Status

Each document on the document selection screen is listed with its status.

- **Not Started**   You haven't started this document. If you choose this document, you will start with a few orientation screens that will familiarize you with what you are about to do. Then your interview will begin.

- **Partially Complete**   You have started this document, but have not entered completed the document's interview. If you reenter this document, you will pick up the interview where you left off the last time you worked on this document.

- **Ready to Print**   You have answered all the questions in the interview for this document and have entered enough information to print out a complete document. If you reenter this document, you will go directly to the "Congratulations" screen, from which you can print, export or review and/or modify your document. (See Section C, below, on what to do when your interview is complete.)

3. Creating Additional Portfolios

With WillMaker you can create as many portfolios as you want. However, WillMaker and its manual are copyrighted, and the licensing agreement prohibits you from preparing wills for people outside your immediate family or for commercial or nonprofit purposes.

To make a will for another person in your immediate family, including your spouse or domestic partner, children or parents, you must make a new portfolio.

There are two ways to do this.

- Choose **New** from the **File** menu.

  or

- Click the **New Portfolio** button on the List of Portfolios screen. (See Section 4 below.)

If you choose the first method, you will come to the first screen of the program, walked through the orientation again, and then be asked for the name the new portfolio.

If you choose the second method, you will be taken directly to a screen where you name the portfolio.

4. Opening Previously Created Portfolios

To open a portfolio that you created earlier with this program, choose **Open** from the **File** menu. This displays the List of Portfolios screen. The portfolios you have already created appear in a list. Click the portfolio you want to open, then click **Continue**.

If you have created more than one set of douments (more than one portfolio), they are listed here.

All portfolio files are kept in the WillMaker Windows directory. Any files in any other directory will not be accessible by the program.

If there is more than one portfolio with the same first name, a number is added to the end of the first name (for example, "JOHN.WW5, JOHN2.WW5, JOHN3.WW5, etc.)

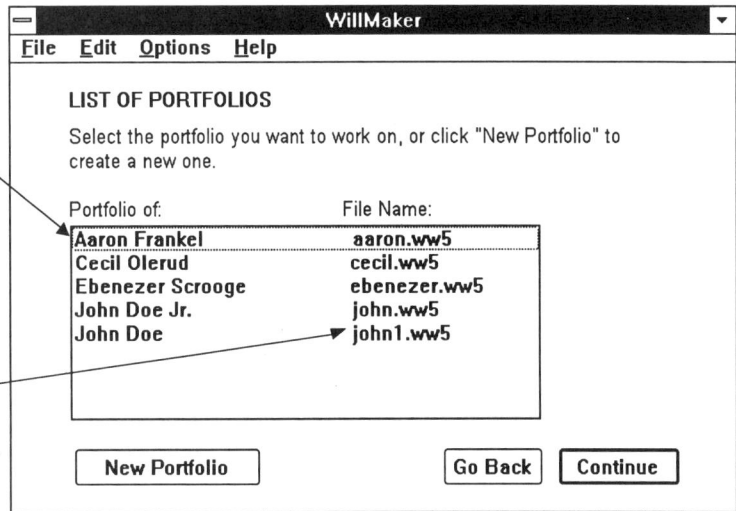

```
┌─────────────────────────────────────────────────┐
│ ▬                      WillMaker                ▼ │
├─────────────────────────────────────────────────┤
│  File   Edit   Options   Help                    │
│                                                   │
│   LIST OF PORTFOLIOS                             │
│                                                   │
│   Select the portfolio you want to work on, or   │
│   click "New Portfolio" to create a new one.     │
│                                                   │
│   Portfolio of:              File Name:          │
│   ┌───────────────────────────────────────────┐ │
│   │ Aaron Frankel              aaron.ww5       │ │
│   │ Cecil Olerud               cecil.ww5       │ │
│   │ Ebenezer Scrooge           ebenezer.ww5    │ │
│   │ John Doe Jr.               john.ww5        │ │
│   │ John Doe                   john1.ww5       │ │
│   │                                            │ │
│   └───────────────────────────────────────────┘ │
│                                                   │
│   ┌──────────────┐        ┌─────────┐ ┌────────┐│
│   │ New Portfolio│        │ Go Back │ │Continue││
│   └──────────────┘        └─────────┘ └────────┘│
└─────────────────────────────────────────────────┘
```

To select a portfolio from the list if you are not using a mouse:

1. Press TAB until a dotted outline appears in the list

2. Use the DOWN or UP arrows to highlight your choice

3. Press ENTER.

▶ ## What's in the Portfolio List
▶
▶   WillMaker saves all portfolio files in the same directory on your hard disk where
▶   the WillMaker program (WMW.EXE) is located. The files in the Portfolio List are
▶   only those files in that directory. If you move a file out of the directory where the
▶   WillMaker program is located, that portfolio will not show up in the Portfolio List.
▶
▶

5. Converting Files Made With Other Versions of WillMaker

WillMaker 5 for Windows can convert files made with WillMaker 5 or 4.0 for DOS or Macintosh.

To convert any of these files:

1. Choose **Convert** from the **File** menu.

A standard Windows file dialog will appear.

2. Locate and select the WillMaker file you want to convert.

WillMaker files in other versions are named as follows.

VERSION	FILE NAME
WillMaker 5 for DOS	All files with ".WM5" extension
WillMaker 4.0 for DOS	The file "WILLDATA.WMK" in the WillMaker 4 directory
WillMaker 5 for Macintosh	The name of person using the portfolio
WillMaker 4.0 for Macintosh	WILL.DAT

3. After you've located the file you want to convert, click **OK**.

At this point, WillMaker automatically reads the old file. The first name of the user in the old file is used to create a new WillMaker 5 for Windows portfolio file, in keeping with the method used for WillMaker 5 portfolios. The new converted file is saved in the directory where WillMaker for Windows is located, and the old file remains intact.

B. The WillMaker Interview: Answering Questions and Entering Information

The WillMaker interview is how the program gets the information from you that it needs to correctly generate your document. There are separate interviews for each of the three documents in your portfolio. You can start or stop an interview at any time, or switch between interviews by choosing **Switch to Other Document** from the **Options** menu. However, we suggest that you work on one interview at a time so as not to get confused.

The interviews consist of several different types of screens.

- **Information screens** introduce each interview topic and explain important legal or practical considerations you should consider when answering questions or making choices.

- **Multiple-choice screens** offer a choice or require you to answer Yes or No to a simple question.

- **Text-entry screens** ask you to type in information, like your name, address or the names of your children.

- **Lists of specific gifts and property managements** (in the Will interview only) where you can make up to 100 gifts of specific property and arrange property management for up to 100 young beneficiaries.

This section explains how to use multiple-choice screens, text-entry screens, and lists of specific gifts and property managements. It also explains how to review and revise your answers if you change your mind or want to make a correction.

1. Multiple Choice Screens

Some multiple-choice screens ask a simple Yes or No question, while others offer three or more choices.

Option Buttons

Below are two examples of screens that require you to choose among several options.

```
┌─────────────────────────────────────────────────────────┐
│ ▬          WillMaker - Portfolio of John Doe Jr.       ▼ │
├─────────────────────────────────────────────────────────┤
│ File   Edit   Options   Help                             │
│                                                          │
│   MARITAL STATUS                                         │
│                                                          │
│   Are you married?                                       │
│                                                          │
│                                                          │
│                                                          │
│                                    ● Yes                  │
│                                    ○ No                   │
│                                                          │
│                                                          │
│                                                          │
│                              ┌──────────┐ ┌──────────┐   │
│                              │ Go Back  │ │   OK     │   │
│                              └──────────┘ └──────────┘   │
└─────────────────────────────────────────────────────────┘
```

This screen requires a Yes or No response.

Make your selection by clicking the correct answer, and then clicking OK.

```
┌─────────────────────────────────────────────────────────┐
│ ▬          WillMaker - Portfolio of John Doe Jr.       ▼ │
├─────────────────────────────────────────────────────────┤
│ File   Edit   Options   Help                             │
│                                                          │
│   WHAT IF THE BENEFICIARY DIES BEFORE YOU DO?           │
│                                                          │
│   If the beneficiary you named to receive this property  │
│   fails to survive you, the property should pass to:     │
│                                                          │
│   ● the children of that beneficiary in equal shares.    │
│                                                          │
│   ○ one or more named alternate beneficiaries.           │
│     You will name these alternates on the next screen.   │
│                                                          │
│   ○ the residuary beneficiaries.                         │
│     You will name the residuary beneficiaries later in   │
│     this program.                                        │
│                              ┌──────────┐ ┌──────────┐   │
│                              │ Go Back  │ │   OK     │   │
│                              └──────────┘ └──────────┘   │
└─────────────────────────────────────────────────────────┘
```

This screen offers a multiple choice.

Make your selection by clicking the appropriate option button.

Click on the appropriate response. A black dot in the circle indicates your choice. You must choose one of the options before you can continue with the interview.

If you are not using a mouse, press the UP or DOWN ARROW KEYS to make your selection, then press ENTER.

Selecting "option buttons"
A black dot in the circle indicates that
the button is selected. A dotted outline
appears around the button you have
moved to. Click a different button or
press the ARROW KEYS to change
your answer.

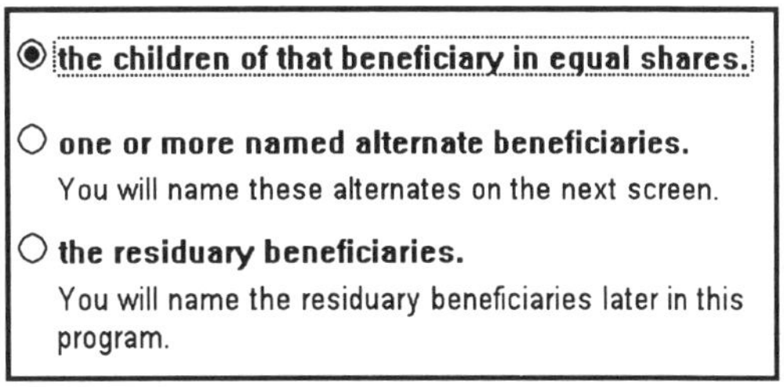

⦿ the children of that beneficiary in equal shares.

◯ **one or more named alternate beneficiaries.**
You will name these alternates on the next screen.

◯ **the residuary beneficiaries.**
You will name the residuary beneficiaries later in this
program.

Check to make sure your answer is correct. If not, change it by clicking on
a different button. When you are sure it's correct, click on the **OK** button or
press the ENTER key.

Check Boxes

A few WillMaker screens have check boxes buttons that allow you to choose
one or more of several choices offered to you. Clicking on a check box marks
the box with an X or clears the X if it is already checked.

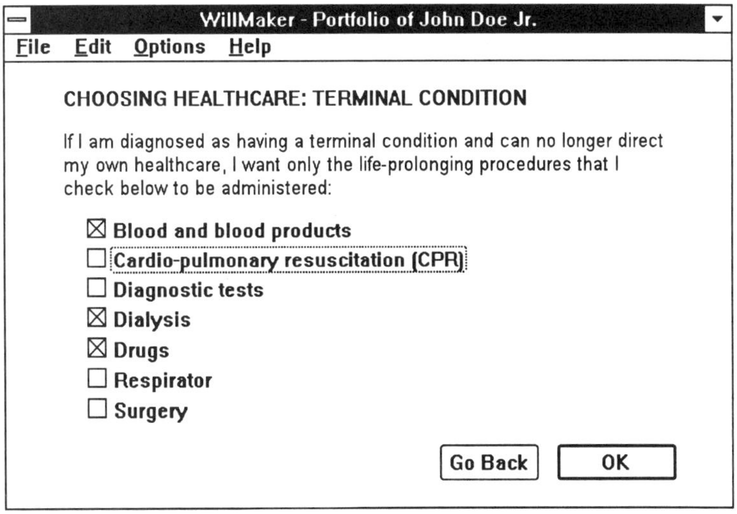

WillMaker - Portfolio of John Doe Jr.

File   Edit   Options   Help

CHOOSING HEALTHCARE: TERMINAL CONDITION

If I am diagnosed as having a terminal condition and can no longer direct
my own healthcare, I want only the life-prolonging procedures that I
check below to be administered:

☒ **Blood and blood products**
☐ **Cardio-pulmonary resuscitation (CPR)**
☐ **Diagnostic tests**
☒ **Dialysis**
☒ **Drugs**
☐ **Respirator**
☐ **Surgery**

Go Back   OK

If you are not using a mouse, use the TAB key (or SHIFT+TAB) to move to a check box (until it has a dotted outline around it), then mark it or unmark it by pressing the SPACE BAR.

Check to make sure your answers are correct. Remember that clicking on a different button does not de-select your first choice. You must select or de-select each choice one at a time. When you are sure your choices are correct, click on the **OK** button or press the ENTER key.

Lists of States

On the screen where you select your state, you make your choice by clicking your state in the list, then clicking **OK**. Use the scroll bar to see the entire list.

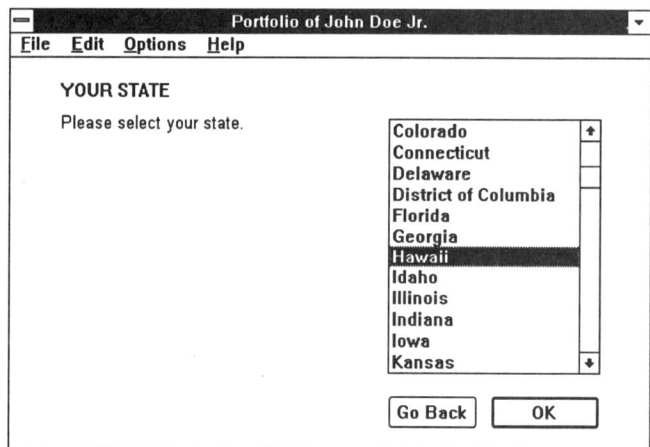

```
┌─────────────────────────────────────────────────────────────┐
│ ▬              Portfolio of John Doe Jr.                  ▼  │
│ File  Edit  Options  Help                                   │
│                                                             │
│    YOUR STATE                                               │
│    Please select your state.      ┌──────────────────┬──┐   │
│                                   │ Colorado         │ ↑ │   │
│                                   │ Connecticut      │  │   │
│                                   │ Delaware         │  │   │
│                                   │ District of Columbia │ │   │
│                                   │ Florida          │  │   │
│                                   │ Georgia          │  │   │
│                                   │ Hawaii           │  │   │
│                                   │ Idaho            │  │   │
│                                   │ Illinois         │  │   │
│                                   │ Indiana          │  │   │
│                                   │ Iowa             │  │   │
│                                   │ Kansas           │ ↓ │   │
│                                   └──────────────────┴──┘   │
│                                   ┌──────────┐ ┌──────────┐ │
│                                   │ Go Back  │ │   OK     │ │
│                                   └──────────┘ └──────────┘ │
└─────────────────────────────────────────────────────────────┘
```

You can only select one state. To change your selection, scroll to your new choice and click on it. Your original selection will be erased.

If you are not using a mouse, use the ARROW KEYS to select the item of your choice, then press the ENTER key.

2. Text-entry Screens

Some screens require you to type in information—such as a name, address or descriptions of items of property. When these screens are displayed, the active field will have a flashing cursor in it. To enter your answer, just start typing.

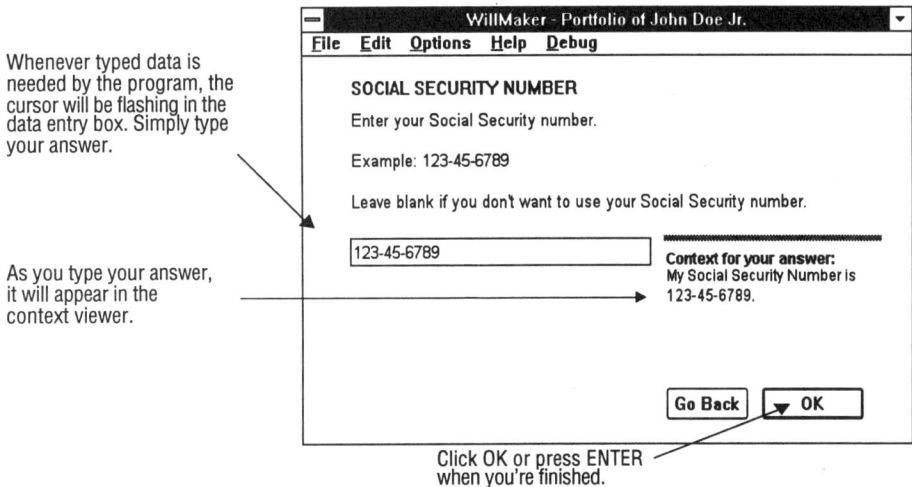

Whenever typed data is needed by the program, the cursor will be flashing in the data entry box. Simply type your answer.

As you type your answer, it will appear in the context viewer.

WillMaker - Portfolio of John Doe Jr.

File   Edit   Options   Help   Debug

SOCIAL SECURITY NUMBER

Enter your Social Security number.

Example: 123-45-6789

Leave blank if you don't want to use your Social Security number.

123-45-6789

Context for your answer:
My Social Security Number is
123-45-6789.

Go Back   OK

Click OK or press ENTER when you're finished.

In the Will portion of the WillMaker program, these input screens allow you to view a short fragment of text from the will—the context in which your current answer will appear when you finally print out your will. This is to help answer questions about how you should word your answers, such as: "Should the names of my children be separated by commas?" or "Should I enter the name of my county as the County of XXX or XXX County or just XXX?" Remember that context-sensitive help is also available at any time by pressing F1.

When you are satisfied with your answer, click on the **OK** button or press the ENTER key.

If you don't use a mouse, you can move around the screen, from text fields to buttons and back, by pressing the TAB key. If you return to the text field this way, the text that was in the text field will now be selected. (Selected text is white with a black background, the reverse of normal text.)

Note   If you start typing while text is selected, the selected text will be replaced by whatever you type. If you do this unintentionally, choose **Undo** from the **Edit** menu or press CTRL+Z immediately to restore the replaced text.

▶
▶
▶ ## Leaving an Entry Blank
▶
▶ Some WillMaker screens do not require an answer and allow you to leave the
▶ entry field blank. If you return to a screen of this type, and have left the field
▶ blank, "*BLANK*" will appear in the text entry box.

```
┌─────────────────────────────────────────────────────────────┐
│ ▭        WillMaker - Portfolio of John Doe Jr.            ▼ │
│ File   Edit   Options   Help                                  │
│                                                               │
│   YOUR ADDRESS                                                │
│                                                               │
│   Enter your address, including city, state and zip code.     │
│                                                               │
│   ┌──────────────────────────────────────┬─┐                │
│   │123 Main Street, Ann Arbor, Michigan  │▲│                │
│   │48104│                                 │ │                │
│   │                                       │ │                │
│   │                                       │ │                │
│   │                                       │▼│                │
│   └──────────────────────────────────────┴─┘                │
│                                                               │
│                                                               │
│                              ┌──────────┐  ┌──────────────┐  │
│                              │ Go Back  │  │     OK       │  │
│                              └──────────┘  └──────────────┘  │
└─────────────────────────────────────────────────────────────┘
```

Most text-entry fields in WillMaker will not accept carriage returns, even if they allow for multiple lines of wrapping text. This is because the text you type will be incorporated within a sentence in final document; a carriage return would create a new paragraph where there shouldn't be one. So, even on screens that allow for scrolling text, do not type a carriage return in your answer. Pressing ENTER to insert a carriage return will, instead, trigger the **OK** button.

Changing Your Answers

You can change any answer you typed while you are still at the screen by backspacing over the characters you have typed.

To delete an entire entry, choose **Select All** from the **Edit** menu (CTRL+A), or TAB around the screen until the text entry field is selected again. You will notice that all of the text is selected and looks "reversed" on the screen—that is, white text on a dark background. Press the DELETE (or BACKSPACE) key to delete the text.

If you mistakenly delete text you didn't mean to, choose **Undo** from the **Edit** menu (CTRL+Z). This will undo your most recent change.

If you start typing while text is selected, the text will be deleted; whatever you type will replace it.

If you don't want to replace the selected text, press the RIGHT ARROW or the END key to move the cursor to the end of the text entry field. Then you can use the BACKSPACE key, the DELETE key and the ARROW KEYS to make whatever changes you want to make.

You can also select text with the mouse by clicking and holding down the mouse button and dragging across the field.

You can also select one word at a time by double-clicking on it. To select additional words, double-click and hold, and then drag across the words. Notice that one word at a time is selected, rather than one character.

To de-select text, click outside the selected text but inside the text field, or press the RIGHT or LEFT ARROW keys.

Changing an Answer After You Have Left the Screen

If you have already passed by a screen but want to change your answer, click the **Go Back** button until you are once again at the screen you want to change. When you arrive at that screen the cursor will be flashing at the beginning of the field containing your data.

If you don't use a mouse, press the TAB key to make **Go Back** the default button, then press ENTER. (See Part 3, Section B2 on using the TAB key to change the default button). Click the mouse to place the cursor where you want or use the arrow keys to edit your answer as desired. When finished, click the **OK** button to again move forward.

Note If "*BLANK*" appears in the box (because you chose not to answer the question), delete the word and the asterisks entirely before entering your answer. (See above on "Changing Your Answers.") If you want to leave your answer blank, click **OK**.

On some data entry screens, you don't have to enter anything if you don't want to.

If you leave a screen like this blank, "*BLANK*" will appear in the data entry box to indicate that it was intentionally left blank.

If later you change your mind and want to enter data in this box, select and delete "*BLANK*" type in your answer, and click OK.

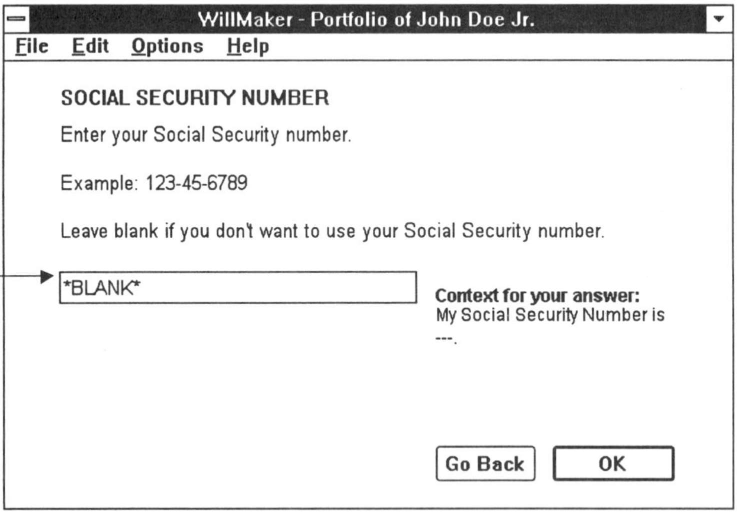
WillMaker - Portfolio of John Doe Jr.
File Edit Options Help
SOCIAL SECURITY NUMBER
Enter your Social Security number.
Example: 123-45-6789
Leave blank if you don't want to use your Social Security number.
BLANK
Context for your answer:
My Social Security Number is
---.
Go Back
OK

3. Specific Bequests and Property Management Lists

In the WillMaker interview for your will, you are given the option of making up to 100 specific bequests of property. In another part of that same interview, you are given the option of setting up property management for up to 100 young beneficiaries you have named.

These parts of the interview are similar in that you can repeat the same portion of the interview up to 100 times, once for each specific bequest or property management arrangement that you want to set up.

Here's a description of how to use these parts of the WillMaker interview.

Specific bequests   You may make up to 100 separate bequests of specific personal or real property in your WillMaker will. Each specific bequest requires you to go through a succession of screens in which you enter:

- the name of a beneficiary
- a description of the beneficiary (person, organization or both)
- a description of the property you are leaving to the beneficiary
- directions for what should happen to the property if the primary beneficiary dies before you do, and
- an optional alternate beneficiary.

Property management for minors and young adults   Later in the WillMaker interview for your will, you are given a chance to name who should manage the property you are leaving to beneficiaries who are too young to responsibly manage property for themselves. You can repeat this part of the interview for up to 100 different young beneficiaries. For each beneficiary, you:

- name the minor or young adult beneficiary that you have named in your will
- choose the kind of management you want (if your state allows more than one kind)
- specify the name of the trustee or custodian for the property the minor beneficiary will receive through your will
- name an alternate trustee or custodian, and
- specify the age at which the management terminates, if applicable.

Each time you finish entering the required information about a specific bequest or property management arrangement, WillMaker displays a list of specific bequests or property management arrangements you have made so far. If you have entered many specific bequests or property, use the scroll bar or the UP and DOWN ARROWS to see the entire list.

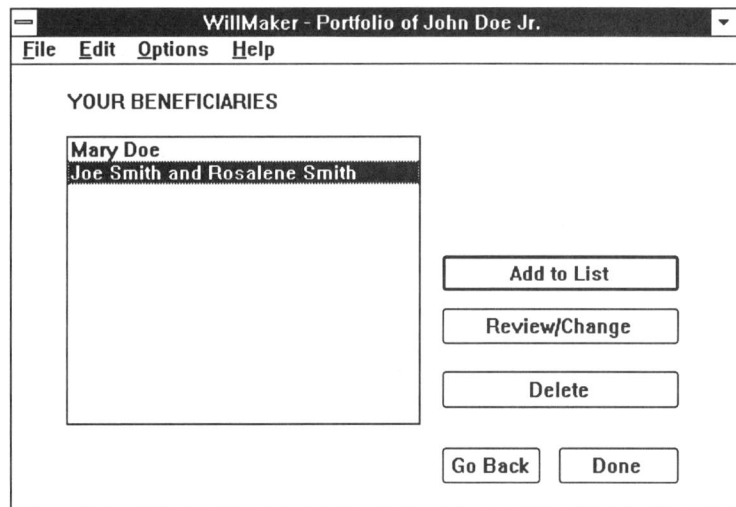

```
┌─────────────────────────────────────────────────────────────┐
│ ▬        WillMaker - Portfolio of John Doe Jr.            ▼ │
│ File   Edit   Options   Help                                 │
│                                                              │
│    YOUR BENEFICIARIES                                        │
│   ┌───────────────────────────────────┐                     │
│   │ Mary Doe                           │                     │
│   │ Joe Smith and Rosalene Smith       │                     │
│   │                                    │                     │
│   │                                    │  ┌─────────────────┐ │
│   │                                    │  │  Add to List    │ │
│   │                                    │  └─────────────────┘ │
│   │                                    │  ┌─────────────────┐ │
│   │                                    │  │ Review/Change   │ │
│   │                                    │  └─────────────────┘ │
│   │                                    │  ┌─────────────────┐ │
│   │                                    │  │    Delete       │ │
│   └───────────────────────────────────┘  └─────────────────┘ │
│                                                              │
│                                    ┌──────────┐ ┌──────────┐ │
│                                    │ Go Back  │ │   Done   │ │
│                                    └──────────┘ └──────────┘ │
└─────────────────────────────────────────────────────────────┘
```

From this list, you can do any one of these operations:

• Add a new item to the list

• Review or change the information contained in an existing item

• Delete an existing item from the list

• Proceed to the next subject of the WillMaker interview when you're done

• Go Back to previous parts of the WillMaker interview.

To add a new specific bequest or property management, click the **Add to List** button to cycle through the questions again. You will be asked the name of this new beneficiary, and so on.

If you need to alter an existing bequest or property management, select it from the list (by clicking it or highlighting it with the UP and DOWN ARROW keys), and click **Review/Change**. You will return to the first screen of the sequence outlined above. From there you can go through each of the screens which make up the bequest or property management..

As you go through each screen, your previous answers are displayed. Change any or all of the answers you wish by typing in a new answer or clicking on a different button than the one that is selected. When you finish with the last screen that makes up the sequence, you will return to the list.

If you wish to delete an existing bequest or property management, select it from the list and click **Delete.**

If you do not wish to make or change any more bequests or property management arrangements, click **Done**.

If you wish to go back to previous portions of the WillMaker interview, click **Go Back**.

If you are not using a mouse, remember that you can move around the screen by using the TAB key.

Example

Your first bequest is your jazz record collection to your nephew Bernard. You would proceed through a sequence of screens in which you: name Bernard as beneficiary, indicate that Bernard is a single person and not an institution, describe the record collection, choose what should happen if Bernard does not survive you and specify alternate beneficiaries.

When you have finished the gift, the name of your first beneficiary, Bernard, appears on the list. You want to make another bequest, so you click on **Add to List** to cycle through the questions again. When you're finished, you click **Done** and continue on with the next portion of the interview.

Unfinished Bequests or Property Management

If you start but don't complete a bequest or property management—for example, you name a beneficiary, and then try to back up before completing the sequence—WillMaker will force you to omit the unfinished item or finish it by putting up this warning:

```
┌──────────────────────────────────────────────┐
│ ▄                WillMaker                     │
├──────────────────────────────────────────────┤
│         Any changes or additions you have  ┌────────┐ │
│   ❓    made to the current bequest will be │   OK   │ │
│         ignored if you Go Back now.        └────────┘ │
│                                                │
│         Are you sure you want to Go Back?   ┌────────┐ │
│                                             │ Cancel │ │
│                                             └────────┘ │
└──────────────────────────────────────────────┘
```

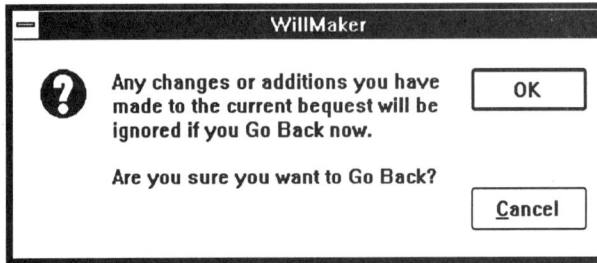

WillMaker will not allow you to leave this gift partially completed, because the program cannot assemble your will with an invalid bequest.

If you quit the program or switch to another document in the middle of making a bequest or arranging for property management, when you next return to this interview, you will return to the point you were when you quit. For this reason, it might be useful for you to make a note to yourself stating what you were doing when you quit, especially if you had to quit in the middle of a complicated part, such as the lists described above.

C. After the Interview Is Finished

Once you have entered all the information necessary to make your document, you will come to a "Congratulations" screen like this. (The screen shown here is for the will document. The other two documents are similar.)

```
┌─────────────────────────────────────────────────────────────┐
│ ▬              Portfolio of John Doe Jr.                   ▼ │
│  File   Edit   Options   Help                                │
│                                                              │
│     CONGRATULATIONS!                                         │
│     Your will is complete.                                   │
│                                                              │
│                                  ┌──────────────────────┐    │
│                                  │    Display Will       │    │
│                                  └──────────────────────┘    │
│                                  ┌──────────────────────┐    │
│                                  │    Print Will...      │    │
│                                  └──────────────────────┘    │
│                                  ┌──────────────────────┐    │
│                                  │    Export Will...     │    │
│                                  └──────────────────────┘    │
│                                  ┌──────────────────────┐    │
│                                  │  Review/Change Answers│    │
│                                  └──────────────────────┘    │
│                                                              │
│   ┌────────────────────────────────┐                        │
│   │  Choose a Different Document    │                        │
│   └────────────────────────────────┘                        │
└─────────────────────────────────────────────────────────────┘
```

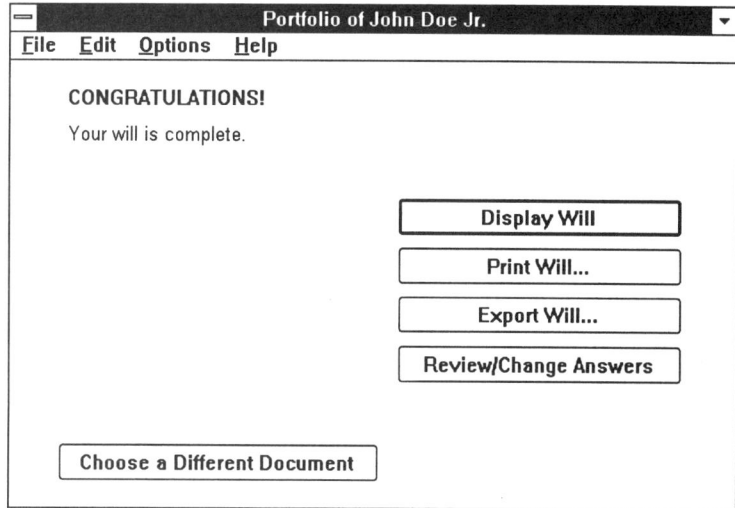

At this point, you can view your document on the screen or print it out.

1. Your Final Documents

Now you're ready to display your final document on the screen. To do this, click the **Display** button. The final documents that will display are as follows:

Your Will   Instructions
                             Will
                             Self Proving Affidavit (if applicable in your state)

Healthcare Directions   Instructions
                             Living Will or Healthcare Directive
                             Healthcare Proxy or Durable Power of Attorney
                                 for Healthcare

Final Arrangements   Instructions
                             Final Arrangements

a. Your Will

When you create a will document, you may end up with more than just one form. In addition to the will itself, WillMaker generates a set of instructions to be printed with the will. The instructions explain what you need to do to make your will legally enforceable in your state.

Depending on your state of residence, WillMaker may also generate a separate self-proving affidavit to be used with your will. (See Chapter 9, Section B2 of the legal guide for more information.)

b. Healthcare Directions

When you create healthcare directions, you may end up with more than just one form. Your directions for medical care is usually called a "declaration" or "living will," although the name used differ by state. WillMaker generates a set of instructions that explain what the form for your healthcare directions is called in your state, and also how to make this form legally enforceable.

If you named somebody to be your healthcare proxy to see to it that your healthcare directions are followed, WillMaker may also generate a separate form, called a "durable power of attorney" in most states. Again, the instructions will explain what this form is called in your state and how to make it legally enforceable. Note that a few states do not have separate healthcare directions and healthcare proxy forms. (See Chapter 13 of the legal guide for more information.)

c. Final Arrangements

When you create a final arrangements document, you will end up with a set of instructions in addition to the letter itself. The instructions explain what you should do with your letter to make sure your wishes are followed. (See Chapter 14 of the legal guide for more information.)

2. Using the Display/Print Window

When a documents is displayed on the screen you can view each page of this document, but you cannot do any editing.

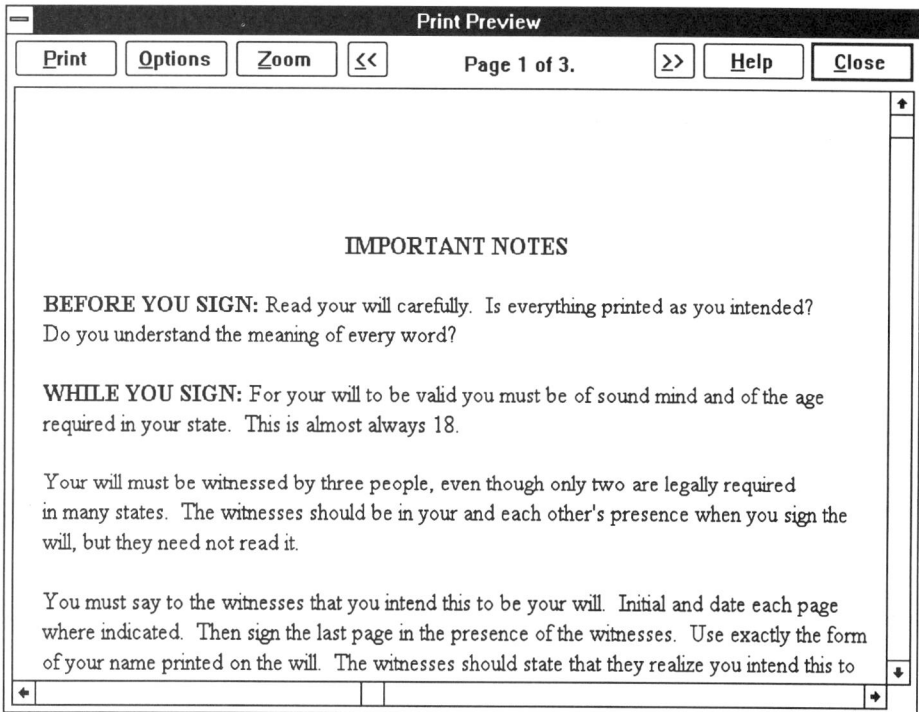

Print Preview
Print	Options	Zoom	<<	Page 1 of 3.	>>	Help	Close

IMPORTANT NOTES

BEFORE YOU SIGN: Read your will carefully. Is everything printed as you intended? Do you understand the meaning of every word?

WHILE YOU SIGN: For your will to be valid you must be of sound mind and of the age required in your state. This is almost always 18.

Your will must be witnessed by three people, even though only two are legally required in many states. The witnesses should be in your and each other's presence when you sign the will, but they need not read it.

You must say to the witnesses that you intend this to be your will. Initial and date each page where indicated. Then sign the last page in the presence of the witnesses. Use exactly the form of your name printed on the will. The witnesses should state that they realize you intend this to

- To move around each page of the displayed document, use the scroll bars or press the UP and DOWN ARROW KEYS or the PAGE UP and PAGE DOWN KEYS.

- To move from page to page, click the << and >> buttons.

```
┌────────────────────────────────────────────────────────────┐
│ ■ ─                    Print Options                         │
├────────────────────────────────────────────────────────────┤
│ Page Margins:                                                │
│                                        ┌─Line Spacing:─────┐ │
│ Top    [1.00"]    Bottom [1.00"]       │ ○ Tight spacing   │ │
│ Left   [1.25"]    Right  [1.25"]       │                   │ │
│                                        │ ◉ Standard spacing│ │
│ □ Footers in smaller type              │ ○ Loose spacing   │ │
│                                        └───────────────────┘ │
│   [ Font... ]   [ Setup... ]        [ Cancel ]   [  OK  ]    │
└────────────────────────────────────────────────────────────┘
```

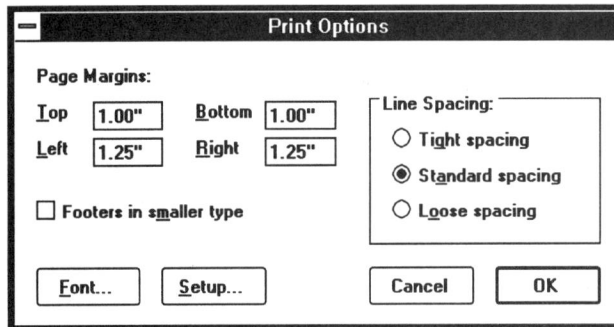

- To change the page margins or line spacing, click the **Options** button. (This will bring up the Print Options dialog pictured above.)

- To close the display windows, and return to the "Congratulations" screen, click the **Close** button.

If you don't use a mouse, you can activate these buttons by pressing the indicated hot key.

While it's displayed on screen, read your document thoroughly, and make sure that the information you typed or selected is correct. If you'd rather proofread from paper, print a copy by clicking the **Print** button.

- **If you want to change the font or margins:**
Click the **Options...** button. This will bring up the Print Options dialog. Make your changes as desired and click OK. Your changes will be reflecetd in the displayed document.

- **If you want to change your answers:**
Click the **Close** button. This will bring you back to the "Congratulations" screen. From there click the **Review/Change** button to change your answers. (See Section 3, below, for more information on reviewing and changing your answers.)

- **If the document is the way you want it:**
Print it out by clicking the **Print** button on the display window. In the print dialog box, just click **OK** to print everything.

Entering page numbers in the **From** and **To** boxes in the print dialog will cause the program to print only the pages you specify. Keep in mind that the program counts from the first page actually printed, which will be the instruction page(s). Be sure to factor this in if you want to print only certain pages of a specific document, because each document restarts the page numbering at page one. Use the "Page x of xx" prompt on the display window to determine precisely which pages you want to print.

After you have printed out the final documents, read the printed instructions and appropriate chapter of the legal manual for information on how to sign your documents and have them witnessed or notarized if necessary.

For your will, see Chapter 9 of the legal manual.

For your healthcare directions, see Chapter 13 of the legal manual.

For your final arrangements, see Chapter 14 of the legal manual.

3. Reviewing or Changing Your Answers

If after displaying or printing your document, you find something that you want to change, click the **Review/Change** button on the Congratulations screen. This will bring you to a Review or Change screen. (The screen shown here is for the will document. The other two documents screens are similar.)

```
┌──────────────────────────────────────────────────────────────────┐
│ ▬              WillMaker - Portfolio of John Doe Jr.            ▼ │
│  File   Edit   Options   Help                                      │
│                                                                    │
│     REVIEW OR CHANGE YOUR WILL                                     │
│    ┌ Introduction ────────────────────────────────────────────┐   │
│    │ ○ Introduction to making your will                        │   │
│    └───────────────────────────────────────────────────────────┘   │
│    ┌ Basics ──────────────┐  ┌ Bequests ──────────────────────┐   │
│    │ ○ Marital status      │  │ ○ Specific bequests             │   │
│    │ ○ Children            │  │ ○ Residuary bequest             │   │
│    │ ○ You and your residence│ │ ○ Cancelling debts             │   │
│    │ ○ Paying debts and taxes│ │ ○ Custodianships and trusts    │   │
│    └───────────────────────┘  └─────────────────────────────────┘   │
│    ┌ Nominations ─────────────────────────────────────────────┐   │
│    │ ○ Personal guardian                                       │   │
│    │ ○ Property guardian                                       │   │
│    │ ○ Personal representative (executor)                      │   │
│    └───────────────────────────────────────────────────────────┘   │
│    ┌──────────────────┐                      ┌─────────────┐      │
│    │ Display/Print    │                      │     OK      │      │
│    └──────────────────┘                      └─────────────┘      │
└──────────────────────────────────────────────────────────────────┘
```

This screen lists the various parts of the your WillMaker interview. To display a particular part, click on the button corresponding to where you want to go, then click **OK.** If you're not using a mouse, press the UP and DOWN ARROW KEYS to highlight a button, then press ENTER.

For example, to go back to the part of the interview concerning where you live, click **You and your residence**, then click **OK**. The program will return to the part of the interview where you entered your name. Your answer will be displayed in the context "I, John Smith, of California, San Francisco County, do hereby . . . ."

If you want to change an answer, you can do so. Click **OK** when you finish changing the answer. At this point, you will cycle through the remaining screens that are contained in that section of the interview, and then return to the Review or Change screen—with one exception. If you have changed an answer that affects other choices you have made in the program, such as changing your state of residence in your will, the program will make you review all of your answers.

Use this Review or Change screen to update your will, healthcare directions, or final arrangements whenever you deem it necessary. (See Chapter 10 of the legal manual for concerns about updating your will.)

4. Exporting to a Text File

WillMaker can store your completed will to a plain text (ASCII) file on your hard disk.

There is really no reason to export your will or healthcare directions to a text file. Most formatting including font, font size and page margins, can be done from within WillMaker itself.

Do not change the language of your documents under any circumstances Even slight changes can seriously affect the usefulness of your documents. Changes in the language can create confusion, contradictions and legal problems. If you have questions about the language in your documents, or if you would like to change the language in them, take the documents to an experienced estate planning attorney and get advice on how to accomplish your goals.

This exported file has no formatting (such as bold and italics) and no headers or footers. You will have to put the headers and footers in manually with your own word processor. All word processors that can read plain text files can load the plain text file produced by WillMaker.

To make a text file, click the **Export** button on the Congratulations screen. Your will clauses will be assembled and saved. The text file will be saved with the name you give it in the Export Text dialog box. The text file will be given a .TXT extension.

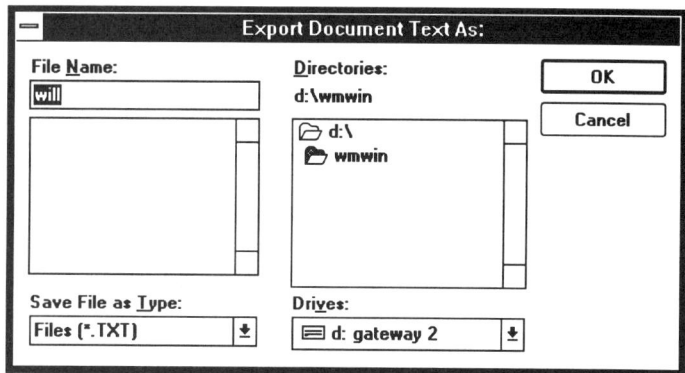

```
┌─────────────────────────────────────────────────────────────────┐
│ ▄  Export Document Text As:                                       │
├───────────────────────────────────────────────────────────────────┤
│  File Name:              Directories:                   ┌──────────┐│
│  ┌─────────────┐         d:\wmwin                       │    OK    ││
│  │will         │                                        └──────────┘│
│  └─────────────┘         ┌─────────────────┐           ┌──────────┐│
│  ┌─────────────┐         │ 📂 d:\           │           │  Cancel  ││
│  │             │         │ 📁 wmwin         │           └──────────┘│
│  │             │         │                 │                        │
│  └─────────────┘         └─────────────────┘                        │
│                                                                     │
│  Save File as Type:      Drives:                                   │
│  ┌─────────────┬──┐      ┌──────────────────┬──┐                  │
│  │Files (*.TXT)│ ↓│      │ 🖥 d: gateway 2   │ ↓│                  │
│  └─────────────┴──┘      └──────────────────┴──┘                  │
└─────────────────────────────────────────────────────────────────┘
```

To print out the exported document, you will have to open the text file with your word processor.

▶ Important Text File Notes

- Do not alter the language of your will.
- Each time you use the text file option, any text file you have previously made with the same name will be erased.
- To use a text file, you must use a word processing program to load the will text file by using the Open feature of the word processing program. Consult your word processor's manual or the directions that follow if you are not sure how to do this.
- Do not call Nolo Press Technical Support for instructions on how to operate your word processor. Consult the manual that came with your word processor on how to do the necessary operations.

Opening the Text File in a Word Processor

If you are making a text file of your will with WillMaker 5, carefully read the information in the exported file about how to place the proper headers and footers to correctly format your will or other document.

After you have made a text file and named it, start your word processing application. The steps for opening and editing a plain text (ASCII) should be found in the manual that came with your word processor.

When you open the file, read the instructions and important notes at the beginning of the file.

Delete the instructions from your exported file before you print out your final document.

D. Backing Up and Restoring Your WillMaker Portfolio Files

As with all important computer files, it is important to keep an extra copy of your WillMaker portfolio files on a floppy disk, stored in a safe place, in case something should happened to the files on your hard disk. (You can reinstall the rest of the program from the installation disks.)

1. Backing Up Your Files to a Floppy Disk

To back up your all of your portfolio files to a floppy drive:

1. Go to the Windows File Manager and double-click on the WM5WIN folder (assuming that is where you installed WillMaker 5 for Windows).

2. Choose **Copy** from the **File** menu.

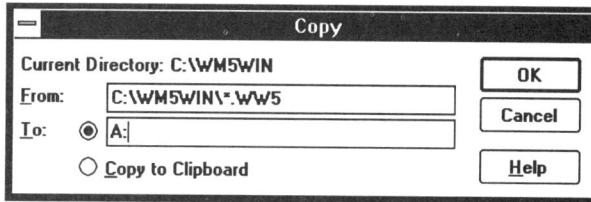

```
┌──────────────────────────────────────────────────────┐
│ ─                         Copy                         │
├──────────────────────────────────────────────────────┤
│ Current Directory: C:\WM5WIN                ┌────────┐ │
│ From:    ┌──────────────────────────────┐   │   OK   │ │
│          │ C:\WM5WIN\*.WW5              │   └────────┘ │
│ To:   ◉ ┌──────────────────────────────┐   ┌────────┐ │
│          │ A:│                          │   │ Cancel │ │
│          └──────────────────────────────┘   └────────┘ │
│       ○ Copy to Clipboard                   ┌────────┐ │
│                                             │  Help  │ │
│                                             └────────┘ │
└──────────────────────────────────────────────────────┘
```

3. When the copy dialog appears type

    C:\WM5WIN*.WW5

   in the "From" box, and

    A:\

   in the "To" box (if you are copying to drive B, type B:\).

4. Insert your floppy in the appropriate drive.

5. Click **OK**. (Copying should only take a second or two. Each portfolio file takes up about 3K on your disk.)

   When the files are copied, remove the disk and put it in a safe place.

2. Restoring Your Files from the Backup Copy

If at some point you need to restore one or more of your files from your backup copy, do the following:

1. Go to the Windows File Manager and double-click on the WM5WIN folder (assuming that is where you installed WillMaker 5 for Windows).

2. Choose **Copy** from the **File** menu.

```
┌──────────────────────────────────────────────────────┐
│ ─                         Copy                         │
├──────────────────────────────────────────────────────┤
│ Current Directory: C:\WM5WIN                ┌────────┐ │
│ From:    ┌──────────────────────────────┐   │   OK   │ │
│          │ A:\JOHN.WW5                  │   └────────┘ │
│ To:   ◉ ┌──────────────────────────────┐   ┌────────┐ │
│          │ C:\WM5WIN\JOHN.WW5│          │   │ Cancel │ │
│          └──────────────────────────────┘   └────────┘ │
│       ○ Copy to Clipboard                   ┌────────┐ │
│                                             │  Help  │ │
│                                             └────────┘ │
└──────────────────────────────────────────────────────┘
```

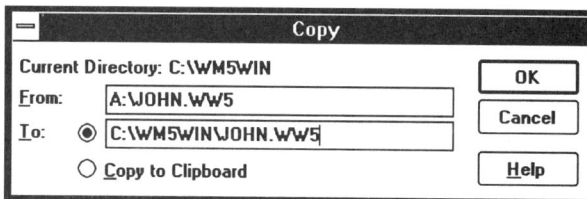

3. When the copy dialog appears, type the name of the file you want to restore from the floppy drive, in the "From" box, like this:

    A:\filename

(if you are copying to drive B, type `B:\filename`).

The file name should be the name of the file you are trying to restore. It should be an eight-character name with a WW5 extension.

Then type:

`C:\WM5WIN\`*filename*

in the "To" box.

4. Insert your floppy in the appropriate drive.

5. Click **OK**. (Copying should only take a few seconds.)

6. When the files are copied, remove the disk and put it in a safe place.

To begin working on the restored files or to check that the files were restored correctly:

1. Start WillMaker

2. Choose **Open** from the **File** menu.

3. Select the restored portfolio from the list.

Part 5. Problems Running WillMaker

A. Troubleshooting

This section of the manual briefly discusses some common technical difficulties you might encounter in running WillMaker on Windows.

On-screen help is also available by pulling down the **Help** menu.

1. Problems Reading the Installation Disk

If you try to run "A:SETUP" from the Program Manager's Run command, and receive a message:

"Application Execution Error", cannot find A:SETUP, or one of its components"

this means that your disk drive cannot read the setup disk—your disk drive is on the blink or the disk is defective.

Remove the disk from the drive.

Check the disk drive by using another disk that you have used before. If the disk drive operates properly, then the disk you have received may be defective. Contact Nolo Press Technical Support.

2. Additional Error Messages

ERROR	WHAT IT MEANS	WHAT TO DO
An error occurred: couldn't find the requested DOS path name	DOS couldn't find the path for a file it wants to open.	Call Nolo Technical Support.
An error occurred while assembling the document	The resource files of the program might be damaged.	Reinstall all program files. Try again. If that doesn't work, call Nolo Technical Support.
An error occurred: couldn't find the requested file	You may have too many files open.	Either quit other applications and TSR's or modify the FILES setting in your CONFIG.SYS file.
Disk access denied	The disk is locked.	Unlock it by sliding back the write-protect tab so that the hole in the top corner of the disk is closed.
Internal error: WillMaker attempted to access nonexistent memory	This shouldn't happen in WillMaker and it is probably a sign of a bug.	Try to remember the steps you did before the error appeared, then call Nolo Technical Support.
Internal error: attempt to overwrite existing file	WillMaker is attempting to overwrite an existing file without permission. This shouldn't happen in WillMaker.	Try to remember the steps you did before the error appeared, then call Nolo Technical Support.
Internal error: bad file number requested	This is a DOS error meaning that a bad file number was passed to one of its routines.	Try to remember the steps you did before the error appeared, then call Nolo Technical Support.
Internal error: memory blocks have been destroyed. (ECONTR.)	Don't worry. Your computer is not damaged. Memory that was allocated to WillMaker has been improperly used by some other application.	Quit WillMaker without saving your changes, as the whole system is probably unstable. Restart your machine.
Sorry, an internal data-module error occurred	Your portfolio file has been corrupted.	Quit and restart the program and attempt to repeat what you did. The problem may clear up on its own. If that doesn't work, contact Nolo Technical Support.

ERROR	WHAT IT MEANS	WHAT TO DO
Sorry, an internal error occurred	Something very serious is wrong with the program, either because of a disk error, memory error, or (gasp!) a bug.	Quit and restart the program and attempt to repeat what you did. The problem may clear up on its own. If not, try reinstalling the application. If that doesn't work, contact Nolo Technical Support.
Sorry, a needed resource cannot be found	The resource files of the program might be damaged.	Reinstall all program files and try again. If that doesn't work, call Nolo Technical support.
Sorry, the file has been corrupted and cannot be read	Your portfolio file has been corrupted.	Use a backup file.
Sorry, the file has been severely corrupted and cannot be read	Your portfolio file has been seriously corrupted.	Use a backup file.
Sorry, this file cannot be read by this version of WillMaker	The version of the file being read in cannot be read by this version of WillMaker.	Try to use the Convert command.
Sorry, this file cannot be read by WillMaker	You are trying to open or convert a file that is not recognized by WillMaker.	If you are sure the file you are attempting to use is a WillMaker data file, try a backup copy. If that doesn't work, contact Nolo Technical Support.
Sorry, WillMaker ran out of memory	The program ran out of memory.	Try quitting any other program running under Windows. Turn on virtual memory (if you are running Windows in Enhanced mode). Buy more RAM.
System Error; Internal XVT Error: XXXXX-XXXXX	Something very serious is wrong with the program, either because of a disk error, memory error, or (gasp!) a bug.	Jot down the numbers that appear in the dialog. Quit and restart the program, then repeat what you did. If that doesn't work, contact Nolo Technical Support.
Sorry, WillMaker was unable to open the resource file	WillMaker couldn't find the file named "WMWRSC.d11."	Make sure "WMWRSC.d11" is in the same directory as WillMaker. Try reinstalling all program files.
WillMaker cannot open any more files	Your computer has too many files open.	Either quit other applications and TSR's or modify the FILES setting in your CONFIG.SYS.
WillMaker cannot open that file (it may be locked)	WillMaker was not allowed to open a file because it didn't have permission to open it, either because it is in use, or it is locked.	Check to make sure you don't have two instances of WillMaker running. Also check that the file (or the disk) is not locked.

WINDOWS USERS' GUIDE

3. Other Problems that Might Arise

Displayed and Printed Document Shows Line After Line of "/////"

These hash marks are there as a precaution. WillMaker has built-in formatting that forces certain blocks of text to stay together on the same page.

For example, it is a requirement for making a legally valid will that a few lines setting out something of substance in your will appear on the same page as your signature and the signatures on your witnesses. Often this results in a page break which leaves less than a full page of text on the previous page. When space is left at the bottom of the page, but there is more text of the document on the next page, it is customary to fill in remaining the "blank" lines with hash marks—the "/////" you see on the page.

This prevents someone from later tampering with your will and filling in the blank space with additional clauses after you have signed it.

Printing Problems Running under Windows

Most Windows printing problems are caused by the Print Setup being set incorrectly. Select the Print Setup from the **F**ile menu. Check to make sure the settings for your printer are correct. For example, if your printer uses a sheet feeder, make sure the print setup for your printer is set for sheet feeding.

B. Calling Nolo Press Technical Support

If you have problems that are not cleared up in the Troubleshooting section, call Nolo Press Technical Support: (510) 549-1976 between 9 am and 5 pm Pacific Time, Monday through Friday.

When you call, try to be in front of the computer with which you are having the problem. And please have the following information ready:

- version of WillMaker (should be 5 or higher)

- the point in the program where the problem occurred

- whether you can duplicate the problem

- version of DOS you are running (which you can get by typing "VER" at the DOS command prompt)

- version of Windows you are running (which you can get by choosing the **About the Program Manager...** command from the **Help** menu)

- the brand and model of computer you are using, and

- the brand and model of printer—if you are having trouble printing.

The following information may also be helpful, which you can get by typing MSD at the DOS command prompt.

- type of BIOS (Brand)

- amount of RAM

- description of any special printer or monitor interface hardware, and

- any TSRs or screen savers you are running. ▲

WILLMAKER®

LEGAL GUIDE

Legal Guide Contents

1 About Wills

2 The Basics

3 About You

4 About Your Property

5 How to Leave Your Property

6 Caring for Children and Their Property

7 Choosing a Personal Representative or Executor

8 Paying Debts and Expenses

9 Making It Legal: Final Steps

10 Keeping Your Will Up-to-Date

11 Explanatory Letters

12 Estate Planning

13 Healthcare Directives

14 Final Arrangements

15 If You Need Expert Help

1 About Wills

Making a will is an excellent way to ensure that your plans for leaving property to family and friends are carried out after you die. You can efficiently and safely write your own legal will using the WillMaker program. But before you start, it is a good idea to read this chapter and Chapter 2, which explain generally what a will can accomplish and how you can use WillMaker to meet your needs.

A. Making It Legal

For a will to be legally valid and to accomplish what you want it to, both you—the person making the will—and the will itself, must meet some technical requirements.

1. Who Can Make a Will

Most states require that a person must be at least 18 and of sound mind before he or she can make a valid will. (These requirements are discussed in more detail in Chapter 3.)

2. Will Requirements

The laws in each state control whether a will made by a resident of the state is valid—and a will that is valid in the state where it is made is valid in all other states. Contrary to what many people believe, a will need not be notarized to be legally valid. (See Chapter 9, Section B, for a discussion of notarizing self-proving affidavits.) There are surprisingly few legal restrictions and requirements in the willmaking process. In most states, a will must:

- include at least one substantive provision—either giving away some property or naming a guardian to care for minor children who are left without parents
- be signed and dated by the person making it

- be witnessed by at least two other people who are not named to take property under the will, and

- be clearly written. No nonsensical, legalistic-sounding language such as: "I hereby give, bequeath and devise" is necessary.

3. Handwritten Wills

In a minority of states, unwitnessed, handwritten wills—called holographic wills—are legally valid. And a few states accept the historical holdover of oral wills under very limited circumstances, such as when a mortally wounded soldier utters last wishes. But handwritten and oral wills are fraught with possible legal problems. Most obviously, after your death, it may be difficult to prove that your unwitnessed, handwritten document was actually written by you and intended to be your will. It may be almost impossible to prove the authenticity of an oral will.

A properly signed, witnessed will is much less vulnerable to challenge by anyone claiming it was forged or fabricated. If need be, witnesses can later testify in court that the person whose name is on the will is the same person who signed it, and that making the will was a voluntary and knowing act.

B. What Happens If You Die Without a Will

If you die without leaving a valid will, money and other property you own at death will be divided and distributed to others according to your state's intestate succession laws. These laws divide all property between a few close relatives according to a set formula—and completely exclude more distant relatives, friends and charities.

These legal formulas are unlikely to mirror most peoples' wishes. Dividing property according to intestate succession laws is likely to be unsatisfactory if you are married and have no children, because most state laws require your spouse to share your property with your parents. And the situation is even worse for unmarried couples. No state's intestate succession law gives an unmarried partner any property.

Also, if you have minor children, another important reason to make a will is to name a personal guardian to care for them. This is an important concern of most parents who worry that their children will be left without a caretaker if both die or are unavailable. Intestate succession laws do not deal with this, leaving it up to the courts and social service agencies to find and appoint a guardian.

C. Basic Decisions about Property and Children

Making a will is not difficult, but it is undeniably a serious and sobering process. Before you begin, get organized and focus on a number of important considerations:

- What do you own?
- Who would you like to get your property?
- Who is the best person to care for your minor children and who is best suited to manage property you leave them?
- Who should you appoint to see that your property is distributed according to your wishes after your death?

This manual offers guidance on how to use WillMaker to implement your decisions in all of these areas. The choices, however, are up to you.

D. A Will Is Not the Only Way to Leave Property

Be aware that a will is not the only way—and in some cases, not the best way—to transfer ownership of your property to another person upon your death. Most property passed by will must go through a legal process known as probate, in which the will is filed with a court, property is located and gathered by an estate executor or administrator, debts and taxes still owed are paid and the remaining property is distributed as the will directs.

Probate has drawbacks. It can be lengthy, commonly taking a year or more. And it can also be expensive, often requiring the services of lawyers or other specialists. In many states, the lawyer handling the probate is paid a percentage of the total value of the estate—that is, the property owned by the deceased person at death. This fee arrangement typically means that a portion of your property you intended for family and friends goes instead to pay lawyers.

In short, if you are making a will—especially if you are older and own a fair amount of property—consider whether it makes sense for you to plan now to pay the least amount in probate fees, and consider how best to use a will as part of a larger estate plan. (See Chapter 12 for an overview of basic estate planning techniques.)

Estate Tax Concerns   Also, if non-tax-exempt property in your estate when you die is worth more than $600,000, the federal government will tax it. Your state may also impose inheritance and estate taxes on the property. Making tax-exempt gifts during your life, along with several other strategies, can reduce the size of your estate and by doing so, reduce its estate and inheritance tax liability. (See Chapter 12, Section D.)

▶ **Is a WillMaker Will Safe?**

Traditionally, wills have been associated with rumpled-suited lawyers, quill pens and offices full of antiques—not with the high tech hum of computers. Times have changed. It is not easy to find a friendly, reasonably-priced family solicitor you can trust these days. Fortunately, the computer has quickly proven to be an ideal tool for assisting informed consumers in making simple wills. It will never betray your confidences or urge you to do anything you do not feel is right. And it will not charge you a cent to revise your will should your needs change.

The reason computers are such efficient willmaking tools is that writing wills involves little more than systematically collecting answers to well-defined questions, then translating the answers into tried and true legal language developed over hundreds of years. WillMaker, which has been in wide and successful use for nearly a decade, prompts you to answer the necessary questions—and produces a will that fits your circumstances and is legal in your state.

E. The Role of Lawyers in Making Wills

As a way to decide who gets your property, the will has been around in substantially the same form for about 500 years. For the first 450 years, self-help was the rule and lawyer assistance the exception. When this country was founded, or even during the Civil War, it was highly unusual for a person to hire a lawyer to set out formally what should be done with his or her property. However, in the past 50 years, the legal profession has scored a public relations coup by convincing many people that writing a will without a lawyer is like doing your own brain surgery. This is nonsense.

But you may have a question about your particular situation that WillMaker does not answer. Or perhaps you have a very large estate—worth over $1 million—and want to engage in some sophisticated tax planning. Or you may simply be comforted by having a lawyer give your WillMaker will a once-over. These are legitimate concerns and it is sensible to act on them. (See Chapter 15 for a discussion of the legal advice available.) ▲

2 The Basics

Because they reflect peoples' intentions of how and to whom they want to leave property, wills can be as complex and intricate as life. While laws broadly regulate the procedures for valid willmaking, you are generally free to write a will to meet your needs. Of course, this freedom can be dizzying to those who are not used to wading in the muck of legal documents.

WillMaker offers considerable guidance, so that the task of willmaking will be understandable and legal rules will not be trampled.

The program works by having you systematically answer questions. As you will soon see, you either already have enough information to answer them easily, or you can quickly get your hands on it.

A. What You Can Do with WillMaker

This chapter gives you a quick survey of what you can and cannot do with the WillMaker program. Each area is discussed in greater detail, both in the program information screens and in other chapters in the manual.

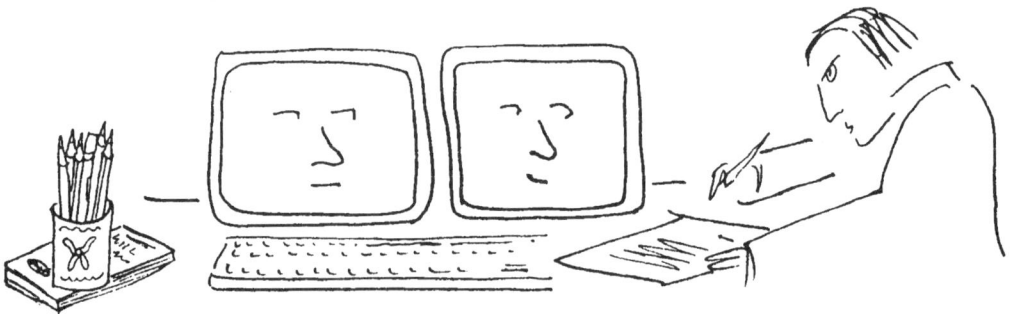

1. Name Beneficiaries to Get Specific Property

WillMaker allows you to make up to 100 separate gifts, called specific bequests, of cash, personal property, or real estate to your spouse, children, grandchildren, or anyone else—including friends, business associates, charities or other organizations.

Example

Using WillMaker, Robin leaves her interest in the family home to her spouse Lee, her valuable coin collection to one of her children, her boat to another child, her computer to a charity and $5,000 to her two aunts, in equal shares.

Example

Raymond, a lifelong bachelor, follows WillMaker's directions and leaves his house to his favorite charity. He divides his personal possessions among 15 different relatives and friends.

Example

Darryl and Floyd have lived together for several years. Darryl wants to leave Floyd all of his property, which includes his car, time-share ownership in a condominium, a savings account and miscellaneous personal belongings. He can use WillMaker to accomplish this.

2. Name Alternate Beneficiaries

Using WillMaker, all beneficiaries you name can inherit property under your will as long as they survive you by 45 days. The reason that WillMaker imposes this 45-day rule is that you do not want to leave your property to a beneficiary who dies very shortly after you do, because that property will then be passed along to that person's inheritors. These beneficiaries are not likely to be the ones you would choose to receive your property.

Also, for every bequest you make using WillMaker, you can specify another beneficiary to take the property if your first choice dies before you do or does not survive by the required period.

Example

Gene wants to leave his house to his daughters, Jenny and Liza, in equal shares. Jenny has two very young children; Liza has two grown children. Gene wants to structure his will so that if Jenny does not survive him by 45 days, her share in the house will go to her husband Greg, and if Liza does not survive him by 45 days, her share will go to her children. Using WillMaker, Gene makes two separate bequests—one to Liza and one to Jenny—of one-half interests in his house. He designates Liza's children as alternate beneficiaries for her bequest and designates Jenny's husband as an alternate beneficiary of her share.

3. Name Someone to Take All Property Remaining in Your Estate

All the property left over after you have made specific bequests of personal property and real estate is called your residuary estate. You can and should use WillMaker to designate a residuary beneficiary to inherit your residuary estate.

Example

Annie wants to make a number of small bequests to friends and charities, but to leave the bulk of her property to her friend Maureen. She accomplishes this by using the specific bequest screens to make the small gifts, and then names Maureen as residuary beneficiary. There is no need for her to list the property that goes to Maureen. The very nature of the residuary estate is that the residuary beneficiary—in this case, Maureen—gets everything that is left over after the specific bequests are distributed.

Fast Use for Simple Estate Plans

If you want all your property to go to only one or to a small group of beneficiaries, you can make efficient use of WillMaker by skipping the specific bequest screens in the program and leaving all your property to one or more loved ones or a favorite charity by naming them as residuary beneficiaries. If you designate more than one residuary beneficiary, each will take an equal share unless you specify differently by listing the percentage in parentheses after each name.

4. Name a Guardian to Care for Your Children

You may use WillMaker to name a personal guardian to care for your minor children until they reach 18 in case there is no natural or adoptive parent to handle these duties. If your children need a guardian after your death, a court will formally review your choice. Your choice will normally be approved unless the person you name refuses to assume the responsibility, or the court becomes convinced that the best interests of your children would be better served if they were left in the care of someone else.

Example

Millicent names her friend Vera to serve as personal guardian in the event that her husband, Frank, dies at the same time she does or is otherwise unavailable to care for their three children. Millicent and Frank die together in an earthquake. The court appoints Vera as personal guardian for all three children since her ability to serve has not been questioned. If Frank had written a will naming another person to serve as guardian, however, the court would have to choose between those nominated.

5. Name Someone to Manage Property Left to Children

You may leave property to your own or other peoples' children. But at your death, property left to minors will have to be managed by an adult until they turn 18. And in many cases, it may be most prudent to have property left to them managed for a longer period.

WillMaker allows you to name a trusted person—or, if no one is available, you can name an institution such as a bank or trust company—to manage property left to a minor. (The management methods available are different from state to state—and are discussed in detail in Chapter 6.)

Management involves safeguarding and spending the property for the young person's education, healthcare and basic living needs, keeping good records of these expenditures and seeing that income taxes are paid.

Management ends at the age you specify. What is left of the property is then distributed to the minor.

Do Not Use WillMaker for Beneficiaries with Special Needs

It is common to set up property management when a beneficiary is mentally or physically disadvantaged, or manages money poorly. The management provided under WillMaker is not sufficiently detailed to provide adequately for disadvantaged people, or those with special problems such as spendthrift tendencies or substance abuse. Management for people in these situations should be custom-tailored to fit their needs. If you need this type of management, consult an experienced attorney. (See Chapter 15 for guidance in finding and using attorneys.)

6. Name a Personal Representative or Executor to Handle Your Estate

With WillMaker, you can name a personal representative for your estate. This person, called an executor in some states, will be responsible for making sure the provisions in your will are carried out and your property distributed as your will directs. The personal representative can be any competent adult. Commonly, people name a spouse or other close relative or friend or—for large estates or where no trusted person is able to serve—a financial institution such as a bank or savings and loan. Because of the risk of disagreement or conflict, WillMaker does not allow you to name two or more people to act as joint personal representatives.

It is also wise to use WillMaker to name an alternate personal representative in case your first choice becomes unable or unwilling to serve.

Example

Rick and Phyllis both use WillMaker to complete wills naming each other as personal representative in case the other dies first. They both name Rick's father as an alternate personal representative to take their property in the event they die simultaneously.

Example

Rick and Phyllis do not wish to burden their relatives with having to take care of their fairly considerable estate. Each names the Third National Bank as personal representative after checking that their estate is large enough so that this bank will be willing to serve.

7. Cancel Debts Others Owe You

You can use WillMaker to relieve any debtors who owe you money at your death of the responsibility of paying your survivors. All you need to do is specify the debts and the people who owe them. WillMaker will then include a statement in your will, canceling the debts. If a debt is canceled in this way, WillMaker also automatically wipes out any interest that has accrued on it as of your death.

Example

Cynthia has lent $25,000 at 10% annual interest to her son George as a downpayment on a house. She uses WillMaker to cancel this debt. At her death, George need not pay her estate the remaining balance of the loan, or the interest accrued on it.

8. Designate How Debts, Expenses and Taxes Are to Be Paid

WillMaker allows you to designate a particular source of money or other specific assets from which your personal representative, or executor, should pay your debts, expenses of probate and any estate and inheritance taxes.

Example

Brent owns a savings account, a portfolio of stocks and bonds, an R.V. and two cars. He uses WillMaker to make a will—leaving his R.V. and stocks and bonds to his nephew, his cars to his niece and his savings account to his favorite charity, River Friends. He also designates the savings account as the source of payment of his debts and expenses of probate. Under this arrangement, River Friends will receive whatever is left in the savings account after debts and expenses of probate have been paid.

Example

Calvin's estate is valued at over $600,000. It is likely that his estate will owe some federal estate taxes when he dies. He uses WillMaker to specify that any estate tax he owes should be paid proportionately from all the property subject to the tax. If there is estate tax liability, the personal representative he designates will require that each of Calvin's beneficiaries pay part of the tax in the same proportion their bequest bears to the value of Calvin's estate as a whole.

B. What You Cannot Do with WillMaker

WillMaker produces a simple will that meets the needs of most people. But there are some common sense restrictions built into the program. Some of the restrictions are designed to prevent you from writing in conditions that may not be legally valid. Others are intended to keep the program simple and easy to use.

1. You Cannot Leave Bequests with Conditions

To ensure that property goes to people you want to have it, WillMaker automatically imposes the condition that, to inherit, your beneficiaries must survive you by 45 days. If they don't survive by that amount of time, the property you had slated for them will pass instead to the person or institution you have named as a residuary beneficiary, or it will go to the one you have named to take your residuary estate.

In addition, you cannot make a bequest that will take effect only if a certain condition comes true—an if, and or but such as "$5,000 to Ted if he stops smoking." Such conditional bequests are confusing and usually require someone to oversee and supervise the erstwhile inheritors to be sure the conditions are satisfied. If you doubt this, consider that someone would have to constantly check up on Ted to make sure he never took a puff.

So, to use WillMaker, you must first decide that you want to leave property to people outright; you cannot make them jump through hoops or change their behavior to get it.

2. You Cannot Make Joint Wills

In the past, it was common for a married couple who had an agreed scheme for how to distribute all their property to write one document together: a joint will. But time has shown that idea to be fraught with difficulties.

WillMaker requires that each spouse make his or her own will, even if both agree about how their property is to be distributed. This limitation is not imposed to annoy people; it has good legal causes.

- Inevitably, one spouse owns some property that the other does not. Should even one of the two die without a will, the state will claim this property, or distribute it to someone in the line of relatives. This is often contrary to what the deceased would have wished.

- Joint wills are intended to prevent the surviving spouse from changing his or her mind about what to do with the property after the first spouse dies. The practical effect is to tie up the property for years in title and probate determinations—often until long after the second spouse dies.

- Many court battles are fought over whether the surviving spouse is legally entitled to revoke any part of the will.

There are still some lawyers who will agree to write joint wills for clients, but they do so in the face of the risk that such wills may become cumbersome or even found invalid in later court challenges. For these reasons, it is best for both spouses to write separate wills—a bit more time-consuming, perhaps, but a lot safer from a legal standpoint.

3. You Cannot Explain the Reasons for Leaving Your Property

Most of the time, the act of leaving property to people—or choosing not to—speaks for itself. Occasionally, however, people making wills want to explain to survivors the reasons they left property as they did. This might be the case, for example, if you opt to leave one of your two children more property than the other to equal out the loan you made during your lifetime to help one of them buy a house. Although the yearning to make such explanations is understandable, WillMaker does not allow you to do it in your will, because of the risk that you might add legally confusing language to the document.

However, there is an easy and legally safe way to provide your heirs with explanations for your bequests. Chapter 11, Section B, of the manual shows you how to draft a letter that you can attach to your will, explaining your reasons for leaving property to some people—or not leaving it to others.

4. You Cannot Name Co-Guardians or Different Guardians for Your Minor Children or Their Property

WillMaker allows you to name one personal guardian to care for all your minor children and one guardian to care for their property. While these guardians may be two different people, you may not name two people to share the job of being a personal or property guardian for your children. (See Chapter 6.) At first glance, it may seem to be a good idea to divide up the job—naming two people or a married couple to agree to take on the responsibility of caring for your children or supervising their property if you die while they are still young.

But a closer look reveals that naming co-guardians often presents more problems than it solves. For example, as life unwinds, the loving couple you named to jointly care for your children may divorce—making it impossible for them to be in the same room together, much less agree on the best way to raise a child. In such cases, courts are often called in to decide who is the most fitting guardian—a process that may be long, costly and very often heart-rending.

Also, WillMaker does not allow you to split up the job and name separate guardians for each of your children. That would render the program too complex for the rare occasions that such an arrangement might be useful. People who jointly own property or have children together should review their wills together to be sure they do not provide conflicting information— such as each parent naming a different guardian for the children in his or her will.

5. You Cannot Control Property Forever

Bequests given in a WillMaker will must take effect as soon as you die. You cannot make a bequest by will with the property to be used for a person's life and then be given to a second person when the first person dies.

Example

Emory wants his grandchildren to inherit his house, but wants his wife to first have the right to live in the house until her death. He cannot use WillMaker to accomplish this. Emory would have to leave his house in trust to his spouse for her life and then to his grandchildren upon his spouse's death. He should consult a lawyer to have the necessary trust prepared.

6. You Cannot Set Up Trusts to Avoid Taxes

If your estate is large—$600,000 or more—or if you are elderly or ill, tax-planning trusts may be important to use to preserve your property for your beneficiaries. WillMaker does not allow you to set up the types of trusts commonly used to lessen federal estate taxes, such as marital life estate trusts or generation-skipping trusts. To do this, you will probably need to consult a lawyer. (See Chapter 12, Section D, for more information on using trusts as part of your estate plan.)

7. You Cannot Require Your Executor or Property Managers to Post Bond

A bond is like an insurance policy that protects the beneficiaries in the unlikely event that the personal representative wrongfully spends or distributes estate property. Because the premium or fee that must be paid for a bond comes out of the estate, leaving less money for the beneficiaries, most wills for small or moderate estates do not require one. Following this general practice, the will produced by the WillMaker program does not require a bond. Instead, you should take care to appoint someone you know to be trustworthy.

C. A Look at a WillMaker Will

You may wish now to take a look at a WillMaker will and instructions that print out with it. Do not be alarmed if the will does not exactly match the one you produce. Your WillMaker will is tailored to your property, circumstances and state laws. Nearly every paragraph—or clause—is explained in the brackets following it.

IMPORTANT NOTES

Before you sign Read your will carefully. Is everything printed as you intended? Do you understand the meaning of every word?

While you sign For your will to be valid you must be of sound mind and of the age required in your state. This is almost always 18.

Your will must be witnessed by three people, even though only two are legally required in most states. The witnesses should be in your and each other's presence when you sign the will, but they need not read it.

You must say to the witnesses that you intend this to be your will. Initial and date each page where indicated. Then sign the last page in the presence of the witnesses. Use exactly the form of your name printed on the will. The witnesses should state that they realize you intend this to be your will and they should then, in your presence, initial each page on the same line you did and sign the last page in the space indicated for witnesses, and include their addresses.

After you sign   Keep your will in a safe place, where it can be readily found. You may make photocopies. However, only the signed original is legally valid and can be probated.

If there are major changes in your life, you should make a new will and have it signed and witnessed. Destroy the original of your old will and all copies. Changes that make it wise for you to make a new will include: having or adopting a child, moving to another state, the death of anyone named in your will, a change of marital status, and a significant change in the property you own.

Keep up-to-date   Fill out the WillMaker registration card in the manual and send it to Nolo Press at the address given. If you do not have a copy of the manual include $69.95 for a full WillMaker package.

WILL OF JAMES MOOREHEAD

PERSONAL INFORMATION

I, James Moorehead, a resident of the State of California, Humboldt County, declare that this is my will. My Social Security Number is 123-45-6789.

REVOCATION OF PREVIOUS WILLS

FIRST: I revoke all wills and codicils that I have previously made.

[This provision makes clear that this is the will to be used—not any other wills or amendments to those wills—called codicils—that were made earlier. All earlier wills and codicils that you have made previously should also be physically destroyed.]

MARITAL STATUS

SECOND: I am married to Wilma Jazmin Moorehead.

[Here you identify your spouse—if you are married. If you are not married, this provision won't appear.]

CHILDREN

THIRD: I have the following child(ren) now living: William Moorehead, Vera Moorehead and Frank Moorehead.

[This part of your will should name all of your natural born and adopted children; your stepchildren should not be included here. By naming all your children, you will prevent a child from claiming that he or she was accidentally overlooked in your will. It will also ward off later claims that they are entitled to a statutory share against your

GRANDCHILDREN

FOURTH: I have the following grandchild(ren) born to a child of mine who is deceased: Gloria Sadowski.

[This clause should list all of your grandchildren whose parent—your child—is deceased. By naming all such grandchildren, you will prevent them from claiming that they were accidentally overlooked in your will. It will also ward off later claims that they are entitled to a statutory share against your wishes.]

Page 1   Initials _____   _____   _____   _____   Date _____

FAILURE TO LEAVE PROPERTY

FIFTH: If I do not leave property in this will to one or more of the children or grandchildren I have identified above, my failure to do so is intentional.

[This clause makes clear that if you did not leave a child—or a child of one of your children who is deceased—any property in your will, that decision was intentional rather than accidental. This language helps protect you against claims by such a child or grandchild that he or she was accidentally overlooked in your will when it came to distributing your property.]

DEFINITIONS

SIXTH: As used in this will, the term "specific bequest" refers to a gift of specifically identified property that I leave in this will. The term "residuary estate" refers to all property subject to this will that is not passed by specific bequest or that is specifically left to or becomes a part of my residuary estate when a beneficiary of a specific bequest does not survive me.

[This language defines the terms specific bequest, residuary estate and residuary bequest as they are used in this will.]

SPECIFIC BEQUESTS OF PROPERTY

SEVENTH: I give $20,000 to William Moorehead. However, if William Moorehead does not survive me, the living children of William Moorehead shall take the property. If there are no children, the property shall go to Michael Reynolds and Ricca Smolinski.

[This language leaves a specific item of property—$20,000—to William Moorehead, the person named to receive it. Moorehead's children will get the property if he does not survive the willmaker—and the two named alternates will get the property if there are no children.]

EIGHTH: I give my rare coin collection to Cynthia Drucelli, Matthew Drucelli and Stephen Price. However, if one of these beneficiaries does not survive me, the surviving beneficiaries shall take his or her share equally. If there are no surviving beneficiaries, the property shall go to Anthony Clark.

[This language leaves a specific item of property to three people and provides that if one of the three do not survive the willmaker, the survivors shall take the deceased person's share. If there are no surviving first choice beneficiaries, the property will go to the named alternate.]

Page 2   Initials _____   _____   _____   _____   Date _____

NINTH: I give my collection of Nash cars to The City Motor Museum and Wilhemina Clark. However, if one of these beneficiaries does not survive me, the surviving beneficiaries shall take that beneficiary's share equally.

[This will leaves specific property to an organization and a person, and provides that if one of the beneficiaries fails to survive the willmaker, the property shall pass to the survivor.]

RESIDUARY BEQUEST

TENTH: I give my residuary estate to Wilma Jazmin Moorehead. However, if Wilma Jazmin Moorehead does not survive me, the living children of Wilma Jazmin Moorehead shall take my residuary estate. If Wilma Jazmin Moorehead does not survive me and leaves no living children, my residuary estate shall go to Lee Moorehead Gwen.

[This clause gives the residuary estate to the person named. Your residuary estate, which is defined in the sixth clause of the will shown here, consists of all your property that is not passed under one of the specific bequest clauses in your will. If the person named here to take the residuary estate does not survive the willmaker, the residuary estate will pass to that person's children. If there are no living children, then the property goes to the alternate beneficiary named. This arrangement reflects choices the willmaker made while using the WillMaker program. There are a number of other ways to leave your residuary estate.]

LIENS AND ENCUMBRANCES

ELEVENTH: All personal and real property I give in a specific or residuary bequest shall pass subject to any encumbrances or liens on the property.

[This language means that whoever inherits any real estate also inherits the mortgage and other legal claims against the property (liens), and anyone who inherits property that is subject to a loan (such as a car loan) gets the debt as well as the property.]

SURVIVORSHIP PERIOD

TWELFTH: When this will states that a beneficiary must survive me to receive a specific bequest or residuary bequest, he or she must survive me by 45 days.

Page 3   Initials _____   _____   _____   _____   Date _____

[This language means that to receive property under your will, a person must be alive for at least 45 days after your death. Otherwise, the property will go to whoever you named as an alternate. This language keeps from defeating your plan for property disposition if a beneficiary dies within a short time of you. It also prevents the confusionassociated with the simultaneous death of two spouses, when it is hard to tell who gets the property they have left each other. Under this clause, property left to a spouse who dies within 45 days of the first spouse, including a spouse who dies simultaneously, will go to whoever has been named as alternate.]

DIVISION OF BEQUESTS

THIRTEENTH: Any specific bequest or residuary bequest made in this will to two or more beneficiaries shall be shared equally among them, unless unequal shares are specifically indicated.

[This language provides that for all specific and residuary bequests that are made to two or more people, the property shall be split equally between the people, unless the bequest itself says otherwise. If you want to give property to be split among people in unequal shares, you need to indicate that when you are describing the bequest by including the percentage share in parentheses after each beneficiary's name. Otherwise, it will be presumed that you wanted the property split equally.]

PERSONAL GUARDIAN

FOURTEENTH: If at my death a guardian is needed to care for my minor child or children, I name Madelyn Cosette as guardian. If this person shall for any reason fail to qualify or cease to act as guardian, I name Pierre Cosette to serve as guardian. No bond shall be required of any personal guardian appointed.

[This clause names someone to provide parental-type care for minor children if there is no natural parent on the scene able to provide it. The clause also provides for an alternate to step in if the first choice is not able or willing to act when the moment comes. When making your own will, be aware that if there is a natural parent on the scene, that parent will be awarded custody of the children, even if you named someone else as personal guardian, unless it is shown that the children would be at risk of harm. The clause also provides that the personal guardian need not provide a bond to secure faithful performance of his or her duties.]

PROPERTY GUARDIAN

FIFTEENTH: If at my death, a guardian is needed to care for any property belonging to my minor child or children, I name Robert Johannson as property guardian. If this person for any reason does not qualify or ceases to act as property guardian, I name Bill Moorehead to serve as property guardian.

No bond shall be required of any property guardian appointed.

[This clause appoints someone to manage property you leave minor children outside of the will, as in a life insurance property or living trust. This person will also manage property left to minor children under a will if the willmaker does not use one of the other property management devices provided by WillMaker for this purpose—that is, the UTMA or the WillMaker children's trust. You may also appoint an alternate property guardian in case your first choice is not able or willing to serve when the time comes. The clause also provides that the personal guardian need not provide a bond—a kind of insurance of good performance—to secure that he or she will act faithfully.]

PROPERTY MANAGEMENT

SIXTEENTH: All specific bequests and residuary bequests made in this will to Frank Moorehead shall be given to Lynette Leander, to be held until Frank Moorehead reaches age 25, as custodian for Frank Moorehead under the California Uniform Transfers to Minors Act. If Lynette Leander cannot serve as custodian of property left to Frank Moorehead under this will, Hank Leander shall serve instead.

[This clause provides that all property given to the minor or young adult named in the clause shall be managed by the person named as the custodian until the minor or young adult turns the age indicated. An alternate custodian is also named in case the first choice custodian is unable or unwilling to serve when the time comes.]

SEVENTEENTH: All specific bequests and residuary bequests made in this will to Vera Moorehead shall be held in a separate trust for Vera Moorehead until he or she reaches age 34. This trust shall be managed under the trust administration provisions set forth in this will. The trustee for the Vera Moorehead trust shall be Wilma Jazmin Moorehead. If Wilma Jazmin Moorehead cannot serve, the trustee shall be Roberta Durango.

No bond shall be required of any trustee.

Page 5   Initials _____ _____ _____ _____   Date _____

[This clause provides that all property given to the minor or young adult named in the clause shall be held in trust—that is, managed strictly for the benefit of the minor or young adult—by the person named as the trustee until the minor or young adult turns the age indicated. An alternate trustee is also named in case the first choice trustee is unable or unwilling to serve when the time comes.]

TRUST ADMINISTRATION PROVISIONS

EIGHTEENTH: All trusts established in this will shall be managed subject to the following provisions:

(a) Any trust income which is not distributed to a beneficiary by the trustee shall be accumulated and added to the principal of the trust administered for that beneficiary.

[Every trust involves two types of property: the property in the trust—called the trust principal—and the income that is earned by investing the principal. This clause assures that the trustee must add to the trust principal any income that is earned on the principal, unless the income is distributed to the trust beneficiary.]

(b) Until a trust beneficiary reaches the age specified for final distribution of the principal, the trustee may distribute some or all of the principal or net income of the trust as the trustee deems necessary for the child's health, support, maintenance and education. "Education" includes, but is not limited to, college, graduate, postgraduate and vocational studies and reasonably-related living expenses.

[This clause lets the trustee spend the trust principal for the minor or young adult's general living, health and educational needs. The clause gives the trustee great latitude in how this is done and what amount will be spent. Because of this discretion, it is appropriate to choose as trustee someone who shares your general attitude about raising children.]

(c) In deciding whether to make a distribution to a beneficiary, the trustee may take into account the beneficiary's other income, resources and sources of support.

[This clause lets the trustee withhold the trust principal from the trust beneficiary if, in the trustee's opinion, the beneficiary has sufficient income from other sources.]

(d) A trust shall terminate when:

(1) the beneficiary reaches the age specified for final distribution of the principal

Page 6   Initials _____   _____   _____   _____   Date _____

(2) the beneficiary dies before the age specified for final distribution of the principal, or

(3) the trust principal is exhausted through distributions allowed under these provisions.

If a trust terminates for reason (1), the remaining principal and accumulated net income of the trust shall pass to the beneficiary. If a trust terminates for reason (2), the principal and accumulated net income of the trust shall pass under the beneficiary's will, or if there is no will, to his or her heirs.

[This clause sets three different conditions for when the trust shall end. The first is when the minor or young adult reaches the age specified for the trust to end. If the trust ends for this reason, the minor or young adult gets whatever trust principal and accumulated income is left. The trust will also end if the minor or young adult dies before the age set for the trust to end. If the trust ends for this reason, the principal and amount accumulated in the trust goes to whoever the young adult named in his or her will to get it, or if there is no will, to the minor or young adult's legal heirs—such as parents, brothers and sisters. A third occurrence that will cause the trust to end is when there is no trust principal left—or so little left that it's no longer financially feasible to maintain it.]

(e) In addition to other powers granted a trustee in this will, a trustee shall have:

(1) all the powers generally conferred on trustees by the laws of the state having jurisdiction over the trust

(2) the powers conferred by this will on the personal representative as to accumulated property and income in each trust, and

(3) the authority to hire and pay from trust assets the reasonable fees of investment advisors, accountants, tax advisors, agents, attorneys and other assistants to administer the trust, manage any trust asset and handle any litigation affecting the trust.

[This clause gives the trustee the authority necessary to manage the trust principal and income for the benefit of the minor or young adult. Because this authority is of the same type as is typically provided trustees under state laws and given to your personal representative later in this will, the trust incorporates or adopts that authority by referring to the trustee authority rather than spelling it all out again here. In addition, subsection 3 gives the trustee authority to hire necessary outside professionals and pay them out of the trust principal.]

(f) It is my intent that any trust established in this will be administered independently of court supervision to the maximum extent possible under the laws of the state having jurisdiction over the trust.

[As a general rule, the management of a trust is a private matter and not subject to very much court supervision. However, to the extent that any state's laws require such supervision, this clause makes clear that supervision is not desired.]

(g) The interests of any beneficiary of a trust established in this will shall not be transferable by voluntary or involuntary assignment or by operation of law and shall be free from the claims of creditors and from attachment, execution, bankruptcy, or other legal process to the fullest extent permitted by law.

[This important clause removes the trust principal and accumulated income from the reach of the minor or young adult's creditors—while it is being held in the trust. Also, this clause prevents the minor or young adult from transferring ownership of the principal or accumulated interest to others—again, while it is in the trust. Once property is distributed to the minor or young adult, however, there are no restrictions on what can be done with it.]

(h) Any trustee serving under the terms set forth in these provisions shall be entitled to reasonable compensation out of trust assets for ordinary and extraordinary services, and for all services in connection with the complete or partial termination of any trust created by this will.

[This provision allows the trustee to be paid out of the trust principal for administering the trust. Typically, however, the trustee is a close relative or friend of the family and performs these services free or for a nominal fee.]

(i) The invalidity of any trust provision of this will shall not affect the validity of the remaining provisions.

[This standard provision makes clear that as much of the trust as possible is to be enforced even if some aspect of it is considered invalid. There is no reason why any part of this particular trust should be considered invalid in any state, but it is still good practice to include a clause like this.]

FORGIVENESS OF DEBTS

NINETEENTH: I wish to forgive all debts specified below, plus accrued interest as of the date of my death: Ben Moorehead, 4/4/90, $250,000.

[Forgiving a debt is equivalent to making a bequest of property and is a common way to equalize what you leave to all your children when you have loaned one of them some money—that is, the amount that you would otherwise leave that child can be reduced by the amount of the debt being forgiven.]

PERSONAL REPRESENTATIVE

TWENTIETH: I name Wilma Jazmin Moorehead as my personal representative. If Wilma Jazmin Moorehead for any reason does not qualify or ceases to act as personal representative, I name Lee Moorehead Gwen as my personal representative.

[This clause identifies your choices for personal representative—that is, your executor— and an alternate representative who will take over if your first choice is unable or unwilling to serve when the time comes.]

PERSONAL REPRESENTATIVE'S POWERS

TWENTY-FIRST: If the probate of this will is necessary, I direct that my personal representative petition the court for an order to administer my estate under the provisions of the Independent Administration of Estates Act.

[This clause sets out the specific authority that your personal representative will have to competently manage your estate until it has been distributed under the terms of your will. In a few states, including California and Texas, this clause invokes a specific statute, called the Independent Administration of Estates Act, that gives a personal representative the maximum authority possible—without court supervision. In all other states, which don't have that statute, the first paragraph expresses your desire that your personal representative work as free from court supervision as possible. This will cut down on delays and expense. The second paragraph lists a number of specific powers that your personal representative will have, if necessary. It also makes clear that the listing of these specific powers does not deprive your personal representative of any other powers that he or she has under the law of your state. The general idea is to give your personal representative as much power as possible, so that he or she won't have to go to court and get permission to take a particular action.]

PAYMENT OF DEBTS

TWENTY-SECOND: Except for liens and encumbrances placed on property as security for the repayment of a loan or debt, I instruct my personal representative to pay all debts and expenses, using the following assets, in the order listed: Account #223-233-03039 in the Independence Bank.

Page 9   Initials _____ _____ _____ _____   Date _____

[This clause states how your debts will be paid. First, it exempts any debt that is attached to a property item. A beneficiary who inherits property that has been pledged for repayment of a debt inherits the debt as well as the property. For all additional debts, you may specify how they should be paid. Depending on the choice you make when operating WillMaker, your debts may be paid from specific assets you designate, from your residuary estate, or according to the law of your state, which may be a combination of these two.]

PAYMENT OF TAXES

TWENTY-THIRD: I instruct my personal representative to pay all estate and inheritance taxes assessed against property in my estate or against my beneficiaries using the following assets, in the order listed: Account #24225-393-1 at Bank Tormeline.

[This clause states how any estate or death taxes owed by your estate should be paid. This will usually only apply to people whose estate has a net value of $600,000 or more. Depending on the choice you make when operating WillMaker, your debts may be paid from specific assets you designate, from your residuary estate, or according to the law of your state, which may be a combination of these three.]

NO CONTEST PROVISION

TWENTY-FOURTH: If any beneficiary under this will contests this will or any of its provisions, any share or interest in my estate given to the contesting beneficiary under this will is revoked and shall be disposed of in the same manner as if that contesting beneficiary had not survived me and left no living children.

[This harsh-sounding clause is intended to discourage anyone who receives anything under your will from challenging the legality of the will for the purpose of receiving a larger share. The clause is often not very effective if a spouse or children are the ones doing the suing, but may be enforced against less closely-related beneficiaries.]

SIGNATURE

I, James Moorehead, the testator, sign my name to this instrument, this _____ day of _____, 19____, at _____. I declare that I sign and execute this instrument as my last will, that I sign it willingly, and that I execute it as my free and voluntary act. I declare that I am of the age of majority or otherwise legally empowered to make a will, and under no constraint or undue influence.

_____

(Signed)

Page 10   Initials _____   _____   _____   _____   Date _____

WITNESSES

We, the witnesses, sign our names to this instrument, and declare that the testator willingly signed and executed this instrument as the testator's last will.

In the presence of the testator, and in the presence of each other, we sign this will as witnesses to the testator's signing.

To the best of our knowledge, the testator is of the age of majority or otherwise legally empowered to make a will, is mentally competent and under no constraint or undue influence.

We declare under penalty of perjury that the foregoing is true and correct, this _____ day of _____,19_____, at _____.

Witness #1:

_____

Residing at:

_____.

Witness #2:

_____

Residing at:

_____.

Witness #3:

_____

Residing at:

_____.

Page 11   Initials _____   _____   _____   _____   Date _____

3 About You

A. Who Can Make a Will

There are a few legal requirements that control who can make a valid will. Before you start your computer and get WillMaker going, make sure you qualify to make a will in the eyes of the law.

1. Age

To make a will, you must either be:

- at least 18 years old,[1] or

- living in a state that permits people under 18 to make a will if they are married, in the military, or otherwise considered legally emancipated. Georgia law, for example, permits people as young as 14 to make their own wills if they are married.

2. Mental Competence

You must also be of sound mind to prepare a valid will. In addition, the laws require that you must:

- know what a will is and what it does and that you are making one

- understand the relationship between you and the people who would normally be provided for in your will, such as a spouse or children

- understand the kind and quantity of property you own, and

- be able to decide how to distribute your belongings.

This threshold of mental competence is not hard to meet. Very few wills are successfully challenged based on the charge that the willmaker was mentally incompetent. It is not enough to show that the person was forgetful or absent-minded.

To have a probate court declare a will invalid usually requires proving that the maker was totally overtaken by the fraud or undue influence of another person—and that person then benefited from the wrongdoing by becoming entitled to a large amount under the will. If the person making the will was very old, ill, senile or otherwise in poor mental condition when he or she made the will, it is obviously easier to convince a judge that undue influence occurred.

---

[1]Wyoming, however, is an exception. There, you must be at least 19 years old to make a will.

If a Contest Seems Possible

If you have any serious doubts about your ability to meet the legal requirements for making a will, or you believe your will is likely to be contested by another person for any reason, consult a lawyer.

B. Information Required by WillMaker

As you go through WillMaker, you will first be asked to answer a number of preliminary questions about yourself and where and how you live.

This chapter discusses those questions. The titles of the manual sections are the same as the titles of the screens in the WillMaker program.

1. Your Name

Enter your name in the same form that you use on other formal documents, such as your driver's license or bank accounts. This may or may not be the name that appears on your birth certificate. If you customarily use more than one name for business purposes, list all of them in your WillMaker answer, separated by aka, which stands for "also known as."

There is room for you to list several names. But use your common sense. Your name is needed here to identify you and all the property you own. Be sure to include all names in which you have held bank accounts, stocks, bonds, real estate or other property. But you need not list every embarrassing nickname from your childhood, or names you use for non-business purposes.

2. Your Social Security Number

WillMaker asks you to enter your nine-digit Social Security number. This is not a legal requirement, and you may choose not to provide it. However, it is a good idea to supply the information, because the number is often helpful to your personal representative and others who must track down your records and property after your death. This is especially true if you have a common name that may be easily confused with others.

3. Your State

Here you are asked to specify the state of your legal residence, sometimes called a domicile. This is the state where you make your home now and for the indefinite future.

This information is important for a number of willmaking reasons, so it is important to doublecheck your answer for accuracy. Your state's laws affect: marital property ownership, property management options for young beneficiaries, how your will can be admitted into probate and whether your personal property and all your real estate located in the state will be subject to state inheritance tax.

If you divide up the year living in two or more states and have business relationships in both, you may not be sure which state is your legal residence. To decide, choose the state where you are the most "rooted"— that is, the state in which you:

- are registered to vote
- register your motor vehicles

- own valuable property—especially property with a title document, such as a house or car
- have checking, savings and other investment accounts, and
- maintain a business.

To avoid confusion, it is best to keep all or at least most of your roots in one state, if possible. For people with larger estates, ideally this should be in a state that does not levy an inheritance tax. (See Chapter 12, Section E, for a list of states that do not tax inheritance.)

If You Live Overseas

If you live overseas temporarily because you are in the Armed Services, your residence will be the Home of Record you declared to the military authorities. Normally, your Home of Record is the state you lived in before you received your assignment, where your parents or spouse live, or where you now have a permanent home. If this is still a close call between two states, consider the factors listed above for determining a legal residence, or get advice from the military legal authorities.

If Your Choice Is Not Clear

If you do not maintain continuous ties with a particular state, or if you have homes in both the U.S. and another country, consult a lawyer to find out which state to list as your legal domicile when using WillMaker.

If you live overseas for business or education, you probably still have ties with a particular state that would make it your legal residence. For example, if you were born in Wisconsin, lived there for many years, registered to vote there and receive mail there in care of your parents who still live in Milwaukee, then Wisconsin is your legal residence for purposes of making a will.

4. Your County

Including your county in your will is optional, but recommended for convenience and as one additional way to help others identify you and to track down your property after your death.

Also, a county name may provide those handling your estate with important direction, because wills are probated through the court system of the county where you last resided, no matter where you died. The one exception is real estate: that property is probated in the court of the county in which it is located.

5. Your Marital Status

If you are married, see Chapter 4, Section C, for a detailed discussion of property ownership laws affecting married people.

For most people, listing the proper marital status does not require much thought. But if you are unsure whether you are married or single according to law, it is important to clarify your status.

Some tips to help you:

- **Divorce decrees**   Do not rely on word of mouth as evidence that you are legally divorced. Make sure you see a copy of the final order signed by a judge. To track down a divorce order, contact the court clerk in the county where you believe the divorce occurred. You will need to give the first and last names of you and your former spouse and make a good guess at what year the divorce became final. If you can't locate a final decree of divorce, it is safest to assume you are still married.

- **Out-of-country divorce decrees**   It is often difficult to verify and evaluate the legality of a divorce that was supposed to have taken place outside the United States. If you have any reason to think that someone you consider to be a former spouse might claim to be married to you at your death because an out-of-country divorce was not legal, consult a lawyer. (See Chapter 15, Section B.)

- **Common law marriages** It is uncommon to have a common law marriage. In most states, common law marriage does not exist. But in some states— Alabama, Colorado, the District of Columbia, Georgia, Idaho, Iowa, Kansas, Montana, Ohio, Oklahoma, Pennsylvania, Rhode Island, South Carolina, Texas and Utah—couples can become legally married if they live together and either hold themselves out to the public as being married or actually intend to be married to one another. Once these conditions are met, the couple is legally married. And the marriage will still be valid even if they later move to a state that does not allow couples to form common law marriages there.

    There is no such thing as a common law divorce; no matter how your marriage begins, you must go through formal divorce proceedings to end it.

    No matter what state you live in, if either you or the person you live with is still legally married to some other person, you cannot have a common law marriage.

- **Same sex marriages** No state currently legally recognizes marriages between people of the same sex—even where a religious ceremony has been performed. However, in several states, including Hawaii and Texas, there is legislation pending to legalize same-sex marriages.

The Importance of Your Marital Status
You should make a new will whenever your marital status changes. (See Chapter 10, Section A.)

For example, if you marry after making a will and do not provide for the new spouse, either in the will or through transfers outside the will, your spouse, in many states, may be entitled to claim up to half your property at your death.

Also, if you name a spouse in a will, then divorce or have the marriage annulled and die before making a new will, state laws will produce different, often unexpected results. In some states, the former spouse will automatically get nothing. In other states, the former spouse is entitled to take the property as set out in the will. And in a few states, courts will consider the entire will invalid.

If You Are Separated

Many married couples, contemplating divorce or reconciliation, live apart from one another, sometimes for several years. While this often feels like a murky limbo while you are living it, for willmaking purposes, your status is straightforward: You are legally married until a court issues a formal decree of divorce, signed by a judge. This is true even if you and your spouse are legally separated as declared in a legal document.

6. Your Spouse's Name

Enter your spouse's full name. As with your own name, list all names used for business purposes, following the tips suggested for entering your own name in Section B1, above. ▲

4 About Your Property

This chapter discusses the grist of willmaking: what you own, how you own it and what legal rules affect how you can leave it. Once you have considered the information about property in this chapter, you will be ready to use WillMaker to leave it to others—a task discussed in detail in Chapter 5.

If you have children, see Chapter 6 for a discussion of their rights to inherit property and your right to disinherit them.

A. Your Property: An Overview

There are a few basic principles about property to keep in mind as you
proceed through this chapter.

1. You Cannot Leave What You Do Not Own

You can only pass property to others if you own it. If you are married or own
property jointly with others, you must be sure of what percentage you actually
own and become familiar with the rules that may restrict what you can do
with it. (See Sections B and C.)

> ► **Making Residuary Bequests:**
> ► **Your Beneficiaries Get Everything You Have**
> ► If you do not make specific bequests in your will but instead pass all your
> ► property through the residuary clause, there is less reason to be concerned about
> ► property ownership rules. All property you own at your death that is not passed
> ► in other ways will simply pass under the residuary clause of your will to the
> ► person or institution you name as residuary beneficiary.

2. You Cannot Pass by Will Property Passed by Another Method

In your will, you cannot leave property that you are passing by another
method. The basic rule is this: Property in a living trust or a pay-on-death
account, in joint tenancy or a retirement account or insurance policy where
you have named the beneficiary, passes under the terms of that arrangement—
not through your will. This is true even if you mention the property in your
will. (These other ways to leave property are discussed in Chapter 12.)

Example
Laverne puts her house into joint tenancy with her daughter Linda. Later, she makes a
will, leaving all of her property to her son Phillip. At Laverne's death, Linda gets the
house.

The following property need not be included in your will:

- Real estate—also called real property—that is held in joint tenancy or tenancy by the entirety. It passes to the other joint owner or owners automatically.

- Joint checking, money market, brokerage or other financial accounts that are held in joint tenancy when you die. They also pass automatically to the surviving joint tenant.

- Life insurance and annuities. These funds automatically go to the person or institution you name as beneficiary, or if your first choice dies before you, the alternate beneficiary. You have no legal right to leave insurance money in your will unless you name your own estate as the beneficiary.

- Bank accounts and U.S. government securities which are held in your name with a direction to pay the balance to another person at your death. You can change this pay-on-death form of ownership while you are alive, but if you die with property owned in this way, the person you have designated will inherit it.

- Property you place in either a revocable or irrevocable trust. It passes automatically to the named beneficiary—not under the terms of your will. This includes property placed in a revocable living trust.

- Property left in personal retirement accounts, such as IRAs, Keoghs and 401K Plans. Such plans allow you to name a beneficiary and alternate beneficiary to take what remains of your account at your death. Once you do, you cannot change the beneficiary in your will.

3. Property Left by Will Goes through Probate

Probate is a court proceeding in which the authenticity of a will is established—and the deceased person's property is distributed to others. The probate process typically takes a year and often costs about 5% to 7% of the value of your estate in money paid to attorneys, appraisers and courts. The greater the value of the property passing through probate, the higher the fees. For this reason, many people choose to pass the ownership of at least their most valuable property to others through methods that do not involve probate—living trusts, joint tenancy, life insurance and pay-on-death accounts. (See Chapter 12, Section B, for an overview of these estate planning devices.)

Probate, of course, does not present a problem until you die. For most people, that will be many years after they write their wills—and they are likely to rewrite their wills several times between now and then. Considering this, many people conclude that in mid-life, it is sensible to leave their property according to a simple will and also use that will to name someone to care for their children and a personal representative (executor) to wind up their affairs in the unlikely event of sudden death. More complicated estate planning, including taking steps to reduce taxes and avoid probate, is usually reserved until the property owner is older.

B. Forms of Property Ownership

▶ **A Roadmap to this Chapter**

If you are single and do not jointly own property with others, you need not worry about the information discussed in this section or in Section C. Go on to the next chapter.

If you are married, do not own property with anyone other than your spouse, and you are leaving all or most of your property to your spouse, you also need not worry about ownership questions. Again, go directly to Chapter 5.

If you are married, do not own property with anyone other than your spouse and your spouse willingly consents to a plan leaving a large part of your estate to others—perhaps children, charities or grandchildren—and you have your spouse's willing consent, you need not worry about the marital property ownership rules discussed here and can go directly to the next chapter. But make sure you and your spouse have a true meeting of the minds, because in most states, your spouse can claim a 1/3 to 1/2 share of your property after your death if he or she asserts that claim. (This is discussed in Section C, below.)

Depending on how you hold title to property, the law often imposes conditions on how you can distribute it at your death. A look at some of the common forms of ownership and the legal repercussions of owning it in that form may help.

1. Owning Property Outright

The simplest form of ownership is when you are the only owner—that is, you do not share ownership and you are not married. Of course, it is possible that a lender has some legal ownership in the property until you pay off the loan— as is true with car notes and mortgages. But for the purpose of making your will, you are the sole owner. Under WillMaker, the beneficiary of any property on which you owe money will inherit the property subject to the loan. This means the beneficiary of the property is responsible for paying off the debt.

2. Community Property

Community property is property belonging to married people in the states that recognize this form of ownership. (It is discussed in more detail in Section C1.) Generally, it includes all earnings and property acquired with those earnings during marriage.

3. Joint Tenancy with Right of Survivorship

Two or more people can own property—real estate or personal property such as securities or a bank account—in joint tenancy with right of survivorship. When one of them dies, his or her share automatically goes to the surviving owner, called a joint tenant. A joint tenant cannot use a will to leave his or her share of the property to someone else.

But during life, joint tenancy is easy to change. Any joint tenant may end a joint tenancy by signing a new deed changing the way the property is held. The effect of this is to change the joint tenancy into a tenancy in common. Each person still owns the same proportional share, but because a tenancy in common does not include any automatic right of survivorship, each owner is then free to leave his or her share of the property by will.

Normally, joint tenancies with right of survivorship are created by language in the document—a deed, title document, or bank account certificate—that controls the form of shared ownership. To find out whether you own property in joint tenancy, see whether the document includes the words "joint tenants" or "joint tenancy." A few states require the document to read "joint tenancy with the right of survivorship," and Oregon, for example, requires the words "tenancy in common with the right of survivorship" to set up this kind of joint ownership.

▶
▶
▶ **States That Have Restricted or Abolished Joint Tenancy**
▶
▶ The following states have limited or abolished joint tenancy. If you live in one of
▶ these states and believe you may have a joint tenancy ownership, make sure you
▶ understand what it means. Pay special attention to the state rules about whether
▶ the joint tenancy property passes automatically at death.
▶
▶ Alaska   No joint tenancy in real estate, except for husband and wife.
▶ North Carolina   No joint tenancy for any property except joint bank accounts.
▶ Pennsylvania   No joint tenancy in real estate. Existing joint tenancy in real
▶   estate has been questioned in court decisions.
▶ Tennessee   No joint tenancy for any property, except for husband and wife.
▶ Texas   No joint tenancy in any property, unless there is a separate
▶   written agreement between joint owners.
▶

4. Tenancy by the Entirety

This form of ownership is basically the same as joint tenancy with right of survivorship discussed above, but is limited to married couples. When one spouse dies, the entire interest in the property then goes automatically to the other. Before tenancy by the entirety property can be changed to some other form of property ownership, both spouses must agree to the change. Nearly half the states now recognize tenancy by the entirety, but several of them—Alaska, Indiana, Kentucky, Michigan, New Jersey, New York, North Carolina, Oregon, Virginia and Wyoming—allow it only for real estate.

▶
▶ **States with Tenancy by the Entirety Ownership**
▶
▶
▶   Alaska   Maryland   Ohio
▶   Arkansas   Massachusetts   Oklahoma
▶   Delaware   Michigan   Oregon
▶   District of Columbia   Mississippi   Pennsylvania
▶   Florida   Missouri   Tennessee
▶   Hawaii   New Jersey   Vermont
▶   Indiana   New York   Virginia
▶   Kentucky   North Carolina   Wyoming
▶

5. Tenancy in Common

This is the most common way for unmarried people to own property together. In a tenancy in common, all owners have equal rights to use the property. Ownership shares are usually equal, but it is possible to arrange for unequal shares by deed or written contract. Each co-owner is free to sell or give away his or her interest during life, and if not disposed of before that time, can transfer it to another at death under the terms of a will.

C. Ownership Rules for Married People

The great majority of married people simply leave all or most of their property to the surviving spouse at death. For them, the willmaking process is simple. The nuances of marital property law do not apply.

But if your plan for your property involves leaving it to many other people instead of or in addition to your spouse, the picture becomes more complicated. Questions of which spouse owns what property may then become important unless your spouse consents to your plan for property disposition, as is most often true when older spouses leave property directly to their children.

Under your state's laws, your spouse may own some property you believe you have the right to leave to others in your will. In some states, your spouse may have the right to inherit the family residence, or at least use it for his or her life. The Florida constitution, for example, gives a surviving spouse the deceased spouse's residence. And another legal rule states that even if you are the owner, your spouse may have the right to claim up to half of your property—whether you like it or not.

So if you are married—and this includes everyone who has not received a final decree of divorce—you should also become familiar with:
- the property ownership laws of the state in which you reside permanently, and
- the property ownership laws of any state in which you own real estate.

Special Procedures for Waiving Inheritance Rights

In some states, one spouse can give up all rights to inherit any property by completing and signing a special document. If you want to make that type of arrangement, see a lawyer.

Fortunately, learning the basics of these rules is not difficult. States are broadly divided into two types for the purpose of deciding what is in your estate when you die: community property states and common law property states.

▶ **Community Property States**

▶ Arizona   New Mexico
▶ California   Texas
▶ Idaho   Washington
▶ Nevada   Wisconsin[1]

▶ **Common Law States**

▶ All other states

1. Community Property States

In community property states, what you own and can leave by will consists of both your own separate property and one-half of the community property you and your spouse own together.

Obviously, then, if you live in a community property state and are making a will in which you plan to leave considerable property to someone other than your spouse, it is essential to learn what property you own separately and what is classified as community property. However, you need not be concerned about these property classifications if you plan to leave all or most of your property to your spouse—or your spouse supports your property disposition plans.

In community property states, a spouse's separate property is:

• all property the spouse owned prior to marriage, any property acquired by the spouse after legal separation, or property the spouse receives during marriage by gift or inheritance, as long as it is kept separate from community property. Note that community property can be transformed into separate property and vice-versa by means of gifts between spouses.

---

[1]While Wisconsin is not technically a community property state, it changed its marital property law on January 1, 1986 to resemble those found in community property states. This law covers all property owned at a person's death even though the property was accumulated before 1986.

Also, one spouse's separate property can be given to the other spouse as his or her separate property. The rules for how to do this differ from state to state.

Community property is:

- all employment income received by either spouse during marriage. The one major exception to this rule is that all community property states except Washington allow spouses to treat income earned during marriage as separate property if they sign a written agreement to do so and then actually keep that income separate—as in separate bank accounts.

  Note also that this rule generally only refers to the period when the two are living together as husband and wife. From the time spouses permanently separate, most community property states consider newly-acquired income and property as the separate property of the spouse receiving it.

- all property acquired with employment income received by either spouse during their marriage—but not after permanent separation, and

- all property that, despite originally being classified as separate property, is transformed into community property under state laws. This commonly occurs where either: one spouse makes a gift of separate property to the community, such as by putting a separately-owned home in community property ownership, or a spouse who owns separate property allows it to get so mixed together—or commingled—with community property that it is no longer possible to tell the difference between the two.

Example

John has $10,000 in the bank when he marries Elsie. This is his separate property. Over the next several years, John deposits a number of community property paychecks in this account and regularly withdraws money to pay bills—some of them for the couple's living expenses, some to pay for John's own optimistic habit of betting in favor of the New England Patriots. The bank account balance fluctuates from a low of $2,000 to a high of $20,000. The separate property money in this account has been so commingled with community property that now the entire account is considered community property. John only owns half of the balance.

▶ **State Differences in Categorizing Property**
▶ The community property states have slightly different rules on what is classified as
▶ community property. One of the biggest differences is that in Idaho and Texas,
▶ income brought in by separate property is considered community property. In
▶ Arizona, California, Nevada, New Mexico and Washington, any income earned by
▶ separate property is also considered separate property.

Property That Is Difficult to Categorize

Normally, classifying property as community or separate is easy enough, but in some situations, it can be a close call. There are several potential problem areas.

Businesses Family businesses can create complications, especially if they were owned before marriage by one spouse and expanded during the marriage. The key is to figure out whether the increased value of the business is community or separate property. If you plan to leave your share of the business to your spouse, or in a way your spouse approves of, you have no practical problem. However, if you and your spouse do not have the same view of what is the best estate plan, it may be worthwhile to get help from a lawyer or accountant.

Money Judgment for Personal Injuries Usually, personal injury awards won in a lawsuit are the separate property of the spouse receiving them. But not always. Whether such a court award is considered separate or community property can vary, especially if the injury is caused by the other spouse. In short, there is no easy way to characterize this type of property. If a significant amount of your property came from a personal injury settlement, research the specifics of your state's law or check with an estate planning expert.

Debts   Generally, either spouse's debts for food, shelter and other necessities of life are considered to be incurred on behalf of the marriage and must be paid from the couple's community property. Each spouse is individually responsible for paying personal debts. Unfortunately, the line between individual and community debts is not always clear. And, under some circumstances, one spouse's separate property may be used to satisfy debts for common necessities incurred by the other. Whether this is true depends on the law of each state, and may also be complicated by nuances of the circumstances.

Pensions   Generally, the proportion of pensions gained from earnings made during the marriage are considered to be community property. This is also true of military pensions. However, some federal pensions—such as Railroad Retirement benefits and Social Security retirement benefits—are not considered community property because federal law deems them to be the separate property of the employee earning them.

Examples of Community and Separate Property

The following examples can help you better understand how community property principles determine what you own.

Example
Ed and Babs are married and living in a community property state and have property consisting of:
- a computer inherited by Babs during marriage
- a car purchased by Ed before marriage
- a boat registered in Ed's name which was purchased during marriage with his income
- a family home which Ed and Babs own together, and
- a loan that Ed's brother owes Ed and Babs.

Property Ed owns and can leave using WillMaker consists of the car, one-half of the boat, one-half the equity in the family home and one-half of the debt owed by Ed's brother. The reasoning is that Ed's car was his before the marriage, so is his separate property; the boat and house were purchased with community property income (income earned during the marriage), and so Ed and Babs each own half-interests in them. The loan to Ed's brother was made from community property funds and belongs half to Ed and half to Babs. The computer, on the other hand, was inherited by Babs and so is her separate property. Ed can leave all his property in his will—and forgive one-half the debt owed by his brother.

Example

James and Sue Ellen are married. They live in Arizona, a community property state. They have $50,000 equity in a house—with a value of $150,000—which the deed specifies they own as "husband and wife," and a joint tenancy savings account containing $15,000. James owns a fishing cabin in Colorado worth $12,000, which he inherited from his father, and an Austin-Healy sports car worth approximately $10,000, which he purchased before he was married. In addition, James and Sue Ellen own $100,000 worth of stock in a blue chip corporation they purchased with savings from Sue Ellen's earnings during marriage.

Property owned by James and which he can leave in his WillMaker will includes:

* his one-half interest in the community property house (worth $25,000, or one-half of the equity)
* his separate property fishing cabin
* his separate property Austin-Healy, and
* one-half of the community property stock.

James should make no provision for his share of the joint tenancy savings account in his will, because full ownership of it will pass automatically to Sue Ellen if he dies before she does. And if she dies before he does, the property will pass as part of his residuary estate.

2. Common Law Property States

Common law property states are all states other than Arizona, California, Idaho, Nevada, New Mexico, Texas, Washington and Wisconsin.

In common law property states, the property you own consists of:

- all property you purchased with your separate property or separate income, and

- property you own separately in your name if it has a title slip, deed or other legal ownership document.

    In common law states, the key to ownership for many types of valuable property is whose name is on the title. If you earn or inherit money to buy a house, and title is taken in both your name and your spouse's, you both own the house. If your spouse earns the money, but you take title in your name alone, you own it. If the property is valuable, but has no title document, such as a computer, then the person whose income or property is used to pay for it owns it. If joint income is used, then ownership is joint—generally considered to be a tenancy in common, unless a written agreement provides for a joint tenancy or a tenancy by the entirety.

Example

Will and Jane are married and live in Kentucky, a common law property state. They have five children. Shortly after their marriage, Jane wrote an extremely popular computer program that helps doctors diagnose a variety of ills. Jane has received royalties averaging about $200,000 a year over a ten-year period. Jane has used the royalties to buy a car, yacht and mountain cabin—all registered in her name alone. The couple also owns a house as joint tenants. In addition, Jane owns a number of family heirlooms which she inherited from her parents. Throughout their marriage, Jane and Will have maintained separate savings accounts. Will works as a computer engineer and has deposited all of his income into his account. The balance of Jane's royalties has been placed in her account, which now contains $75,000.

    Property owned by Jane alone consists of:

- the car, yacht and cabin, since there are title documents listing the property in her name. If there were no such documents, she would still own them because they were purchased with her income

- the savings account that is listed in her name alone

- the family heirlooms, and

- one-half of the interest in the house. Note that although the half-interest in house is in Jane's estate, it would go to Will outside of the probate estate because of its joint tenancy status. However, if the house was in Jane's name alone, it would be her property, even if purchased with money she earned during the marriage, or even if purchased with Will's money.

Example

Martha and Scott, who are married, have both worked for 30 years as schoolteachers in Michigan, a common law state. Generally, Scott and Martha pooled their income and jointly purchased a house, worth $200,000 (in both their names as joint tenants), cars (one in Martha's name, worth $5,000 and one in Scott's, worth $3,000), a share in a vacation condominium, worth $23,000 (in both names as joint tenants), and household furniture. Each maintains a separate savings account (approximately $15,000 in each), and they also have a joint tenancy checking account containing $2,000. In addition, Scott and his sister own a piece of land as tenants in common.

Property owned by Scott and which he can leave by will includes: his car, savings account, one-half the land he owns with his sister and half the furniture. Martha owns her car, her savings account and half the furniture and can use WillMaker to leave it. Scott and Martha jointly own the house and condo, but unless they take this property out of joint tenancy, the survivor automatically gets both and neither one can pass the property in his or her will.

Your Spouse Is Entitled to a Share of Your Property

Despite property ownership rules, if you intend to leave your spouse very little or no property, you may run into some legal roadblocks. All common law property states protect a surviving spouse from being completely disinherited—and most assure that a spouse has the right to receive a substantial share of a deceased spouse's property. Some states provide additional, relatively minor protection devices such as family allowances and probate homesteads. These vary from state to state in too much detail to discuss here. Generally, however, these devices attempt to assure that your spouse and children are not totally left out in the cold after your death, by allowing them temporary protection, such as the right to remain in the family home for a short period, or funds—typically, while an estate is being probated.

But a shortchanged surviving spouse usually has the option of either taking what the will provides, called taking under the will, or rejecting the gift and instead taking the minimum share allowed by state law, called taking against the will. Of course, these are just options; a spouse who is not unhappy with the share he or she receives by will is free to let it stand.

Laws protecting spouses are similar, but are not exactly alike in any two states. In most common law property states, a spouse is entitled to one-third of the property left in the will. In a few, it is one-half. The exact amount of the spouse's minimum share often depends on whether there are also minor children and whether the spouse has been provided for outside the will by trusts or other means.

Example

Leonard's will gives $50,000 to his second wife, June, and leaves the rest of his property, totaling $400,000, to be divided between May and April, his daughters from his first marriage. June can choose instead to receive her statutory share of Leonard's estate, which will be far more than $50,000. To the probable dismay of May and April, their shares will be substantially reduced; they will split what is left of Leonard's property after June gets her statutory share.

How a Spouse's Share Is Calculated

In many common law states, the property share that the surviving spouse is entitled to receive is measured both by what that spouse receives under the will and outside of the will by transfer devices such as joint tenancy and living trusts. The total of both of these is called the augmented estate.

While the augmented estate concept is rather complicated, its purpose is easy to grasp. Basically, all property of a deceased spouse, not just the property left by will, is taken into account in determining whether a spouse has been left the minimum statutory share. In determining whether a surviving spouse has been provided for adequately, the probate court will compute the value of the property the spouse has received outside of probate, and will also count the value of the property that passes through probate. This makes sense because many people devise ways to pass their property to others outside of wills to avoid probate fees.

Example

Alice leaves $10,000 to her husband, Mike, and $7,000 to each of her three daughters in her will. However, Alice also leaves Mike real estate worth $500,000 through a living trust. The total Mike receives from the augmented estate—$510,000—is more than one-half of the value of Alice's total property, so he would have nothing to gain by exercising his option of ignoring the will and taking his statutory share instead.

Moving from State to State

Complications may set in when a husband and wife acquire property in a common law property state and then move to a community property state. California and Idaho treat the earlier-acquired property as if it had been acquired in the community property state. The legal jargon for this type of property is quasi-community property.

The other community property states do not recognize the quasi-community property concept for willmaking purposes, and instead go by the rules of the state where the property was acquired. Thus, if you and your spouse move from a non-community property state into California or Idaho, all of your property is treated according to community property rules. However, if you move to any of the other community property states from a common law state, you must assess your property according to the rules of the state where the property was acquired.

Couples who move from a community property state to a common law state face the opposite problem. Generally, each spouse retains one-half interest in the community property the couple accumulated while living in the community property state. However, if there is a conflict after your death, it can get messy; the reasoning of the courts in dealing with the problem has not been consistent.

If You Move

If you have moved from a community property state to a common law state, and you and your spouse have any disagreement as to who owns what, it may be wise to check with a lawyer.

The following chart provides a cursory outline of the basic rights that states give to the surviving spouse. It does not set out the specifics of every state's law, as the laws in many states are quite complex in this area.

Spouse's Share in Common Law States

1. Surviving spouse receives right to use one-third of the deceased spouse's real property for the rest of his or her life

Connecticut	Rhode Island	Virginia
Kentucky	South Carolina	West Virginia
Ohio	Vermont	

2. Surviving spouse receives percentage of estate

a. Fixed percentage

Alabama	1/3 of augmented estate
Alaska	1/3 of augmented estate
Colorado	1/2 of augmented estate
Delaware	1/3 of estate
District of Columbia	1/2 of estate
Florida	30% of estate
Hawaii	1/3 of estate
Iowa	1/3 of estate
Maine	1/3 of augmented estate
Minnesota	1/3 of augmented estate
Montana	1/3 of augmented estate
Nebraska	1/2 of augmented estate
New Jersey	1/3 of augmented estate
North Dakota	1/3 of augmented estate
Oregon	1/4 of estate
Pennsylvania	1/3 of estate
South Dakota	1/3 of augmented estate
Tennessee	1/3 of estate
Utah	1/3 of augmented estate

b. Percentage varies if there are children (usually one-half if no children, one-third if children)

Arkansas	Michigan	North Carolina
Illinois	Mississippi	Ohio
Indiana	Missouri	Oklahoma
Kansas	New Hampshire	Virginia
Maryland	New York	Wyoming
Massachusetts		

Leaving Little to a Spouse

If you do not plan to transfer at least one-half of your property to your spouse in your will and have not provided for him or her generously outside your will, consult with a lawyer. ▲

5 How to Leave Your Property

People who have worked hard to accumulate a fair amount of property understandably want to decide who it goes to after they die. Accomplishing this as efficiently as possible is what using a WillMaker will is all about.

WillMaker uses two approaches to passing property.

- You can make specific bequests in which you name specific beneficiaries to get specific property. As part of every specific bequest, you have the option of naming an alternate beneficiary in case your first choice does not survive you. If you wish to make one or more specific bequests, the program leads you step-by-step through that process—up to 100 times.

- You can designate a residuary beneficiary to take your residuary estate—all property you have not passed either in a specific bequest or by some other legal method. You can also name an alternate residuary beneficiary who will take the property if your first choice does not survive you. If you wish to leave your entire estate to one or a few beneficiaries, you may skip the specific bequests entirely and just leave all your property in the form of one residuary bequest.

A. Specific Bequests

A specific bequest is a gift of named property—for example, a house, cash, an heirloom, a car—to one or more individuals or organizations that you designate. WillMaker lets you make up to 100 specific bequests.

For each specific bequest, you encounter screens that ask you to:

- name one or more beneficiaries
- identify the number of beneficiaries and whether they are people or organizations
- describe the property being left
- describe what happens to the property if one or more beneficiaries does not survive you, and
- identify one or more alternate beneficiaries.

For specific bequests to organizations, you will encounter only the first three of these screens—since it is presumed that the institution will survive you.

The number of items you may leave in each specific bequest is limited only by the space available in the program for describing them. For example, "my silver engraved watch, antique gold locket and watchslide bracelet to Lucy Morant" qualifies as one specific bequest to Lucy.

Because it makes sense to group similar items of property left to one beneficiary—"all my clothing," "my woodworking tools," "my carrier pigeons"—there should be plenty of room for you to include all the property you wish to in each specific bequest.

1. Property Not Covered by Your Will

If you have already arranged to leave property outside your will by using legal devices such as life insurance, pay-on-death bank accounts or living trusts, you do not need to include that property in your will. Some people worry that one of these alternative forms of property disposition might fail to do the job for some reason, and want to include this property as a specific bequest as a failsafe. There is no need to do this. As long as you use WillMaker to name a residuary beneficiary, the person or place you named will be entitled to all property you do not dispose of in some other way. (See Section G, below, for a detailed discussion of the residuary estate and how it functions.)

2. Don't Place Conditions on Bequests

WillMaker warns against placing conditions on bequests. Sometimes this sort of bequest is illegal. Often, placing conditions on gifts risks making a confusing and even unenforceable will.

▶
▶
▶   ## A Beneficiary Must Survive 45 Days to Inherit
▶   WillMaker automatically puts one condition in your will; all beneficiaries must
▶   survive you by 45 days.
▶   This survivorship condition is essential because 45 days is the minimum
▶   amount of time it usually takes to turn property over to beneficiaries. WillMaker
▶   assumes that if a beneficiary only survives you by a few days or weeks, you would
▶   prefer the property to pass to an alternate or residuary beneficiary named in your
▶   will.

Other than this one exception, WillMaker does not allow you to leave bequests that depend on the beneficiaries meeting some condition you place on them or on the property. For example, you cannot leave: "My gold Rolex to Andres, but only if he divorces his current wife, Samantha." Such a gift would not be considered legally valid, since it actually encourages the break-up of a family.

Another unacceptable gift would be: "My dental office equipment to Claude, as long as he sets up a dental practice in San Francisco." The reason this bequest is unwieldy becomes obvious once you think ahead to the need for constant supervision. Who would be responsible for tracking Claude's dentistry career and making sure he ends up in San Francisco? What if Claude initially practices orthodontia in San Francisco, using the equipment he was willed, then moves north to grow wine grapes in the Napa Valley? Must he give the equipment back? To whom?

WillMaker also asks you not to place conditions on the property you give in your will to others, such as: "My vintage Barbie Doll collection to Collette, if the dolls are still in good condition." Again, there would be a problem with someone making an assessment. Who is to judge whether the collection is in good condition?

If You Still Want to Make a Conditional Gift
So much for WillMaker rules. Despite the inherent problems, some people are determined to place conditions on beneficiaries or property. Occasionally, this can be sensibly accomplished with a custom-drafted clause. If you feel you must make a bequest with conditions, consult a

lawyer who is experienced in drafting bequests that will adequately address these complex "what if" arrangements.

B. Naming a Beneficiary

The first step to making a specific bequest when using WillMaker is to name who is to receive it.

This is easy when the bequest you are making is to one individual: Type in the full name by which he or she is commonly known. This need not be the name that appears on a birth certificate; as long as the name you use clearly identifies the person in the context of your will, all is well.

Naming multiple beneficiaries to take one bequest is usually simple, too. Just list the names. However, in some circumstances, naming more than one beneficiary to take a specific bequest can be more complex. For instance, you may wish to:

• name beneficiaries to take property in unequal shares, or
• name one or more organizations as beneficiaries.

1. Leaving Property in Equal Shares

If you want two or more beneficiaries to share a specific bequest equally, simply list their names. WillMaker will automatically specify in your will that the beneficiaries should share the property equally.

▶ **Running Out of Room**
▶
▶ A very few people will find they are limited by the space allowed in the specific
▶ bequest screens in the WillMaker program. However, if you name many multiple
▶ beneficiaries, or beneficiaries with very long names, you may wish to be creative.
▶
▶

Example

When naming a group of twenty beneficiaries with the last name of Wyszymerinsky to inherit your cabin—which you will identify in a later screen—you might put "Chuck Wyszymerinsky, Isadora Wyszymerinsky, Ismerelda Wyszymerinsky, Salvator Wyszymerinsky and Natoli Wyszymerinsky" and so on. It is equally acceptable—and far less exhausting—to list these beneficiaries as "Chuck, Isadora, Ismerelda, Salvator and Natoli Wyszymerinsky."

2. Giving Property in Unequal Shares

As noted, if you name a group of beneficiaries without specifying the shares each should take, WillMaker automatically makes their shares equal. If you want one or more beneficiaries to receive a greater share of a particular item of property than the others, the best way to do this is to put the percentage in parentheses directly after each beneficiary's name. Make sure that:

• each beneficiary is assigned a percentage, and

• the portions you specify add up to 100%.

Example

Fred Wagner wants to leave his ownership interest in an undeveloped real estate parcel to his three children—Mary, Sue and Peter. Because he has already paid for Mary's graduate school education, he wants to give Sue and Peter greater percentages of the property in case they want to go back to school, too. He lists his children and the share of his property to which they are entitled this way: Mary Wagner (20%), Sue Wagner (40%) and Peter Wagner (40%).

Alternatives for Multiple Beneficiaries

In most cases, you will not want to split up portions of a bequest by using several different screens. However, doing this can be extremely useful in multiple beneficiary situations if:

- you want to have a predeceased beneficiary's share go directly to a named alternate beneficiary instead of to his or her children, to the remaining beneficiaries, or to the residuary estate, or

- you want to have one predeceased beneficiary's share pass to his children, another's share go to any remaining beneficiaries and another's share go to an alternate beneficiary.

Example

Pat wants to leave her cabin to her two children, Mike and Jim, and her sister Mary Lou. However, she wants each child to receive a 40% share and her sister a 20% share. In the event her children do not survive her by 45 days, she wants their shares to go first to their children, if they have any, and otherwise to Mike or Jim, whoever is the survivor. However, if her sister predeceases her, Pat wants that 20% share to pass to her brother Roger rather than to either her sister's children or to Mike and Jim.

Using WillMaker, if Pat left her cabin to her children and her sister as multiple beneficiaries in one specific bequest, she could not accomplish her plan. If, however, Pat uses WillMaker to leave the cabin in three separate specific bequests, she can accomplish her goals with ease.

Pat would first name Mike as the beneficiary of a specific bequest. She would then use the property description screen to leave Mike a 40% interest in her cabin. Next, she would have this interest pass to Mike's children if Mike did not survive her by 45 days. After finishing the bequest to Mike, Pat would do the same for Jim. Finally, Pat would name Mary Lou as the beneficiary of a specific bequest, specify the property as 20% interest in the cabin, choose to have Mary Lou's share pass to a named alternate, and name Roger as the alternate. The following chart demonstrates this approach:

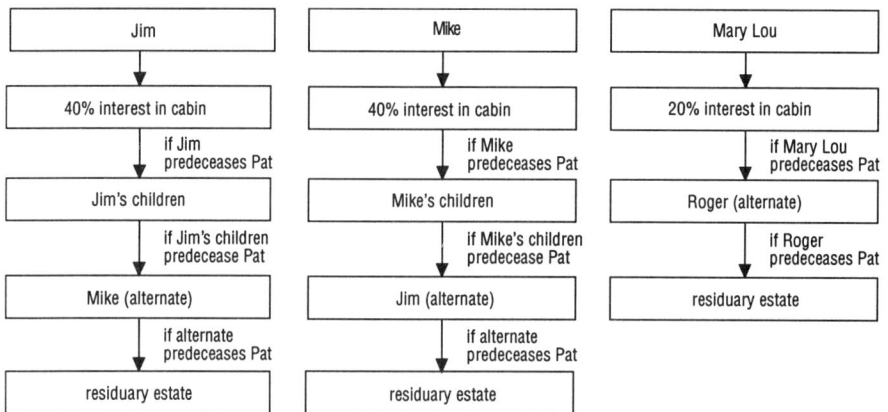

Jim		Mike		Mary Lou
↓		↓		↓
40% interest in cabin		40% interest in cabin		20% interest in cabin
if Jim predeceases Pat ↓		*if Mike predeceases Pat* ↓		*if Mary Lou predeceases Pat* ↓
Jim's children		Mike's children		Roger (alternate)
if Jim's children predecease Pat ↓		*if Mike's children predecease Pat* ↓		*if Roger predeceases Pat* ↓
Mike (alternate)		Jim (alternate)		residuary estate
if alternate predeceases Pat ↓		*if alternate predeceases Pat* ↓		
residuary estate		residuary estate		

3. Organizations as Beneficiaries

You may want to name a charity or a public or private organization to take property in a specific bequest—for example, the American Red Cross, the Greenview Battered Women's Shelter, the University of Kansas.

The organization you name need not be set up as a nonprofit, unless you wish your estate to qualify for a charitable estate tax deduction. (See Chapter 12, Section C.) It can be any organization you consider worthy of your bequest. The only limitation is that the organization must not be set up for some illicit or illegal purpose. For example, courts would likely find that the Downtown Center for Vice and Prostitution would not be eligible to take property under a will.

When naming the organization you wish to take the bequest, be sure to enter its complete name, which may be different from the truncated version by which it is commonly known. Several different organizations may use similar names—and you want to be sure your bequest goes to the one you have in mind.

4. Describing Your Beneficiary

After you name each beneficiary, WillMaker asks you for a description. But it is not looking for a long-winded response. To answer, you need only type in the number next to the phrase that best describes your beneficiaries:

1. One individual

2. Two or more individuals

3. One or more organizations

4. A mixture of individuals and organizations

WillMaker needs this information so that it can give you the opportunity to plan for the appropriate contingencies.

- If you have named only individuals to inherit the property, WillMaker will ask you to name an alternate beneficiary to take the property if your first choice does not survive you by the required period.

- If you have named an organization as your first choice beneficiary, you will not be presented with the option of naming an alternate beneficiary. WillMaker assumes that the organization will survive you—that is, it will still exist after your death.

- Finally, if you have named a mixture of individuals and organizations as beneficiaries of a specific bequest, you need not name an alternate beneficiary. In such cases, WillMaker makes the assumption that even if the individuals you want to take the bequest do not survive, the institution will survive to take over all the property.

▶
▶
▶ **Providing for Pets**
▶
▶ You cannot legally name a pet as a beneficiary in your will; the law considers pets
▶ to be property. But if you own a pet, you may well be concerned that it receives a
▶ good home and good care after your death. Because of WillMaker's proscription
▶ against leaving bequests with conditions on them (see Section A2, above), you
▶ cannot leave, for example, "$100 to Suzy Anderson, to be spent for my cat, Felix."
▶
▶   However, because a pet is legally considered to be property, you can leave it
▶ to another person in your will. It is also permissible—and common practice—to
▶ leave some money to the caretaker, explaining in a letter attached to your will that
▶ you want the money to be used for the pet's care. (See Chapter 11, Section B5, for
▶ a sample letter.) Of course, you should get the caretaker's agreement first—or he
▶ or she could end up as the unwilling recipient of an animal that needs care and a
▶ good home.
▶

C. Describing Property in Bequest

Once you have described your beneficiaries, you are asked to describe the
property you are leaving to them.

When describing a specific bequest, be as concise as you can. But use
enough detail so that people will be able to identify and find the property.
Most often, this will not be difficult: "my Baby Grand piano," "my collection of
blue apothecary jars," "my llama throw rug" are all the description you will
need for tangible items that are easy to locate.

► Do You Owe Money on Property You Are Leaving?

It is common to pay for major assets such as a house, car, major appliances or a business over a period of time. For such assets, full payment is normally required to obtain full ownership. Also, assets you already own such as household furniture may be pledged as security for a loan or extension of credit.

If you are leaving property in your will that carries an associated debt, you will naturally be concerned about whether the debt as well as the property should pass to the beneficiary, or whether the debt should be paid instead by your estate. WillMaker's handling of such concerns is discussed in detail in Chapter 8, but briefly:

- WillMaker passes all debts owed on real estate, including mortgages, deeds of trust and tax liens, to the beneficiary of that real estate
- WillMaker passes all debts owed on personal property in connection with its purchase to the beneficiaries of the property, and
- WillMaker provides that all debts owed on personal property for reasons other than its purchase—such as money you borrow from a finance company with your furniture pledged as collateral—shall be paid by your estate as you provide in your will.

If the property you leave as a bequest is very valuable or could be easily confused with other property, make sure you include identifying characteristics such as location, serial number, color or unique feature.

Here is some help in how to identify different types of property with enough detail to prevent confusion.

- **Household furnishings** You normally need not get very specific here, unless some object is particularly valuable. It is enough to list the location of the property: "all household furnishings and possessions in the apartment at 55 Drury Lane."

- **Real estate** You can simply provide the street address, or for unimproved property, the name by which it is commonly known: "my condominium at 123 45th Avenue," "my summer home at 84 Memory Lane in Oakville," "the vacant lot next to the McHenry Place on Old Farm Road." You need not provide the legal description from the deed.

- **Bank, stock and money market accounts** List financial accounts by their account numbers. Also, include the name and location of the organization holding the property: "$20,000 from savings account #22222 at Independence Bank, Big Mountain, Idaho," "my money market account #23456 at Beryl Pynch & Company, Chicago, Illinois," "100 shares of General Foods common stock."

- **Personal items** As with household goods, it is usually adequate to briefly describe personal items and group them, unless they have significant monetary or sentimental value. For example, items of extremely valuable jewelry should normally be listed and identified separately, while a drawer full of costume jewelry and baubles could be grouped.

What If There's Not Enough Space?

If you run out of room when describing a bequest you wish to give to the same beneficiaries, split it into two or more specific bequests.

Example

You want your collection of vintage coats to be shared by your two nieces, Doris and Natasha. Because each coat is special and valuable, you do not want to group them as "all my coats."

If the coats can be entered on the specific bequest screen, you can list them all on one screen. However, if there are too many to fit on one WillMaker screen, you can deal with the problem as follows: Begin one bequest by naming Doris and Natasha as beneficiaries and describe several of the coats in the WillMaker screen titled Description of Bequest—"the aubergine silk smoking jacket, rose lace theater cape, paisley velvet blazer, red velour hunting jacket, handpainted kimono," and so on. After cycling through the options for naming alternate beneficiaries of this specific bequest, begin another bequest—again naming Doris and Natasha as beneficiaries and then listing the remainder of the coats.

▶ **WillMaker's Context Box:**
▶ **A Good Way to Check Your Wording**
▶ For short bequests, it is a good idea to doublecheck the wording of your bequest
▶ in the box at the bottom of the WillMaker screen to be sure the language you have
▶ chosen flows gracefully in the context of your completed will. If your bequest is
▶ too long to appear in the context box in its complete form, check the wording
▶ when you display your will on the screen or when you print it out.
▶

D. What If a Beneficiary Dies Before You Do?

After you describe the property that you are leaving in a bequest, WillMaker
asks you to indicate your broad plan as to who gets your property if your first
choice beneficiary does not survive you by 45 days. If this involves naming an
alternate beneficiary, you will have the opportunity to do that.

E. Alternate Beneficiaries

When using WillMaker, you can name one or more alternate beneficiaries to
take the bequest if your first choice—and back-up choices, if you named
them—do not survive for the required period.

Example
Joan leaves her horse to her brother Pierre. In case Pierre does not survive her by 45
days to take this bequest, Joan names her sister Carmen to get the horse as the
alternate beneficiary.

Example
Gideon leaves his house to his three nephews in equal shares. In case one or more of
the nephews does not survive him by 45 days, Gideon specifies that the house should
then go to the surviving nephews in equal shares. He names his brother Morris as
alternate beneficiary. Morris will get the house only if none of the nephews survive
Gideon by 45 days.

If you want two or more people to share one piece of property but want to name different alternate beneficiaries for any of them, use separate screens to break apart the bequest.

Example

Marcia wants to leave her home to her two children, Emily and Robb. If Emily does not survive to take the bequest, Marcia wants Emily's share to go to Emily's two children. If Robb, who is unmarried and has no children, does not survive, Marcia wants his share to go to the Red Cross. The best way for her to put this plan in place using WillMaker would be to make two separate specific bequests to each of her children. The property in each bequest would be described as: "1/2 my home at 271008 SE Moss Street." Then she could name different alternate beneficiaries for each bequest.

F. List of Beneficiaries

When you complete a specific bequest—that is, you have named the beneficiary, identified the property and named an alternate beneficiary— WillMaker will display the first choice beneficiary's name on the screen. You can then add, review or change and delete any one of the bequests by following the instructions at the bottom of the screen.

Assuming you wish to make a second specific bequest, choose the "add" option. Then complete the cycle again until you have made all your specific bequests—up to 100 in all.

G. Leaving Your Residuary Estate

Your residuary estate is all the property you own at your death but for which you have not named a beneficiary in your will and have not arranged to pass to anyone outside the will by means of a probate avoidance technique, such as joint tenancy or a living trust. (See Chapter 12 for an overview of these techniques.) Your residuary estate can include property you overlook when making your will, property that comes into your hands after you make your will and property that does not go to the person you named to get it in a specific bequest, for example, because that person dies before you do and you have not named an alternate beneficiary to receive the property.

If you make few specific bequests, your residuary estate can contain a great deal of property—the value of which can increase substantially from the time you write your will until the time you die. But it can also decrease in value because you spend or give away the property that would have been passed in it.

▶ **Debts and Taxes: Your Residuary Estate Often Must Pay**
▶ After your death, property in the residuary is often what is used to satisfy
▶ unsecured debts, unpaid income taxes and estate taxes you owe at your death
▶ unless you specify otherwise in your will. Secured debts such as mortgages and
▶ car payments pass with the specific item of property. (See Chapter 8 for a
▶ thorough discussion of debts and taxes and why it is often wise to use your will to
▶ identify specific funds to pay them.)

You can name one or more individuals, one or more organizations or a combination of individuals and organizations to take your residuary estate. If more than one residuary beneficiary is named, WillMaker will make the assumption that you intend for them to share the residuary property equally. If you want them to take unequal shares, you must specify that after their names.

Example

Maurice Fuhrmann leaves his residuary estate to his five children—Clara, Heinrich, Franz, Lise and Wiebke. He wants Lise and Wiebke each to receive 35% of the property and the other three children to receive 10% each. He should list the children this way on the screen asking him to name his residuary beneficiary: Clara Fuhrmann (10%), Heinrich Fuhrmann (10%), Franz Fuhrmann (10%), Lise Fuhrmann (35%) and Wiebke Fuhrmann (35%).

If you use this approach, make sure every beneficiary is followed by a percentage share and that the shares add up to 100%.

Example

Ted and Mary Edwards, a married couple with two children, make no specific bequests in their wills. Instead, they each name the other as residuary beneficiary, which means the survivor takes all of the property when the first spouse dies. Each names the two children as alternate residuary beneficiaries.

1. Describing Your Residuary Beneficiaries

WillMaker asks you to describe the beneficiaries you named to take your residuary estate.

If you indicate that you have chosen an individual or two or more individuals to take your residuary estate, WillMaker will ask you to think ahead and indicate your broad plan as to who gets your property if your first choice does not survive you by 45 days. If this involves naming an alternate residuary beneficiary, you will have the opportunity to do that next.

Example

Alfredo leaves his residuary estate to his daughter Vanessa. He then specifies that if Vanessa does not survive him, her share should go to her two children—Alfredo's grandchildren. If Vanessa dies before Alfredo, and he does not write a new will, Vanessa's children would each inherit one-half of Alfredo's residuary estate.

Example

Jack writes a WillMaker will, making a few specific bequests to relatives and leaving his residuary estate to his friend Joe. He names another friend, Josette, as alternate residuary beneficiary. Josette will inherit property under Jack's will only if Joe does not survive 45 days longer than Jack.

If you have chosen a charitable institution to take all or part of your residuary estate, you need not worry about naming any alternate to take your residuary estate. WillMaker simply assumes the institution will survive—that is, be in operation longer than 45 days after you die, so will take your residuary estate.

2. Alternate Residuary Beneficiaries

It is a good idea to name one or more people or organizations as alternate residuary beneficiaries to provide a kind of insurance for your property plans against the bleak scenario that all other beneficiaries die before you. Your alternate residuary beneficiaries will take the property left in your residuary estate if no other named beneficiaries survive to take it.

H. If Your First Choice Does Not Survive

Making a will is easy if your primary concern is to designate who should get your property as a first choice. But things can get murky in a hurry if you want to provide for the fateful possibility that your first choice or choices do not survive you by the required period—45 days.

Not everyone is concerned about this issue. Younger people in reasonably good health are usually confident that they can address a beneficiary's premature death by updating their will. However, married people are commonly concerned about what will happen if they die in close proximity. And older people in poor health are concerned that they will not have an opportunity to update their wills if their first choice beneficiaries die before they do.

This section provides some examples of how you can use WillMaker to plan for the contingency of a beneficiary's death.

1. Specific Bequests to an Individual Beneficiary

After you have made a specific bequest of property to an individual beneficiary, WillMaker offers a choice as to what happens in the event that beneficiary does not survive you by 45 days. You can choose to have the property pass:

1. to the first choice beneficiary's children in equal shares

2. to one or more alternate beneficiaries you name on a later screen, or

3. to those you name to take your residuary estate.

Option #1: Property First to Children and Then to Alternate

Example

Janie makes a will leaving most of her estate to her husband and certain family heirlooms to their child Ellen. Janie designates Ellen's children to inherit the heirlooms if Ellen doesn't survive her, and names her husband as the alternate beneficiary. Ellen does not survive Janie by 45 days, but leaves three children of her own.

Assuming Janie does not change her will, the grandchildren inherit the heirlooms in equal shares. However, if none of the grandchildren survive Janie by 45 days, her husband, as alternate beneficiary, receives the heirlooms. If no alternate had been named or the alternate (Janie's husband) did not survive Janie, the heirlooms would have gone into Janie's residuary estate. The following chart shows how this works:

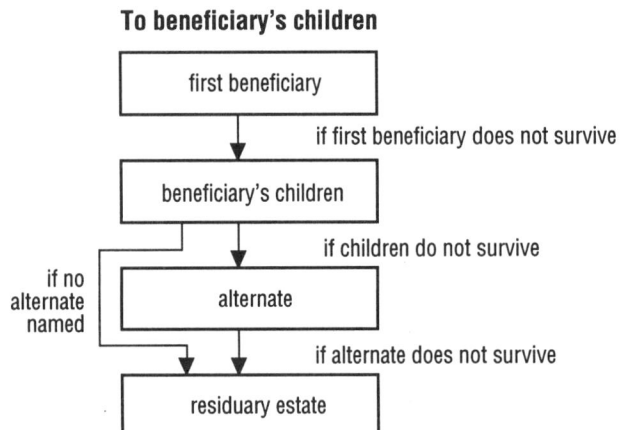

To beneficiary's children

```
              ┌─────────────────────────┐
              │     first beneficiary    │
              └─────────────────────────┘
                          │
                          │   if first beneficiary does not survive
                          ▼
              ┌─────────────────────────┐
              │   beneficiary's children │
              └─────────────────────────┘
                          │
                          │   if children do not survive
                          ▼
    if no     ┌─────────────────────────┐
  alternate   │        alternate         │
   named      └─────────────────────────┘
                          │
                          │   if alternate does not survive
                          ▼
              ┌─────────────────────────┐
              │     residuary estate     │
              └─────────────────────────┘
```

Option #2: Property Directly to Alternate

As mentioned, if you do not choose to have your beneficiary's children take the property if the beneficiary predeceases you, but instead direct it to go to the alternate, you merely shorten the chain of potential beneficiaries. The basic scheme is the same, but the property will go directly to the alternate beneficiary you choose if the first beneficiary is unavailable. If the alternate also does not survive you, the property will become part of your residuary estate.

Example

Sal makes out a will leaving one specific bequest of her antique piano to her brother Tim. She then names her daughter Justine as residuary beneficiary, which means Justine receives everything but the piano. Sal does not want Tim's children to receive the piano in the event Tim does not survive her, so she does not choose WillMaker option #1, but instead makes choice #2 and names her sister Val as alternate beneficiary.

If Tim does not survive Sal by 45 days, the piano will go to Val. Tim's children will not get it. If Val also does not survive Sal, the piano will go to Justine, Sal's residuary beneficiary.

To alternate beneficiary

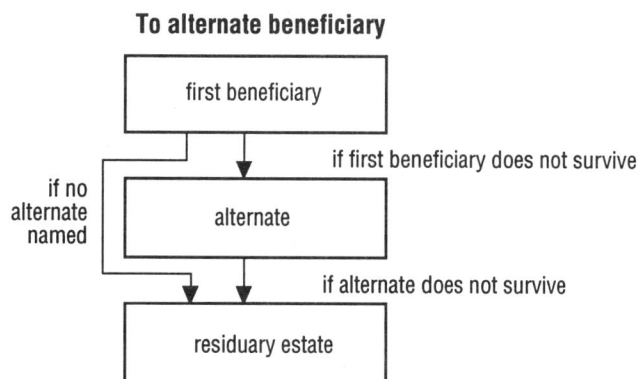

Option #3: Property Directly to Residuary Estate

You may choose to leave your property to just a few people. Your willmaking scheme will then be very simple, but less flexible—since you will not have set up alternative plans if your beneficiaries die before taking their share of your property.

Example
David leaves his apartment complex to his daughter Lurlene. If Lurlene does not survive him by 45 days, David wants the apartment to go directly to his wife Agnes, who he has named as his residuary beneficiary. If neither Lurlene nor Agnes survive, the property would go to whomever David has named as alternate residuary estate beneficiary. If he has not named a back-up residuary taker, David's apartment complex will pass as if he had left no will.

2. Specific Bequests to Multiple Beneficiaries

When the original bequest is made to two or more beneficiaries, choosing alternate beneficiaries becomes slightly more complicated. If one of a group of beneficiaries dies, WillMaker gives you two options.

Option #1: Property First to Children, Then to Alternates

Under the first option, the property goes first to the surviving children, if any exist, of the deceased beneficiary, in equal shares. If there are no surviving children, the property goes to any surviving beneficiaries in equal shares. If there are no other surviving beneficiaries, the property goes next to an alternate if one has been named. If none has been named, the property passes into the residuary estate.

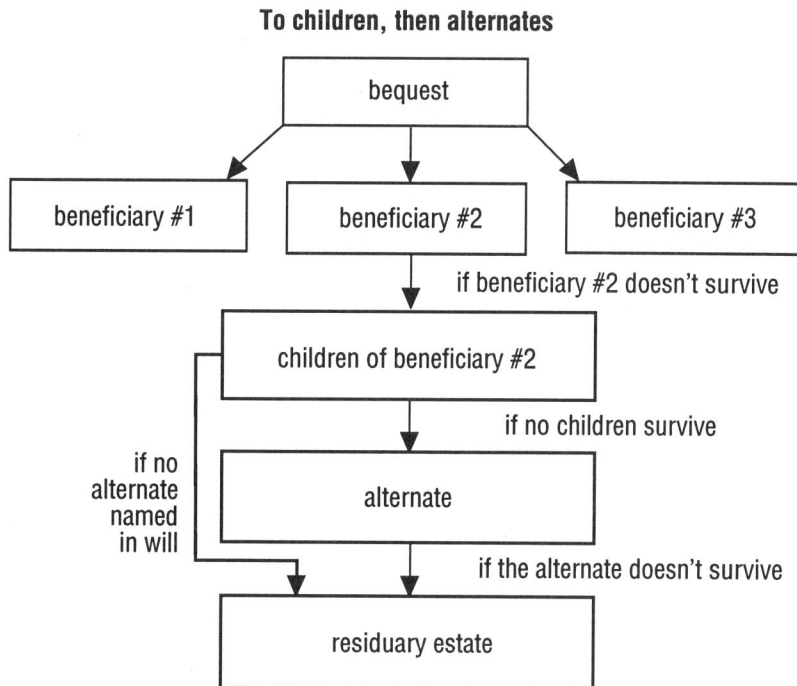

To children, then alternates

```
                        ┌──────────────────────┐
                        │       bequest        │
                        └──────────────────────┘
          ┌────────────────────┼────────────────────┐
          ▼                    ▼                    ▼
┌──────────────────┐ ┌──────────────────┐ ┌──────────────────┐
│  beneficiary #1  │ │  beneficiary #2  │ │  beneficiary #3  │
└──────────────────┘ └──────────────────┘ └──────────────────┘
                              │   if beneficiary #2 doesn't survive
                              ▼
                   ┌──────────────────────┐
                   │ children of          │
                   │ beneficiary #2       │
                   └──────────────────────┘
                              │   if no children survive
        if no                 ▼
        alternate    ┌──────────────────────┐
        named        │      alternate       │
        in will      └──────────────────────┘
                              │   if the alternate doesn't survive
                              ▼
                   ┌──────────────────────┐
                   │  residuary estate    │
                   └──────────────────────┘
```

Example

Pat leaves her vacation cabin in the mountains to her children Mike and Jim and her sister Mary Lou. Should neither Jim nor Mary Lou survive Pat by 45 days, Pat chooses to specify that the children of named beneficiaries receive their shares. This means that if Jim and Mary Lou do not survive Pat, Jim's two children would take his share, and Mary Lou's son takes Mary Lou's share.

If neither the named beneficiaries nor any of their children had survived Pat, the person Pat named as the alternate beneficiary would take the bequest. If no alternate was named, the cabin would have become part of Pat's residuary estate.

Example

Myrna has three children, Abby, Ben and Charlotte. She leaves her savings account to them in equal shares. Myrna uses WillMaker to specify that should any of her children not survive her by 45 days, that child's share will go to his or her surviving children (Myrna's grandchildren) and that, if there are no surviving children, the property should go to the remaining named beneficiaries—for example, if Ben dies before Myrna, the money goes to Abby and Charlotte. At Myrna's death, the savings account contains $30,000. First, assume that Ben predeceased Myrna and left no children. His share would be split between Abby and Charlotte, who will each get $15,000. Abby and Charlotte have two children each, who will receive nothing; the only grandchildren entitled to Ben's share are his children, and none survived him.

Now assume that both Abby and Ben predeceased Myrna. In that case, Abby's one-third share would be split equally by her children. Charlotte, the only surviving child, would receive $20,000—her share and Ben's share, since she is the sole surviving named beneficiary.

Next assume that Abby, Ben, Charlotte and one of Charlotte's children predeceased Myrna. In this case, because all three primary beneficiaries have predeceased Myrna, only the surviving grandchildren inherit. Abby's kids would split her original $10,000 share, Charlotte's kids would take her entire share, and Ben's share would pass to the alternate taker Myrna had named.

Finally, if all of the children and grandchildren had predeceased Myrna, the named alternate would take the $30,000. If no alternate had been named, the money would go into the residuary estate.

Grandchildren Not Part of this Scheme When you choose the multiple beneficiaries option, you can specify only children, not grandchildren, of a named beneficiary to take their parent's share of a bequest. If your will becomes so out-of-date that not only a beneficiary, but all the beneficiary's children predecease you, any grandchildren of the beneficiary are out of luck. They will not inherit anything; the beneficiary's share will go to surviving named beneficiaries, the alternate, or the residuary estate.

Option #2: Property Directly to Surviving Beneficiaries

Under this approach, a deceased beneficiary's share is divided among the other multiple beneficiaries. If none of the original multiple beneficiaries survives, the bequest passes to the alternate beneficiary named in the will. In the unlikely event that none of the named beneficiaries or the alternate survives you, the property becomes part of the residuary estate.

To surviving beneficiaries

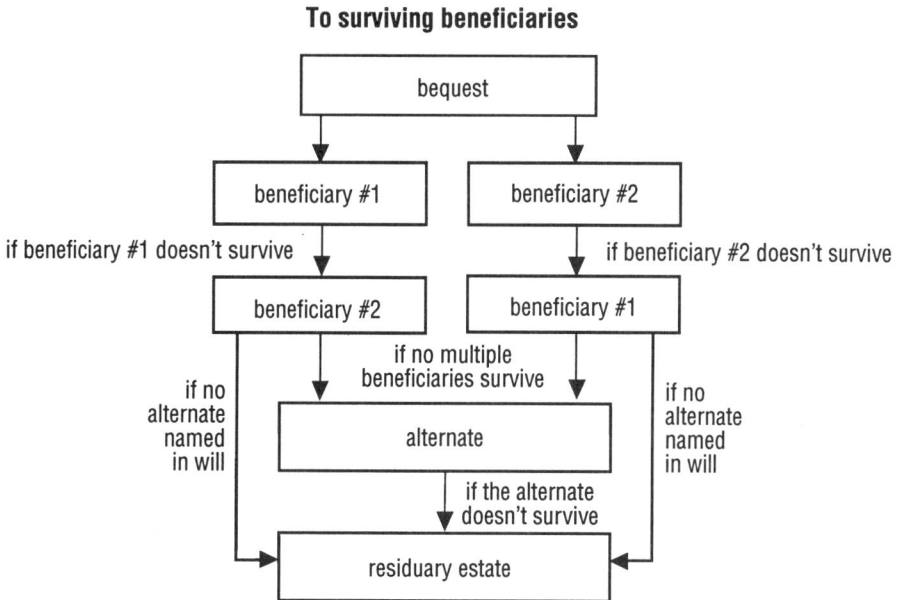

Example

Brandy uses WillMaker to provide in her will that her house will be divided equally between her brother Zeke and her daughter Maria. Her will also specifies that if one of the beneficiaries dies within 45 days after Brandy's death, his or her share will go to the other beneficiary, not to his or her children. Brandy chooses her friend Sabrina as the alternate beneficiary. Maria dies before Brandy, leaving two children.

Zeke, the surviving beneficiary, gets Maria's share of the property. Maria's children take nothing. If Zeke and Maria had both died before Brandy—and Brandy had not made a new will—Sabrina would inherit the property. If Sabrina had not survived Brandy, the property would go to the residuary estate.

Option #3: Property Directly to the Residuary Estate

Under this approach, a deceased beneficiary's share goes directly to the people or organizations you named to get your residuary estate.

To residuary estate

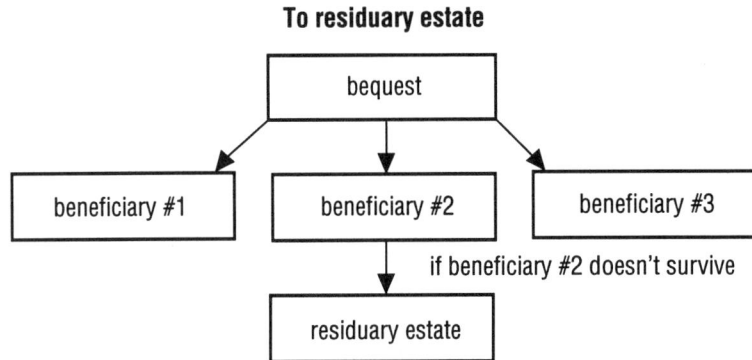

Example

Ken leaves his substantial savings account to his friends Patrick, Bill and Evan. Since none of his friends intends to have children and Ken wants to treat them all equally, his WillMaker will provides that if one of the beneficiaries dies within 45 days after his death, his share should go to the Center City Hospice, named as the residuary beneficiary.

When Ken and Patrick are killed in a plane trip together, Patrick's share of the account money passes directly to the hospice.

3. Simultaneous Death of Spouses

Many married couples with children are concerned about what will happen to their property and their children in the unlikely event that they both die at the same time.

The concern for children can best be met by taking advantage of the personal guardian and property management parts of the program. The people you choose as personal and alternate personal guardians will be available to care for your minor children. And your choices for property managers will be available to handle their property.

To take care of concerns about what happens to property that one spouse leaves to another, look to the 45-day survivorship clause that WillMaker automatically inserts into every will. This clause provides that, to receive property under a will, a beneficiary must survive the person making the will by 45 days. If the beneficiary does not survive that long, the property will pass to whoever has been named as an alternate beneficiary.

For example, if a husband's will leaves property to his wife, and both spouses die at the same time, the wife's estate will not take the property because of the 45-day survivorship requirement. Instead, the property will go to any named alternate beneficiary.

There is, however, one situation where this solution to simultaneous death will not work: when there are no alternate beneficiaries to take a deceased spouse's share. In that case, the rules of each state will determine who gets the property.

Fortunately, WillMaker provides many opportunities to specify alternate beneficiaries, so you need not fret over losing control over who receives property under your will in this unlikely event. ▲

6 Caring for Children and Their Property

Becoming a parent is what may have motivated you to buckle down to the task of writing your will in the first place. Although contemplating the possibility of your early death can be wrenching, it is important to face up to it and adopt the best contingency plan for the care of your young children. If the other parent is available, then he or she can handle the task. But life is full of possibilities—some of them rather bleak. You and the other parent might die close together in time. Or you may currently be a single parent, and need to come to terms with what will happen if you do not survive until your children become adults.

When planning for the possibility of your early death, consider:

- who will care for your minor children, and
- who will manage property you leave them.

WillMaker lets you make these decisions separately. This gives you the opportunity to place the responsibilities in the hands of the same person, or if need be, different people.

If your minor children may inherit valuable property from you, you must face another issue. Except for items of little value, minors are not permitted by law to have control over property. Instead, that property will have to be managed by a responsible adult. It is of vital importance to your children's interests that you arrange for this management yourself, in your will, rather than leave it up to a court to appoint and supervise a property manager.

WillMaker enables you to establish management for property that your minor children receive from you:

- under your will, or
- outside of your will—for example, through a living trust or a life insurance policy.

For property received under your will, this management may last until the minor turns an age you choose, up to 35 years old. For property that your minor children receive outside of your will, the management provided by WillMaker lasts until the children become adults.

It also makes good sense to establish management for property you plan to leave to other minor children in your will—your grandchildren, nieces and nephews. That way, you free their parents, or other adults responsible for them, from the expensive and time-consuming burden of having to go to court to get legal authority to manage the property on behalf of the minor. Here, too, you can use WillMaker to provide property management that lasts until the young beneficiary is 35 years old.

And those considering young adults as beneficiaries may also want to defer distribution of inherited property until a later age. As with minors, you can use WillMaker to postpone distributing property left to any young adult— yours or someone else's—until the beneficiary reaches an age you choose, up to and including 35.

▶ **Explaining Your Bequests to Your Children**

WillMaker, of course, allows you to divide up your property among your children as you see fit. If your children are already responsible adults, your prime concern will likely be about fairness—given the circumstances and the children's needs. Often, this will mean dividing your property equally among your children. Sometimes, however, the special health or educational needs of one child, the relative affluence and stability of another or the fact that you are estranged from a child will be the impetus for you to make an uneven distribution.

Doing this can sometimes raise serious worries—a child who receives less property may conclude that you cared for him or her less. To deal with this, you may wish to explain your reasons for dividing your property unequally. Because of the risk of adding illegal or confusing language, WillMaker does not allow you to make this explanation in your will. Fortunately, there is a sound and sensible way to express your reasons and feelings. Simply prepare a separate letter to accompany your will. (See Chapter 11, Section B2, for a sample letter.)

A. Identify Your Children in Your Will

It is important to name all your children when making your WillMaker will. This warning is backed by strong legal reasoning: If a minor or adult child is neither named in a will nor specifically disinherited, the law of most states assumes that you accidentally forgot to include that child. The effect is that the overlooked child has a right to the same share of your estate he or she would be entitled to had you left no will. This amount varies from state to state, often depending on your family composition, but would likely be a significant percentage of your property.

These laws are intended to protect both the interests of the accidentally forgotten child—termed a "pretermitted heir"—and the person making the will. This rule applies no matter how old your children are when you die—and no matter whether you specifically plan to leave them any property in your will.

Example

Bruno leaves nothing to his daughter Portia in his will because they have been estranged for years. He neither names her nor specifically disinherits her. When Bruno dies, Portia is 66 years old. Portia is entitled to sue for a share of Bruno's estate as a pretermitted heir.

WillMaker protects you against the pretermitted heir rule by asking you to name all your children and then including the statement in your will that if you do not leave any property to one or more of these children, that decision is intentional. However, to go the last inch to make sure that no child can challenge your will under the pretermitted heir rule, it also makes excellent sense to leave each child some amount of property, no matter how small.

When WillMaker asks whether or not you have any children and, if so, it asks that you name all of them, including:

- children born to or adopted by you while you were married to your current spouse

- children born to or adopted by you when you were married to a previous spouse, and

- children born to or adopted by you when you were not married, and

If you are the parent of a child who has been legally adopted by another person—or you have otherwise given up your parental rights—then you need not name that child in your will.

It is not necessary to name stepchildren that you have not adopted, but you may leave them property in your will if you wish to do so.

To list your children, enter their full names in the sequence and format you want the names to appear in your will.

Example

Peter John Jones, Sophie Elizabeth Jones and Harold Portnoy Jones.

There should be enough room on the screen to list all your children in this manner. If, however, you have many children and they have long names, causing space problems, identify them by eliminating their middle names—or listing all their first names and then putting the common last name at the end of the sequence.

Example

Peter, Sophie, Harold, Rubin, Julian, Stanley, Robert, Ralph, Jennifer and Jill Jones.

⚠ Don't Use "All My Children"

Some people want to skip naming their children individually and put in "all my children," "my surviving children," "my lawful heirs," or "my issue." Don't do it. It can be confusing and may lead to pretermitted heir problems down the line.

B. Identify Children of a Deceased Child

WillMaker asks you to name the children of a deceased child. Name all such grandchildren—including children your child legally adopted and those born while he or she was not married.

This question is asked because the rule that allows pretermitted children to sue to get a share of your estate also applies to grandchildren you may have overlooked in your will if their parent (your child) is dead.

As it does for your own children, WillMaker automatically provides the statement that if you have not left any property to that grandchild, that is intentional—and therefore eliminates the problem. Again, you are free to leave the grandchild property if you choose.

▶
▶ **Keep Your Will Up-To-Date**
▶
▶ You should make a new will in the following two situations:
▶
▶ • If a child is born to or legally adopted by you after you make your will. You
▶   must change your will to list the new child. If you do not, that child may
▶   challenge your will as a pretermitted heir and sue to receive a share of what
▶   you leave.
▶
▶ • If one of your children dies before you do and leaves children of his or her
▶   own. The laws of many states require that you name and provide for the
▶   children of deceased children. If you do not, they are considered pretermitted
▶   heirs. To protect against this, make a new will, naming these grandchildren so
▶   that you can signal that you are aware that these grandchildren exist. You are
▶   still free to leave them as little or as much property as you wish in your will.
▶ (See Chapter 10 for information on updating your will.)

C. Name a Personal Guardian for Your Minor Children

This section discusses using WillMaker to choose a personal guardian to care for the children's basic health, education and other daily needs. Choosing someone to manage your children's property is discussed in Section D, below.

1. Why Name a Personal Guardian?

Among the most pressing concerns of parents with minor children is who will care for the children if one or both of them die before the children reach 18. The general legal rule: If there are two parents willing and able to care for the children, and one dies, the other will take over physical custody and responsibility for caring for the child. In many states, the surviving parent may also be given authority by a court to manage any property the deceased parent left to the children—unless the deceased parent has specified a different property management arrangement in a will.

But what if both parents of a minor child die, or in the case of a single parent, there is not another parent able or willing to do the job? Using WillMaker, you can tackle these concerns by naming a personal guardian and an alternate. The person you name will normally be appointed by the court to act as a surrogate parent for your minor children if:

- there is no surviving natural or adoptive parent able to properly care for the children, and
- the court agrees that your choice is in the best interests of the children.

If both parents are making wills, they should name the same person as guardian—to avoid the possibility of a dispute and perhaps even a court battle should they die simultaneously. But remember, if one spouse dies first, the other will almost always assume custody and will then be free to make a new will naming a different personal guardian if he or she wishes. In short, in a family where both parents are active caretakers, the personal guardian named in a will cares for the children only if both parents die at the same time or close together.

WillMaker allows only one person to be named as personal guardian and one person as alternate personal guardian for all of a parent's minor children. While it is legally permissible to name co-guardians, it is normally a poor idea because of the possibility that the co-guardians will later disagree or go separate ways.

2. Choosing a Personal Guardian

To qualify as a personal guardian, your choice must be an adult—18 in most states—and competent to do the job. For obvious reasons, you should first consider an adult with whom the child already has a close relationship—a stepparent, grandparent, aunt or uncle, older sibling, close friend of the family or even a neighbor. But, whoever you choose, be sure that person is mature, goodhearted and willing and able to assume the responsibility.

3. Choosing an Alternate Personal Guardian

WillMaker lets you name a back-up or alternate personal guardian to serve in case your first choice either changes his or her mind or is unable to do the job at your death. The considerations involved in naming an alternate personal guardian are the same as those you considered when making your first choice: maturity, a good heart, familiarity with the children and willingness to serve.

4. Explaining Your Choice for Personal Guardian

If you are separated or divorced, you may have strong ideas about why the child's other parent, or perhaps a grandparent, should not have custody of your minor children. In an age when many parents live separately, the following predicaments are sadly common:

"I have custody of my three children. I don't want my ex-husband, who I believe is emotionally destructive, to get custody of our children if I die. Can I choose a guardian to serve instead of him?"

"I have legal custody of my daughter and I've remarried. My present wife is a much better mother to my daughter than my ex-wife, who never cared for her properly. What can I do to make sure my present wife gets custody if I die?"

"I live with a man who's been a good parent to my children for six years. My father doesn't like the fact that we aren't married and may well try to get custody of the kids if I die. What can I do to see that my mate gets custody?"

There is no definitive answer to these questions. If you die while the child is still a minor and the other parent disputes your choice in court, the judge will likely grant custody to the other natural parent, unless that parent:

- has legally abandoned the child by not providing for or visiting the child for an extended period, or

- is clearly unfit as a parent.

It is usually difficult to prove that a parent is unfit, absent serious and obvious problems such as chronic drug or alcohol abuse, mental illness, or a history of child abuse. The fact that you do not like or respect the other parent is never enough, by itself, for a court to deny custody to him or her. But if you honestly believe the other natural parent is incapable of caring for your children properly, or simply will not assume the responsibility, follow the procedure below.

Step 1

In your will, name the person you want to be your child's personal guardian.

Example

Susan and Fred, an unmarried couple, have two minor children. Although Susan loves Fred, she does not think he is capable of raising the children on his own. She uses WillMaker to name her mother, Elinor, as guardian. If Susan later dies, Fred, as the children's natural parent, will be given first priority as personal guardian over Elinor, despite Susan's will, assuming the court finds he is willing and able to care for the children. However, if the court finds that Fred should not be personal guardian, Elinor would get the nod, assuming she was fit.

Example

Susan and Fred live together with Susan's minor children from an earlier marriage. The natural father is out of the picture, but Susan fears that her mother, Elinor, who does not approve of unmarried couples living together, will try to get custody of the kids if something happens to her. Susan wants Fred to have custody because he knows the children well and loves them. She can use WillMaker to name Fred as personal guardian and attach a separate letter to her will making the reasons for this choice clear. (See Step 2, below.) If Susan dies and Elinor goes to court to get custody, the fact that she named Fred will give him a big advantage. If he is a good parent, he is likely to get custody in most states.

Step 2

Explain in a letter that you attach to your will the reasons for making your choice. (See Chapter 11, Section B4, for a sample letter that you can modify to suit your circumstances.)

▶
▶
▶ **Custody Difficulties for Lesbians and Gay Men**
▶
▶ Many lesbians and gay men are parents. If only one of the couple is a lesbian or
▶ gay, and there is later an acrimonious divorce, who gets custody of the children
▶ often involves a difficult legal battle. In a court fight over custody, judges are
▶ supposed to consider all factors and arrive at a decision in the "best interests of the
▶ child." This means that virtually any information about a parent's lifestyle, sexual
▶ identity and behavior can be brought out in court. In many states, especially in the
▶ south and midwest, evidence of a parent's lesbian or gay sexual identity is still
▶ legally accepted reason for denying custody. If you anticipate a contested custody
▶ case, you will find guidance in *A Legal Guide for Lesbian and Gay Couples,* by
▶ Curry, Clifford and Leonard (Nolo Press).
▶

D. Property Management: An Overview

WillMaker allows you to think ahead and establish management for property you leave in your will to any beneficiaries who may be minors or young adults when you die. Management established under WillMaker may last until an age you choose—up to and including age 35.

This section presents an overview of basic property management considerations. Section E discusses how to use WillMaker to put your management choices into your will.

Property management consists of naming a trusted adult to be in charge of caring for and accurately accounting for the property a young beneficiary inherits under your will until the beneficiary turns a specific age. The property being managed for the young beneficiary must be held, invested or spent in the best interest of the beneficiary. In other words, someone other than the young beneficiaries will decide if their inheritances will be spent on college tuition or a new sports car.

1. Property Management for Minors—Generally

Except for property of little value—usually under $1,000—minors may not directly control property they inherit under a will. The property must be managed by an adult for the minor's benefit until he or she turns 18. If you do not provide this management in your will, the court will do it for you—an expensive, public and time-consuming alternative requiring court supervision of how the guardian manages and spends the money.

In addition, you may want to provide that management for property left to a minor continues beyond age 18—the age at which a guardianship ends. WillMaker allows this management to last up to and including age 35.

2. Property Management for Young Adults—Generally

If you are leaving valuable property to someone who is in his or her late teens or early twenties, you may justifiably wish to delay the time the young beneficiary actually gets to use and control it. WillMaker lets you extend the time property left to young adults is managed until they reach an age up to and including 35.

3. Leaving Property to Your Own Minor Children

If you are married, you may choose to leave your property directly to your spouse and trust him or her to use good judgment in providing for your children's current and future needs. Even if you do this, however, you are not necessarily freed from the need to provide property management. To plan for the possibility that your spouse dies close in time to you, you may want to name your children as alternate beneficiaries. And then you will want to appoint a trusted adult as manager for the property they could inherit.

Finally, once you choose a person to manage the property, you must decide what you want to happen when your children reach the age of 18. You can choose to have the property left them handed over in one lump sum, or instead have the property management continued until the children are somewhat older.

4. Property Management for Other Children

If it is possible that other people's children—such as your grandchildren—will take property under your will, you must also address how and whether this property is to be managed. This is important. If the child is a minor and you do not provide management for the property, the child's parent will usually be required to establish a time-consuming and relatively expensive court-supervised property guardianship. It is much wiser to use WillMaker to name the child's parent or some other person or institution as property manager.

▶ **What Happens If the Minor Does Not Inherit Property**

▶ If you arrange for property management for a minor, but the minor never inherits
▶ the property, no harm is done. The management provisions for that minor are
▶ ignored. For instance, suppose you identify a favorite niece to take property as an
▶ alternate beneficiary, and provide management for that property until the niece
▶ turns 25. If the niece never gets to take the property because your first choice
▶ beneficiary survives you, no property management will be established for her,
▶ since none will be needed.

E. Property Management Under WillMaker

WillMaker offers three basic legal approaches to property management for minors and young adults:

• the Uniform Transfers to Minors Act—for property left in your will

• the WillMaker children's trust—for property left in your will, and

• a property guardianship—for property that passes to your minor children outside of your will.

1. The Uniform Transfers to Minors Act

The Uniform Transfers to Minors Act (UTMA) allows you to name a custodian to manage property you leave to a minor. The management ends when the minor reaches age 18 to 25, depending on state law.

States are free to adopt or reject the UTMA, which is a model law proposed by a group of legal scholars who make up the Uniform Law Commission. So far, over half the states have adopted the UTMA—many making minor changes to it. There is every reason to believe that the UTMA will be universally adopted, but that will take a few more years. Since adoption means that it is built into the legal framework, if the UTMA is already on the books in your state, all banks, insurance companies, brokers and other financial institutions should already be familiar with it.

▶ **States That Have Not Adopted the UTMA**

At present, the UTMA has not been adopted in these states: Connecticut, Delaware, Michigan, Mississippi, New York, Pennsylvania, South Carolina, Texas and Vermont.

If you are a resident of one of these states, you can set up property management for any minor or young adult beneficiary using the WillMaker children's trust, discussed in Section 2, below.

If the UTMA has been adopted in your state, you may use it to specify a custodian to manage property you leave a minor in your will until the age at which the laws of your state require that it be turned over to the minor. Depending on your state, this varies from 18 to 21; Alaska, California and Nevada allow you to extend management until 25. The WillMaker program keeps track of the state you indicate as your residence and tells you whether the UTMA is available, and if so, the age at which property management under it must end.

► Age Limits for Property Management in UTMA States

Property Management Must End at Age 18 in:

   District of Columbia, Kentucky, Oklahoma, Rhode Island and

   South Dakota

Property Management Must End at an Age You Choose Between Age 18 and 21 in:

   Arkansas, Maine, New Jersey, North Carolina and Virginia

Property Management Must End at Age 21 in:

   Alabama, Arizona, Colorado, Florida, Georgia, Hawaii, Idaho, Illinois,

   Indiana, Iowa, Kansas, Maryland, Massachusetts, Minnesota, Missouri,

   Montana, Nebraska, New Hampshire, New Mexico, North Dakota, Ohio,

   Oregon, Tennessee, Utah, Washington, West Virginia, Wisconsin and

   Wyoming

Property Management Must End by Age 25 in:

   Alaska, California and Nevada

Among the powers the UTMA gives the custodian are the right, without court approval, "to collect, hold, manage, invest and reinvest" the property, and to spend "as much of the custodial property as the custodian considers advisable for the use and benefit of the minor." The custodian must also keep records so that tax returns can be filed on behalf of the minor and must otherwise act as a prudent person would when in control of another's property.

► Special Rule for Life Insurance

Often the major source of property left to children comes from a life insurance policy naming the children as beneficiaries. If you want the insurance proceeds for a particular child to be managed, and you live in a state that has adopted the UTMA, instruct your insurance agent to provide you with the form necessary to name a custodian to manage the property for the beneficiary under the terms of this Act.

2. The WillMaker Children's Trust

The WillMaker children's trust, which can be used in all states, is a legal structure you establish in your will. If you create a trust, any property inherited by a minor beneficiary will be managed by a person or institution you choose to serve as trustee until the beneficiary turns an age you choose—through age 35. The trustee's powers are listed in your will. The trustee may use trust assets for the education, medical needs and living expenses of the minor or young adult beneficiary. All property you leave to a beneficiary for whom a trust is established will be managed under the terms of the trust.

Because management under the WillMaker children's trust can be extended through age 35, it is also suitable to use for property left to young adults. (The pros and cons of the two management options are discussed in Section 3, below.)

Property Management Needs Not Covered by WillMaker

The property management features offered by WillMaker—the UTMA and children's trust—are similar and provide the property manager with broad management authority adequate for most minors and young adults. However, they are not designed to:

- provide skilled long-term management of a business

- provide for management of funds beyond age 35 for a person with spendthrift tendencies or other personal habits that may impede sound financial management beyond young adulthood, or

- meet a disadvantaged beneficiary's special needs. A physical, mental or developmental disability will likely require management customized to the beneficiary's circumstances, both to perpetuate the beneficiary's way of life and to preserve the property, while assuring that the beneficiary continues to qualify for government benefits.

For all these situations, specific trust provisions custom-tailored to the needs of the beneficiary and your wishes should be drafted by an attorney experienced in this type of work.

3. Should You Use the UTMA or WillMaker Children's Trust?

For each minor or young adult to whom you leave property in your will, you must decide which management approach to use—the UTMA or the children's trust. Because both are safe, efficient and easy to put in place, either can be used for many situations. This section helps you decide which is best for you and yours.

▶ **When to Use the UTMA**

As a general rule, the less valuable the property involved and the more mature the child, the more appropriate the UTMA is because it is simpler to use than the children's trust. There are a couple of reasons for this.

Because the UTMA is built into state law, financial institutions know about it and should make it easy for the custodian to carry out property management duties. To set up a children's trust, the financial institution would have to be given a copy of the trust document and may tie up the proceeding in red tape to be sure the trustee is acting under its terms.

Also, a custodian acting under the UTMA need not file a separate income tax return for the property being managed; it can be included in the young beneficiary's return. However, with a children's trust, both the beneficiary and the trust must file returns.

Because the UTMA requires termination of the management at a relatively young age, if the property you are leaving is worth $50,000 or less—or the child is likely to be able to handle more than that by age 21 (25 in Alaska, California and Nevada), use the UTMA. After all, $50,000 is likely to be used up long before management under the UTMA ends—at least in most states.

▶
▶
▶ **When to Use the WillMaker Children's Trust**
▶
▶ As a general rule, the more property is worth, and the less mature the young
▶ beneficiary, the better it is to use the children's trust, even though doing so is a bit
▶ more work for the property manager than using the UTMA. For example, if a
▶ minor or young adult stands to inherit a fairly large amount of property—such as
▶ $200,000 or more—you might not want it all distributed by your state's UTMA cut-
▶ off age, which is usually 18 or 21. In such circumstances, you will be better off
▶ using the WillMaker children's trust. Remember, under the children's trust,
▶ management can last until an age you choose—through age 35.

4. Property Guardianship

The UTMA and the WillMaker children's trust are good management for
property that minor or young adult beneficiaries receive under your will.
However, if you have minor children and they receive property of significant
value outside of your will, the court will usually have to step in and appoint a
guardian to manage the property under court supervision until the children
turn 18.

The two most common ways that children receive property outside of a
will are from life insurance or through a living trust. (See Chapter 12, Section
B.) While it is possible to provide for management of this type of property
through your life insurance agent under the UTMA or within the living trust
itself, often no such management is established and a property guardianship is
required.

In addition, property received by your children from other sources—the
lottery, a gift from an aunt or uncle, earnings from playing in a rock band—
may also need to be managed by a property guardian.

It is always better to specify who will be managing any such property that
your minor children come to own. Otherwise, the court will appoint someone
who may or may not have your children's best interests in mind. The same
person you chose to be personal guardian can be a good choice as property
guardian if you think he or she will handle the property wisely for the benefit
of the minor. Otherwise, you may wish to choose someone else. (See Section
F for more discussion of good choices for property management.)

F. Choosing a Property Manager

You may name one person and one successor, who will take over if your first choice is unable to serve, to manage the property. If you use the UTMA, these people will be called the custodian and successor custodian. If you use the WillMaker children's trust, they will be called the trustee and successor trustee.

▶ **Selecting an Institution as Property Manager**

If you are using the UTMA, you must name a person as custodian; you cannot name an institution. The WillMaker children's trust, however, allows an institution to serve as trustee. Still, it is rarely a good idea to pick a bank or other institution as trustee. Most banks will not accept a trust with less than $200,000 worth of liquid assets.

When banks do agree to take a trust, they charge large management and administrative fees. All trustees are entitled to reasonable compensation for their services—paid from trust assets. But family members or close friends often waive payments or accept far less than banks when chosen to act as trustee. If you cannot find an individual you think is suitable for handling your assets and do not have enough property to be managed by a financial institution, you may be better off not creating a trust.

Also, note that it is common for banks to manage the assets of all trusts worth less than $1,000,000 as part of one large fund, while charging fees as if they were individually managed. Any trustee who invests trust money in a conservatively-run mutual fund can normally do at least as well at a fraction of the cost.

Choosing someone to manage your children's finances is almost as important a decision as choosing someone to take custody of them after your death. Name someone you trust, who is familiar with managing the kind of assets you leave to your children, and who shares your attitudes and values about how the money should be spent.

As a general rule, your choice for custodian or trustee should also live in or near to the state where the property will be managed. Some states require trustees to live in the state where the trust is created. If you are using the trust option and wish to select a trustee who lives in a different state than you do, try to select an in-state person as the successor trustee. Then, if your first choice is prevented by the law of your state from serving, the alternate trustee will be able to step in and do the job.

You need not worry about finding a financial wizard to be your property manager. Under both the UTMA and the WillMaker children's trust, the property manager—custodian or trustee—has the power to hire professionals to prepare accountings and tax returns and to give investment advice. Anyone hired for such help may be paid out of the property being managed. The custodian or trustee's main jobs are to manage the property honestly, make basic decisions about how to take care of the assets wisely and sensibly mete out the money to the trust beneficiary.

Whoever you choose as custodian or trustee, it is essential to get his or her consent first. This will also give you a chance to discuss, in general terms, how you would like the property to be managed to be sure the manager you select agrees with your vision and fully understands the beneficiary's needs.

Example

Ralph and Ariadne agree that Ariadne's sister, Penny, should be guardian of their kids should they both die, but that the $100,000 worth of stock the three kids will inherit might better be handled by someone with more business experience and who will be better able to resist the children's urgings to spend the money frivolously. In each of their wills, they name Penny as personal guardian of the children, but also create trusts for the property they are leaving to their children. They name each other as trustees, and Ralph's mother, Phyllis, who has investment and business knowledge and lots of experience in handling headstrong adolescents, as the alternate trustee, after obtaining her consent. Ralph and Ariadne also decide that one of their children, who is somewhat immature, should receive his share of the estate—at least the portion not already disbursed for his benefit by the trustee—upon turning 25, and the other two children should get their shares when they turn 21.

▶
▶ ### General Rules for Naming a Property Manager
▶
▶ Here are a few general principles to follow when choosing a property manager.
▶
▶ • It is usually preferable to combine the personal care and property management
▶   functions for a particular minor child in the hands of one person. Think first
▶   who is likely to be caring for the children if you die, and then consider if that
▶   person is also a good choice for property manager. If you must name two
▶   different people, try to choose people who get along well; they will have to
▶   work together.
▶
▶ • If you believe that the person who will be caring for the minor is not the best
▶   person to handle the minor's finances, consider an adult who is capable and is
▶   willing to serve.
▶
▶ • If you are married and leaving property directly to your minor children,
▶   consider naming your spouse as first choice as property manager.
▶
▶ • For property being left to young adults, select an honest person with business
▶   savvy to manage the property.

G. Choosing an Age to End Management

If you choose a property guardian to manage property received by your minor children outside of your will, that management will terminate when each child turns 18.

For management under the UTMA, the age at which management terminates is seldom an issue. In all but a few states, the management terminates automatically at age 18 or 21, depending on the state; in Alaska, California and Nevada, it can be from 21 to 25. (See Section E1, above.)

Under the WillMaker children's trust, however, you may select any age up to 35 for the management to terminate. There is no general rule that will direct you in choosing an age for a particular beneficiary to get whatever trust property has not been spent on the beneficiary's health, welfare and educational needs. That will depend on:

• the amount of money or other property involved

• how much control you would like to impose over it

- the beneficiary's likely level of maturity as a young adult. For small children, this may be difficult to predict, but by the time most youngsters reach their teens, you should have a pretty good indication, and

- whether the property you leave, such as rental property or a small business, needs sophisticated management that a young beneficiary is unlikely to master.

H. Examples of Choosing Property Management Options

Here are some examples of how the WillMaker property management options might be selected. The following scenarios are only intended as suggestions. Remember, if you live in a state that has not adopted the UTMA, your only property management option is the WillMaker children's trust.

Example 1

Married

Adult children age 25 and older

You want to leave all your property, worth $150,000, to your spouse and name surviving children as alternate beneficiaries. As long as you think the children are all sufficiently mature to handle their share of the property if your spouse does not survive you, answer no when WillMaker asks if you wish to set up property management.

Example 2

Married

Children aged 19, 21 and 23

You want to leave all your property, which is worth $300,000, to your spouse and name your surviving children as alternate beneficiaries. You sensibly opt for property management in case the children get the property—if you and your spouse both die—and establish a children's trust for each child, to end at age 30. You name your financially experienced brother as trustee. You can leave each of the children the same amount of property, or you can leave varying amounts. You would not want to use the UTMA even if available in your state because it requires that property management end at age 21, or 25 in a few states.

Example 3

Married

Children aged 2, 5 and 9

You want to leave all your property, which is worth $150,000, to your spouse and name your children as alternate beneficiaries. You use the property management feature and select the UTMA option for all property each child inherits under your will. You name your wife's mother—the same person you have named as personal guardian—as custodian, and name your brother as alternate guardian and successor custodian. The property will be managed by the custodian until the age allowed under the UTMA—18, 21, or 25, depending on the state.

You also name your wife's mother as property guardian if management is needed for property your minor children receive outside of your will.

Later, when your children are older and you have accumulated more property, you may wish to make a new will and switch from the UTMA approach to the children's trust, to extend the age of management until a later age (up to age 35) for one or more of the children. Also, you may wish to name different property managers for each child.

If you are in a state that has not adopted the UTMA, use the trust option and set the distribution ages to a later time than permitted by the UTMA.

Example 4

Single or married

Two minor children from a previous marriage and one minor child with your present partner

You want to leave all your property, which is worth $150,000, directly to your children. You can use either the UTMA or the trust for each child, and name separate custodians or trustees, if you wish. You should also name a property guardian to manage any property your minor child might get outside of your will.

> ⚠ If you are married, your spouse has a right to claim a portion of your property, so it is usually unwise to leave it all to your children unless your spouse agrees with that plan. (See Chapter 4, Section C.)

Example 5

Single or married

Two adult children from a previous marriage—ages 23 and 27—and one minor child with your present partner

You decide to divide $300,000 equally among the children. To accomplish this, you establish a trust for each child from the previous marriage and put the termination age at 30. You name your current spouse, who gets along well with the children, as trustee and a local trust company as alternate trustee. Because your third child is an unusually mature teenager, you choose the UTMA for this child and select 21 as the age at which this child takes any remaining property outright. You appoint your wife as custodian and the trust company as successor custodian.

Example 6

Married or single

One daughter of your own, age 32, and three minor grandchildren

You want to leave $50,000 directly to each of the grandchildren. You establish a custodianship under the UTMA for each grandchild, and name your daughter as custodian and her husband as successor custodian. ▲

7 Choosing a Personal Representative or Executor

Using WillMaker, you can name a personal representative—also called an executor. Your personal representative will have legal responsibility, after your death, for safeguarding and handling your property, seeing that debts and taxes are paid and distributing what is left to your beneficiaries as your will directs.

A. Duties of a Personal Representative

Serving as a personal representative is a job that can be fairly easy or it can require a good deal of time and patience, depending on the amount of property involved and the complexity of the plans for it.

▶
▶ **Make Your Will and Records Accessible**
▶ As the willmaker, you can help with the personal representative's first task:
▶ locating your will. Keep a copy in a fairly obvious place—a desk, file cabinet, safe
▶ deposit box. And make sure your personal representative has access to it.
▶   Should you need help in getting organized, *Nolo's Personal RecordKeeper* by
▶ Pladsen and Warner (Nolo Press) is an easy-to-use software program that helps
▶ you keep a complete inventory of all your legal, financial and personal records. It
▶ also offers an overview of how to reduce estate taxes and avoid probate.
▶

Your personal representative will have a number of duties—which do not
require special expertise and can usually be accomplished without outside
help. A personal representative typically must:

- obtain certified copies of the death certificate

- locate will beneficiaries

- examine and inventory the deceased person's safety deposit boxes

- collect the deceased person's mail

- cancel credit cards and subscriptions

- notify Social Security and other benefit plan administrators of the death

- learn about the deceased person's property—which may involve examining
  bankbooks, deeds, insurance policies, tax returns and many other records

- get bank·accounts released or, in the case of pay-on-death accounts, get
  them transferred to their new owner, and

- collect any death benefits from life insurance policies, Social Security,
  veterans' benefits and other benefits due from the deceased's union,
  fraternal society or employer.

In addition to these mundane tasks, however, the personal representative
will typically have to:

- file papers in court—usually called a probate court—to start the probate
  process and obtain the necessary authority to act as personal representative

- handle the court-supervised probate process—which involves transferring
  property and making sure the deceased's final debts and taxes are paid,
  and

- prepare final income tax forms for the deceased, and if necessary, file estate tax returns for the estate.

For these tasks, it may be necessary to hire an outside professional who will be paid out of the estate's assets—a lawyer to initiate and handle the probate process and an accountant to prepare the necessary tax forms. But in some states, because of simplified court procedures and adequate self-help law materials, even these tasks can be accomplished without outside assistance.

B. Naming a Personal Representative

Glancing through the list of the personal representative's duties in Section A above should tip you off about who you know that might be the best person for the job: the prime characteristics are honesty, good organization skills and a finesse with keeping track of details. Obviously, for many tasks, such as collecting mail and finding important records and papers, it is most helpful to name someone who lives nearby and who is familiar with your business matters.

1. Guidance in Choosing a Personal Representative

The most important guideline in naming a personal representative is to choose someone you trust and who you don't mind having access to your personal records and finances after your death. Many people choose someone who is also named to inherit a substantial amount of property under their will. This makes sense because a person with an interest in how your property is distributed—a spouse, mate, child, or close family member—is also likely to do a conscientious job as personal representative. And he or she will probably also come equipped with knowledge of where your records are kept and an understanding of why you want your property split up as you have directed.

Whoever you select, make sure the person is willing to do the job. Discuss what the job requires with your choice as personal representative before naming him or her in your will.

While it is almost always best to choose a trusted person for the job, you may not know anyone who is up to the task—especially if your estate is large and complicated and your beneficiaries are very old, very young, or just inexperienced in financial matters. If so, you can select a trust management firm to act as your personal representative.

If that is your leaning, first be sure the institution you choose is willing to act. Most will not accept the job unless your estate is fairly large—worth at least $250,000 and often more. Also, understand that institutions charge a hefty fee for acting as personal representative—usually both a percentage of the value of property to be managed and a number of smaller fees for routine services such as buying and selling property.

2. Choose Only One Personal Representative

WillMaker requires that you name only one person or institution as your primary choice for personal representative. You may also name one person or institution as alternate in case your first choice is unable or refuses to act when the time comes.

While some people want to name two or more personal representatives to serve jointly, this is usually not wise, which is why WillMaker does not provide for it. If you name joint personal representatives and they later disagree, your estate may be the loser because of lengthy probate delays and litigation expenses.

While it is possible to set out in your will how disagreements between joint personal representatives should be resolved, this type of advance planning should be done with the assistance of a knowledgeable lawyer or estate planner.

3. How Your Personal Representative— and Outside Experts—Get Paid

The laws of every state provide that a personal representative may be paid out of the estate. Depending on your state law, this payment may be:

- based on what the court considers reasonable

- a small percentage of the gross or net value of the estate, or

- set according to factors set out in your state's statutes.

When the personal representative either stands to inherit a large portion of the estate or is a close family relative, it is common for him or her to do the work without being paid. Some willmakers opt to leave their personal representatives a specific bequest of money in appreciation for serving.

However, any outside experts who are used will almost always be paid out of the estate. The amount outside experts—including lawyers—are paid is totally under the control of the personal representative. However, most states set out maximum fees that may be charged by lawyers and other professionals—usually a percentage of the value of the estate.

Beware of Lawyers' Fees

Lawyers commonly misrepresent to prospective clients that the maximum fee allowed by statute is the statutory fee that they charge for their services. In fact, lawyers are perfectly free to charge by the hour or a flat fee that is unrelated to the size of the estate. One of the most important tasks that your personal representative can perform is to negotiate a reasonable fee with any lawyer he or she may pick to probate your estate. Be sure you explain this to your choice for personal representative.

4. If You Do Not Name a Personal Representative

If for some reason you do not name a personal representative in your will, the document will still be valid as a will. But your decision will not have been a wise one. It will most often mean that a court will have to scurry and scrounge to come up with a willing relative to serve. If that fails, the court will probably appoint someone to do the job who is likely to be unfamiliar with you, your property and your beneficiaries. People appointed by the court to serve are called administrators.

The laws in many states provide that anyone who is entitled under the will to take over half a person's property has first priority to serve as personal representative. If no such person is apparent, courts will generally look for someone to serve among the following groups of people, in the following priority:

Surviving spouse
Children
Grandchildren
Greatgrandchildren
Parents
Brothers and sisters
Grandparents
Uncles, aunts, first cousins
Children of deceased spouse
Other next of kin
Relatives of a deceased spouse
Conservator or guardian
Public administrator
Creditors
Any other person

C. Naming an Alternate Personal Representative

In case you name someone to serve as executor who dies before you do or for any other reason cannot take on the responsibilities, you should name an alternate to serve instead.

In choosing an alternate personal representative, consider the same factors you did in naming your first choice. (See Section B1, above.) ▲

8 Paying Debts and Expenses

► **When You Need Not Plan to Pay Debts and Death Taxes**

► You need be concerned about how to cover your debts and death taxes only
► when your willmaking plan involves dividing up your property among a number
► of beneficiaries.

► If you plan to leave all of your property to your spouse, or equally to two or
► more people without specifying what property goes to which person, there is no
► real need to plan how your debts, expenses and death taxes should be paid. Your
► spouse or the co-beneficiaries should be able to agree with your personal
► representative—who will likely be one of these people—as to which of your assets
► should be used.

A. Liabilities of Your Estate

If you live owing money, chances are you'll die owing money. If you do, your
personal representative will be responsible for rounding up your property and
making sure all your outstanding debts are satisfied before any of the property
is put in the hands of those you have named to get it. Your estate will be
liable for: several types of debts, expenses and taxes.

• **Debts you owe when you die—personal loans, credit card bills, mortgage loans,
  income taxes**   Whether such debts pass to the beneficiary along with the
  property, or must be paid out of the estate depends upon how the debt is
  characterized. (See Section B.)

• **Expenses incurred after your death—costs of funeral, burial and probate**
  Probate and estate administration fees typically run about 5% to 7% of the
  value of the property you leave in your will. Unless you specify otherwise,
  the fees will be paid according to the law of your state. Typically, this
  means they come from your residuary estate. This may mean your residuary
  beneficiary will receive less than you intended, especially if you have relied
  on your residuary clause to pass most of your estate. (See Chapter 14 for a
  discussion of other death-related expenses.)

- **Death taxes** If your net estate is more than $600,000 at death, it will likely owe federal estate taxes. It may also owe state death taxes; some states tax estates and some do not. (See Chapter 12, Section E, for a list.) Unless you specify otherwise in your will, the taxes will normally be paid proportionately out of the estate's liquid assets. This means that beneficiary's property will be reduced by the percentage that the property bears to the total liquid assets. Liquid assets include bank accounts, money market accounts and marketable securities. Real estate and tangible personal property such as cars, furniture and antiques are not included. This could cause a problem if, for example, you left your bank account with $50,000 in it to a favorite nephew and your death tax liability—most of which resulted from valuable real property left to another beneficiary— gobbled up all or most of it.

B. Debts and Expenses of Probate

There are two basic kinds of debts with which you need be concerned when making a will—secured and unsecured.

1. Secured Debts

As used here, secured debts are any debts owed on specific property that must be paid before title to that property fully belongs to its owner.

One common type of secured debt occurs when a major asset such as a car, appliances or a business is paid for over a period of time. Usually, the lender of credit will retain some measure of legal ownership in the asset— termed a security interest—until it is paid off. This type of debt is called a purchase money secured debt because it is incurred to purchase the property that serves as security for repayment.

Another common type of secured debt occurs when a lender, as a condition of the loan, takes a security interest in property already owned by the person applying for the money. For instance, most finance companies require their borrowers to agree to pledge "all their personal property" as security for the loan. The legal jargon for this type of security interest is a non-purchase money secured debt—that is, the debt is incurred for a purpose other than purchasing the property that secures repayment.

Other common types of secured debts are mortgages and deeds of trust owed on real estate in exchange for a purchase or equity loan, tax liens and assessments that are owed on real estate, and in some instances, liens or legal claims on personal and real property created as a result of litigation or home repair.

If you are leaving property in your will that is subject to a secured debt, you will naturally be concerned about whether the debt will pass to the beneficiary along with the property, or whether it must be paid by your estate.

How WillMaker Handles Secured Debts

- **Debts owed on real estate** WillMaker passes all secured debts owed on real estate along with the real estate.

Example

Paul owes $50,000 under a deed of trust on his home, signed as a condition of obtaining an equity loan. He leaves the home to his children. The deed of trust is a non-purchase money secured debt on real property and passes to the children along with the property.

Example

Steve and Catherine, a married couple, borrow $100,000 from the bank to purchase their home, and take out a deed of trust in the bank's favor as security for the loan. They still owe $78,000. In separate wills, Steve and Catherine leave their ownership share to each other and name their children as alternates to take the home in equal shares. The deed of trust is a purchase money secured debt and, if the children get the property, they will also get the mortgage.

Example

All is as set out in the example above, but Steve and Catherine are two years behind on their property taxes. The property taxes would also pass to the children along with the home and the deed of trust obligation.

- **Debts owed on personal property** All purchase money secured debts owed on personal property pass to the beneficiaries of the personal property. However, non-purchase money secured debts owed on personal property do not pass with the property and are payable by your estate.

Example
Phil drives a 1985 Ferrari. Although the car is registered in Phil's name, the bank holds legal title pending Phil's payment of the outstanding $75,000 car note. Phil uses WillMaker to leave the car to his long-time companion Paula. The car note is a purchase money secured debt and will pass to Paula with the car.

Example
Carla borrowed $10,000 from a finance company to pay her income taxes. To get the money, she signed an agreement pledging "all her property" as collateral for repayment. Carla has a daughter, Juliet, and a son, Mark. Carla uses WillMaker to leave Juliet a precious doll house collection that has been passed down through the family for five generations, and leaves Mark the rest of her property. When Carla dies, she still owes $9,000 on the loan. The $9,000 debt is a non-purchase money secured debt and is payable out of Carla's estate. Carla can either provide how this—and any other debts—should be paid, or she can leave this decision up to her personal representative.

▶ **What If a Beneficiary Cannot Pay Off a Debt That**
▶ **Comes with the Property?**
▶ Because the property is usually worth more than any debt secured by it, an
▶ inheritor who does not want to owe money can sell the property, pay off the debt
▶ and pocket the difference. However, at times, relying on this approach is not
▶ satisfactory—especially when it comes to houses. For example, if you leave your
▶ daughter your house with the hope that it will be her home, you will probably not
▶ want her to have to sell the house because she cannot meet the mortgage
▶ payments. If you think a particular beneficiary will need assistance with paying a
▶ debt owed on property, try to leave the beneficiary the necessary money or
▶ valuable assets as either a specific or residuary bequest.

2. Unsecured Debts

Unsecured debts are all debts not tied to specific property. Common examples
are medical bills, most credit card bills, student loans, utility bills and probate
fees. Under WillMaker, these debts and expenses must be paid by your
personal representative or executor, either according to instructions in your
will, or as required by the laws of your state if you provide no instructions.

C. Canceling Debts Others Owe You

You can choose to release anyone who owes you a debt from the responsibility of paying it back to your estate after you die. You can cancel any such
debt—oral or written. If you do, your forgiveness functions much the same as
giving a gift; those who were indebted to you will no longer be legally
required to pay the money they owed.

Of course, keep in mind that the gift you are giving to the person or
institution owing the debt will diminish the property that your beneficiaries
may receive under your will.

Forgiving Debts May Be Tricky for Married Willmakers

If you are married and forgiving a debt, first make sure you have the full power to do so. For example, if the debt was incurred while you were married, you may only have the right to forgive half the debt. There is a special need to be cautious about this possibility in community property states. If your debt is a community property debt, you cannot cancel the whole amount due unless your spouse agrees to allow you to cancel his or her share of the debt—and puts that agreement in writing.

D. Paying Debts and Probate Expenses

WillMaker offers three basic options for paying unsecured debts, including the expenses of probate. You can:

- leave no instructions, which will mean that your personal representative will pay the debts and expenses as required by the laws of your state

- specify a particular asset or assets to be used or sold to pay debts and expenses, or

- specify that debts and expenses be paid out of your residuary estate.

1. Leaving No Instructions

If you do not specify in your will how you want your debts and expenses to be paid, your personal representative will be instructed by your will to follow your state's laws.

Some states require that debts and expenses be paid first out of property in your estate that does not pass under your will for some reason—for example, neither your residuary beneficiary nor alternate survive you—and next from the residuary of your estate. In other states, your debts and expenses must first be paid out of liquid assets such as bank accounts and securities, then from tangible personal property, and as a last resort, from real estate.

If you decide not to use either of the debt payment options offered by WillMaker, your personal representative will be instructed by your will to follow your state's rules. Typically, you don't need to leave instructions about debts if:

- your debts and expenses are likely to be negligible—or to represent only a tiny fraction of a relatively large estate

- you are leaving all your property to your spouse or specify that it should be shared among a very few beneficiaries, without divvying it up in specific bequests. In this situation, your debts will be paid first and then the beneficiaries will receive what's left, or

- you know and approve of how your state law deals with debts and expenses.

But you need to plan more carefully if debts payable by your estate are likely to be large enough to cut significantly into bequests left to individuals and charitable institutions. The danger, of course, is that unless you plan carefully, the people whose bequests are used to pay debts and expenses may be the very people who you would have preferred to take your property free and clear.

Example

Ruth has $40,000 in a money market account and several valuable musical instruments, also worth $40,000. She makes a will leaving the money market account to her daughter and the instruments to her musician son, but doesn't specify how her debts and expenses should be paid. Due to medical bills and an unpaid personal loan from a friend, Ruth dies owing $35,000. After Ruth's death, her personal representative must follow state law which first requires that debts be paid out of the residuary estate. But because there is no residuary—all property is used up by specific bequests—a second rule applies that requires that debts be paid out of liquid assets. As a result, the personal representative pays the $35,000 out of the money market account, leaving the daughter with only $5,000. The son receives the $40,000 worth of musical instruments.

▶ **Covering Your Debts with Insurance**

One way to deal with the problem of large debts and small assets is to purchase a life insurance policy in an amount large enough to pay your anticipated debts and expenses and have the proceeds made payable to your estate. You can then specify in your will that these proceeds should be used to pay your debts and expenses—with the rest going to your residuary beneficiary or a beneficiary named in a specific bequest.

But be careful. If large sums are involved, talk with an estate planner or accountant before adopting this sort of plan. Having insurance money paid to your estate subjects that amount to probate. A better alternative is often to provide that estate assets be sold, with the proceeds used to pay the debts. Then have the insurance proceeds made payable directly to your survivors free of probate.

2. Designating Specific Assets

One good approach to taking care of unsecured debts and expenses your estate owes is to designate one or more specific assets that your personal representative must use to pay them. If you designate a savings or money market account, for example, to be used for paying off your debts and expenses, and the amount in the account is sufficient to meet these obligations, the other bequests you make in your will not be affected by your estate's indebtedness.

Of course, if the source you specify is insufficient to pay all the bills, your personal representative will still face the problem of which property to use to make up the difference. For this reason, it is often wise to list several resources and specify the order in which they should be used. Also, make sure that they are worth more than what is likely to be required.

Example

Ella, a widow, makes a will that contains the following bequests:

- My house at 1111 Soto Street in Albany, New York to Hillary Bernette (The house has an outstanding mortgage of $50,000, for which Hillary will become responsible.)
- My coin collection (appraised at $30,000) to Stanley, Mark and Belinda Bernette
- My three antique chandeliers to Herbert Perkins

- The rest of my property to Denise Everread. Although not spelled out in the will, this property consists of a savings account ($26,000), a car ($5,000), a camera ($1,000) and stock ($7,000).

Using WillMaker, Ella specifies that her savings account and stock be used in the order listed to pay debts and expenses. When Ella dies, she owes $8,000; the expenses of probating her estate total $4,000. Following Ella's instructions, her personal representative would close the savings account, use $12,000 of it to pay debts and expenses, and turn the rest over to Denise along with the stock and camera.

Example

Now suppose Ella has only $6,000 in the savings account. When she dies, her personal representative, following the same instructions, would close the account ($6,000) and sell enough stock to make up the difference ($6,000). The remaining $1,000 worth of stock, the camera and the car would pass to Denise.

Selecting Specific Assets to Pay Debts

If you select specific assets to pay your debts and expenses, here are some tips on what assets to choose.

- **Select liquid assets over non-liquid assets**   Liquid assets are those easily converted into cash at full value—bank and deposit accounts, money market accounts, stocks and bonds. On the other hand, tangible assets such as motor vehicles, planes, jewelry, stamp and coin collections, electronic items and musical instruments must be sold to raise the necessary cash. Hurried sales seldom bring in anywhere near the full value, which means the net worth of your estate will also be reduced.

Example

Harry writes mystery books for a living. He has never produced a blockbuster but owns fifteen copyrights, which produce royalties of about $70,000 a year. During his life, Harry has traveled widely and collected artifacts from around the world. They have a value of $300,000 if sold carefully to knowledgeable collectors. Harry makes a will leaving his copyrights to his spouse and the artifacts to his children. He also designates that the artifacts should be used to pay his debts and expenses—which total $150,000 at death. Harry's personal representative, who is not a collector and has little time or inclination to sell the artifacts one by one, sells them in bulk for $140,000—less than half of their true value. To raise the extra $10,000, two of the copyrights are sold, again at less than their true value. As a result, Harry's children receive nothing and his spouse gets less than Harry intended. It would have been far better for Harry to purchase insurance to pay his debts or to sell some of his artifacts before his death for full value and pay off the debt.

- **Avoid designating property you have left to specific beneficiaries** WillMaker allows you to make up to 100 separate specific bequests as well as name a residuary beneficiary to take the rest of your property. It is important to review your specific bequests before designating assets to pay debts and expenses. If possible, designate liquid assets that have not been left to specific beneficiaries. Only as a last resort should you earmark a tangible item also left in a specific bequest for first use to pay debts and expenses.

  One exception to this general recommendation occurs if you believe you are unlikely to owe much when you die, and that the expenses of probate will be low. Then, it makes sense for you to designate a substantial liquid asset left as a specific bequest to also pay debts and expenses.

Describe Property Consistently

Property designated both as a specific bequest and as a source for paying your debts should be described exactly the same in both instances to avoid confusion.

3. Designating Your Residuary Estate

Using this WillMaker option, you direct your personal representative to pay all your debts and expenses out of your residuary estate—leaving it up to him or her which assets to use, and in which order. This option makes sense if you are leaving the bulk of your estate through specific bequests, and are using your residuary as a catch-all for property that comes into your estate after you make your will but before you die. But be sure there will be enough assets in your residuary to pay likely debts.

If your residuary bequest is an important part of your will—you make lots of bequests of specific property items and leave the bulk of your estate to your spouse through the residuary clause—then designating your residuary to pay debts may make less sense, especially if they are large enough to eat into the residuary. Instead, you may prefer to use the specific asset option discussed in Section 1, above. That would permit you to designate a specific asset for paying your debts and expenses and allow your spouse to receive the full amount in your residuary estate.

Designating your residuary to pay debts also makes sense if your residuary beneficiary is the same as one or more of the beneficiaries to whom you have already left specific bequests. For example, this would be the case if you leave the bulk of your estate to your spouse or children in a specific bequest and also name them as your residuary beneficiaries.

E. Paying Estate and Inheritance Taxes

Before you concentrate on how you want your estate and inheritance taxes to be paid, consider whether you need to be concerned about these types of taxes at all. Most people do not.

▶ Arranging to Pay Other Taxes

This discussion does not include back income or real property taxes owed by your estate. Real property taxes are secured debts, and pass to the beneficiary along with the real property. Income taxes must be paid out of your estate as discussed earlier in this chapter.

Basically, if the net worth of your estate is less than $600,000 when you die— or you are leaving property of greater value all to your spouse—there will likely be no federal estate tax unless you made substantial gifts during your life. As is explained in more detail in Chapter 12, Section D, if you give property worth more than $10,000 to an individual other than your spouse during a year, the excess is subtracted from your $600,000 exempt amount.

And while some states impose separate taxes on estates of lesser value, the taxes normally do not take a deep enough bite to cause serious concern unless your estate is very large. In fact, many states impose no significant death taxes. Among those that do, the taxes are technically imposed on the beneficiaries of the estate rather than on the estate itself. However, your personal representative has an obligation to pay the taxes and will therefore deduct the taxes from each bequest unless you specify differently in your will, as you can do when using WillMaker. (For a list of states that impose death taxes, see Chapter 12, Section E.)

If the value of your estate is well below the federal and state tax range, and you have no reasonable expectation that your estate will grow to that level between the time you make your will and the time you die, skip the following discussion of your options for paying taxes. And, when asked by the WillMaker program whether you wish to plan for the payment of taxes, answer no.

Getting Help with Large Estates

As you might imagine, financial planning experts have devised many creative ways to plan for paying estate and inheritance taxes. If your estate is large enough to warrant concern about possible federal estate and state inheritance taxes, it is large enough for you to afford a consultation with an accountant, estate planning specialist, or lawyer specializing in estates and trusts. Again, the threshold at which you need to worry about taxes is normally at least $600,000, and often much higher if you plan to leave much of your property to your spouse. (See Chapter 12 for an overview of estate planning techniques.)

If you are a relatively young, healthy person and your estate is only slightly larger than $600,000, you may want to adopt one of the WillMaker tax payment options now and worry about more sophisticated tax planning later. After all, by the time you die, federal and state tax rules will probably have changed many times.

WillMaker offers the following options for paying your estate and inheritance taxes. You can:

1. leave no instructions

2. designate specific assets

3. specify that the tax burden should be shared equitably among beneficiaries, or

4. specify that your tax liability be paid out of the residuary estate.

1. Leaving No Instructions

If you choose not to leave instructions on how estate and inheritance taxes should be paid, WillMaker directs your personal representative to pay them as required by the laws of your state. As with your debts and expenses, your state law controls how your personal representative is to approach this issue if you do not establish your own plan. Some states leave the method of payment up to your personal representative, while others provide that all beneficiaries must share equitably in the tax burden. Depending on your financial and tax situation and the law of your state, more variables set in than can reasonably be covered here.

2. Designating Specific Assets

As with payment of debts and expenses, it may be a good approach to designate one or more specific property items to satisfy paying your taxes. Again, if you designate a bank, brokerage or money market account to be used for paying taxes, and the amount in the account is adequate to meet these obligations, the other bequests you make in your will should not be affected.

Of course, if the resource you specify for payment of your estate and inheritance taxes is insufficient to cover the amount due, your personal representative will still face the problem of which property will be used to make up the difference. So, again, it is a good idea to list several resources which should be used to pay estate and inheritance taxes in the order listed.

Guidance for Selecting Specific Assets

If you do choose to select specific assets to be used to pay your taxes, follow the general rules set out in Section C, above.

3. Specifying That Tax Payments Be Shared

For the purpose of computing estate and inheritance tax liability, your estate consists of all property you legally own at your death, whether it passes under the terms of your will or outside of your will—under a joint tenancy, living trust, savings bank trust or life insurance policy. Because your estate's tax liability will be computed on the basis of all this property, you may wish to have the beneficiaries of the property share proportionately in the responsibility for paying the taxes.

Example

Julie Johanssen, a widow, owns a house (worth $500,000), stocks ($200,000), jewelry ($150,000) and investments as a limited partner in a number of rental properties ($300,000). To avoid probate, Julie puts the house in a living trust for her eldest son Warren, the stocks in a living trust for another son Alain, and uses her will to leave the jewelry to a daughter Penelope and the investments to her two surviving brothers, Sean and Ivan. She specifies that all beneficiaries of property in her taxable estate share in paying any estate and inheritance taxes.

When Julie dies, the net worth of her estate, which consists of all the property mentioned, is $1,150,000. Because this taxable estate is over $600,000, there is federal estate tax liability.

Each of Julie's beneficiaries will be responsible for paying a portion of this liability. Each portion will be measured by the proportion that beneficiary's inheritance has to the estate as a whole. Under this approach, Warren will be responsible for approximately 43% of the tax, Penelope for 13%, and so on. For Warren, this would mean a tax liability of $175,139. Penelope would owe $52,949.

While this option may be the most equitable way to have your taxes paid, it may not be the best approach in some circumstances. For instance, if Warren is ill and cannot raise the money without selling the house, Julie may want to provide that at least his portion of the taxes should be paid from another designated source.

4. Designating Your Residuary Estate

In this option, you direct your personal representative to pay your estate and inheritance taxes out of your residuary estate—leaving it up to him or her to decide which assets are to be used, and in which order. This can be a wise choice if the money and property in the residuary estate is specifically placed there for this purpose.

Sometimes, however, it can be a mistake. It is particularly unwise when:

- your taxable estate is fairly large, with a number of assets being passed outside of probate, and

- you intend the residuary to be used for other purposes—such as to leave property to your children or to pass large sums to your spouse.

The problem, of course, is that if many valuable assets such as a house are passed outside the will—in a living trust, for example—there will be a hefty estate tax liability but little property in the residuary estate. If all taxes are to be paid by the residuary estate, there may be no money left for the residuary beneficiaries. You will likely want to plan so that taxes will not wipe out the residuary beneficiary's share while recipients of other property get off tax-free.

▲

9 Making It Legal: Final Steps

Once you have proceeded through all the WillMaker screens and responded to all the questions the program poses, your will is complete. There are just a few more steps you must take to make your WillMaker will legally effective so that the directions you expressed in it can be carried out after your death.

> ▶ **Note for Perfectionists: No Accents or Umlauts**
> ▶
> ▶ WillMaker does not allow you to use special characters, such as an accent mark or
> ▶ an umlaut. You may be tempted to ink one in where your name, or the name of a
> ▶ beneficiary, carries the mark in question. Do not. The fact that the character is
> ▶ missing may be displeasing to you, but it will have no adverse impact on your
> ▶ will's legality or effectiveness. Minor spelling errors, typos and even awkward
> ▶ wording in text that you enter also will not adversely affect the legality of your
> ▶ will.

A. Before You Sign

Before you sign your will, take some time to scrutinize it and make sure it
accurately expresses your wishes.

You can do this either by calling it up on the screen or by printing out a
draft copy. Or if you believe in the need for both a belt and suspenders, read
both the screen and printed versions.

To see the will on the screen or print out a draft, follow the directions on
the screen titled "Document Choices." (Consult the Users' Guide, Part 4, if you
need additional guidance.) If, after you review the wording of your will, you
want to make changes, use the review/modify option, also on the Document
Choices screen.

> ▶ **Having Your Will Checked by an Expert**
> ▶
> ▶ You may want to have your will checked by an attorney or tax expert. This makes
> ▶ good sense if you are left with nagging questions about the law or implications of
> ▶ your choices, or if you own a great deal of property or have a complicated idea of
> ▶ how you want to leave it. But keep in mind that you are your own best expert on
> ▶ what property you own, your relation to family members and friends and your
> ▶ own favorite charities—in short, most issues and decisions involved in making a
> ▶ will. Also, few attorneys support the self-help approach to making a will; you may
> ▶ be hard-pressed to find one who is cooperative. (See Chapter 15 for information
> ▶ on how to find and use a lawyer.)

B. Sign Your Will and Have It Witnessed

To be valid, a will must be legally executed. This is not as bloody as it sounds. It means only that you must sign your will in front of witnesses. These witnesses must not only sign the will in your presence, but also in the presence of the other witnesses.

While state laws vary as to how many witnesses are required, three meets the minimum requirement of every state. Even if your state requires only two, it is preferable to have three witnesses for your will. That will ensure that there is one more person to establish that your signature is valid if it is later contested in court.

1. Requirements for Witnesses

There are a few legal requirements for witnesses. They need only be:

- adults—in most states, 18 or older

- of sound mind, and

- people who will not take any property under the will. Anyone to whom you leave property under your will, even as an alternate or residuary beneficiary, should not be a witness.

As a matter of common sense, the people you choose to be witnesses should be easily available when you die. While this bit of future history is impossible to foretell with certainty, it is best to choose witnesses who are in good health, younger than you are and who seem likely to remain in your geographic area. However, the witnesses do not have to be residents of your state.

2. Self-Proving Wills

For a will to be accepted by a probate court, the executor must show that the will really is the will of the person it purports to be—a process called proving the will. In the past, all wills were proved either by having one or two witnesses come into court to testify or swear in written, notarized statements called affidavits that they saw you sign your will.

▶ **States without Standard Self-Proving Laws**

The self-proving option is not available in the District of Columbia, Maryland, Michigan, Ohio and Vermont. In these states, your personal representative will be required to prove your will.

And to comply with New Hampshire law, WillMaker handles the self-proving option a little differently for its residents. They are asked on a separate screen whether they wish to make their will self-proving. If so, the program prints out an affidavit as part of the will. The will should be witnessed and signed in front of a Notary Public.

In California, the self-proving feature does not require a separate affidavit. Instead, the fact that the witnesses sign the will under oath is sufficient to have the will admitted into probate, unless a challenge is mounted.

Today, most states allow people to make their wills self-proving—that is, they can be admitted in probate court without the hassle of herding up witnesses to appear in court or sign affidavits. This is accomplished when the person making the will and the witnesses all appear before a Notary Public and sign the will while under oath.

If you live in a state that has the option of self-proving a will, WillMaker automatically produces a self-proving affidavit that is suitable for your state, with accompanying instructions. In most states, the self-proving affidavit is not part of your will, but a separate document. To use it, you and your witnesses must first sign the will as discussed above. Then, you and your witnesses must sign the self-proving affidavit in front of a Notary Public. This may be done any time after the will is signed, but obviously, it is easiest to do it while all your witnesses are gathered together to watch you sign your will.

Many younger people—who are likely to make a number of wills before they die—decide not to make their wills self-proving, due to the initial trouble of getting a Notary to attend the signing. If you are one of these people, file the uncompleted affidavit and instructions in a safe place in case you change your mind later.

3. Signing Procedure

You need not utter any magic words when signing your will and having it witnessed, but a few legal requirements suggest the best way to proceed.

- Gather all three witnesses together in one place.

- Inform your witnesses that the papers you hold in your hand are your last will and testament. This is important, because the laws in many states specifically require that you acknowledge the document as your will before the witnesses sign it. The witnesses need not read your will, however, and there is no need for them to know its contents. If you want to ensure that the contents of the will stay confidential, you may cover all but the signature portion of your will with a separate sheet of paper while the witnesses sign.

- Initial each page of the will at the bottom on the lines provided. The purpose of initialing is to prevent anyone from challenging the will as invalid because changes were made to it by someone else.

- Sign the last page on the signature line *in the witnesses' presence*. When you sign the will, use the same form of your name as you provided when WillMaker asked you to input your name on the screen. Again, this should be the form of the name you most commonly use to sign legal documents such as deeds, checks and loan applications.

- Ask the witnesses to initial the bottom of each page on a line there, then watch as they sign and fill in their addresses on the last page where indicated. Their initials act as evidence if anyone later claims you changed your will without going through the proper legal formalities.

▶ **Make Sure Witnesses Sign on a Page with Text**
▶
▶ If the final page of your will contains only spaces for the signatures of your
▶ witnesses, and no text of your will, it is remotely possible that after your death
▶ someone might claim that the witness page was illegally added later and that the
▶ will itself was not properly signed and witnessed.
▶   To avoid this, change the number of lines printed per page by a line or two
▶ on the print set-up screen to alter the way the will prints out, so that either:
▶ • some text of the will appears on the last page before the witness lines, or
▶ • at least one of the witness lines appears on the next-to-last page.
▶ (See the Users' Guide, Part 4, for instructions on how to do this.)

C. Do Not Change Your Will

Once you have produced and printed a will using WillMaker, it is extremely important that you do not alter it by inserting handwritten or typed additions or changes—either before or after you sign it. Do not even correct misspellings. The laws of most states require that after a will is signed, any additions or changes to it, even clerical ones, must be made by following the same signing and witnessing requirements as for an original will.

Although it is legally possible to make handwritten corrections before you sign, it is a bad idea, since after your death, it will not be clear to the probate court that you made the corrections before the will was signed. The possibility that the changes were made later may throw the legality of the whole will into question.

▶
▶ **WillMaker Does Not Allow Codicils**
▶
▶ If you want to make changes once your will has been signed and witnessed, there
▶ are two ways to accomplish it: You can either make a new will, or make a formal
▶ addition, called a codicil, to the existing one.
▶ One of the great advantages of WillMaker is that you can conveniently keep
▶ up-to-date by simply making a new will. This does away with the need to tack in
▶ changes to the will in the form of a codicil. Codicils are not allowed when using
▶ WillMaker because of the possibility of creating a conflict between the codicil and
▶ the original will.

D. Storing Your Will

Once your will is properly signed and witnessed, your main consideration is that your personal representative can easily locate it at your death. Here are some suggestions.

- Store your printed and witnessed will in an envelope on which you have typed your name and the word "Will"—or use the preprinted envelope that comes with the WillMaker program.

- Place the envelope in a fireproof metal box, file cabinet or home safe. An alternative is to place the original copy of your will in a safe deposit box. But before doing that, learn the bank's policy about access to the box after your death. If, for instance, the safe deposit box is in your name alone, the box can probably be opened only by a person authorized by a court and, then, only in the presence of a bank employee. An inventory may even be required if any person enters the box or for state tax purposes. All of this takes time, and in the meantime, your will is locked away from those who need access to it.

> ▶ **Helping Others Find Your Will**
> ▶ Your will should be easy to locate at your death. You want to spare your
> ▶ survivors the anxiety of having to search for your will when they are already
> ▶ dealing with the grief of losing you. Make sure your personal representative, and
> ▶ at least one other person you trust, know where to find your will.
> ▶ And while you're at it, making a clear record of all your property, its location
> ▶ and the location of any ownership documents that relate to it will make your
> ▶ executor's job easier. *Nolo's Personal RecordKeeper*, a software program by
> ▶ Pladsen and Warner (Nolo Press) offers an excellent way to do this.

E. Making Copies of Your Will

Some people are tempted to prepare more than one signed and witnessed
original of their will in case one is lost. While it is legal in most states to
prepare and sign duplicate originals, it is never a good idea. Common sense
tells you why: If you later want to change your will, it can be difficult to locate
all the old copies to destroy them.

It can sometimes be a good idea, however, to make several unsigned
copies of your current will. Give one to your proposed personal representative
or executor. And, if it is appropriate, give other copies to your spouse, friends
or children. In a close family, it can be a relief to everyone to learn your plans
for distributing your property. But obviously, there are many good reasons
why you may wish to keep the contents of your will strictly confidential until
your death. If so, do not make any copies.

F. Give the WillMaker Disk a Good Home

Once you have printed out your will, you should make a copy of it in
electronic form—on your disk. Follow the instructions in Part 4 of the User's
Guide on backing up your documents to a floppy disk. Find a safe, private
place to store the disk so that you can use it to restore or update your will if
that becomes necessary. Others should not have access to the disk without
your permission.

▶
▶   **Copies Are Not Valid**
▶   As with other unsigned and unwitnessed copies, the copy of your will stored on
▶   the WillMaker disk does not constitute a valid will until it is printed out and
▶   formally signed and witnessed as discussed above. ▲
▶

10 Keeping Your Will Up-to-Date

Your will is an extremely personal document. Your marital status, where you live, what kind and how much property you own and whether you have children are all examples of life choices that affect what you include in your will and what laws will be applied to enforce it.

But your life changes. You may sell one house and buy another. You may divorce. You may have or adopt children. Eventually you will face the grief associated with the death of a loved one. Not all life changes require that you also change your will. However, significant ones often do. This chapter alerts you to life changes that require you to make a new will.

A. When to Make a New Will

There are several occurrences that signal that you should make a new will.

1. If Your Marital Status Changes

Suppose that after you use WillMaker to leave all or part of your property to your spouse, you get divorced. Under the law in many states, the divorce automatically cancels the bequest to the ex-spouse. The alternate beneficiary named for that bequest, or, if there is none, your residuary beneficiary, gets the property. In some states, however, your ex-spouse would still inherit as directed in the will. If you remarry, state legal rules become even more murky.

Rather than deal with all these complexities, follow this simple rule: Make a new will if you marry, divorce or if you are separated and seriously considering divorce.

If you indicate a change in marital status when using WillMaker, the program does not return you directly to the review menu. Instead, it takes you back through your previous answers and asks you to verify them. The reason for this is that many willmaking decisions are based on marital status. If your marital status changes, you should carefully review whether your property is going to the people you want to get it—and whether your spouse is receiving an adequate share.

Beware of State Laws on Spouse's Shares

If you leave your spouse out of your will because you are separated, and you die before you become divorced, it is possible that the spouse could claim a statutory share of your estate. (Statutory shares are explained in Chapter 4, Section C.) Consult a lawyer to find out how the laws of your state apply to this situation.

2. If Your Property Ownership Changes

If you leave all property through your residuary clause, there is no need to change your will if you acquire new items of property or get rid of existing ones—your residuary beneficiary takes all of your property at your death.

But if you have made specific bequests of property that you no longer own, it may be wise to make a new will. If you leave a specific item to someone—a particular Tiffany lamp, for example—but you no longer own the item when you die, the person named in your will to receive it is out of luck. He or she obviously cannot have the actual item, and is not entitled to receive another item or money in lieu of it.

The legal word for a failure of a bequest is ademption. People who do not inherit the property in question are often heard to use an earthier term.

However, in some circumstances, if a specific item has merely changed form, the original beneficiary may still have a claim to it. Examples of this are:

- a promissory note that has been paid and for which the cash is still available, and

- a house which has been sold in exchange for a promissory note and deed of trust.

A problem similar to the ademption situation occurs when there is not enough money to go around. For example, if you leave $50,000 each to your spouse and two children, but there is only $100,000 in your estate at your death, the gifts in the will must be reduced. In legal lingo, this is called an abatement. How property is abated under state law is often problematic; adjust the amount of your bequests to the size of your estate to avoid this.

3. If You Adopt or Have Additional Children

Each time a child is born or legally adopted into your family, the new child should be named in the will—where you are asked to name your children—and provided for according to your wishes. If you do not do this, the child might later challenge your will in court, claiming that he or she was overlooked as an heir and is entitled to a substantial share of your property. (See Chapter 6, Section A.)

When using WillMaker, if you indicate that you now have a minor child, the program does not return you directly to the review menu. Instead, it takes you back through your previous answers and asks you to verify them. It also will ask you to name a personal guardian and alternate personal guardian to care for the child if he or she is a minor when you die and the child's other parent is dead or unavailable.

4. If Your Child Dies, Leaving Children

If any of your children die before you, and leave children (your grandchildren), those grandchildren should also be named in your will. In the WillMaker program, you should type in their names on the screen where you are asked to name the children of a deceased child. If they are not mentioned in your will, they might later be legally entitled to claim a share of your estate.

5. If You Move to a Different State

WillMaker applies several state-specific laws when it helps you create your will. These laws are especially important in two situations.

- If you have set up one form of management for young beneficiaries and then move to a different state, you may find when making a new will that WillMaker presents you with different management options. This is because some states have adopted the Uniform Transfers to Minors Act and others have not. If you want to see whether your new state offers different management options, see Chapter 7, Section E.

- If you are married and do not intend to leave all or most of your property to your spouse, review Chapter 4, Section C, that discusses the rules if you move from a community property state to a common law state or vice-versa.

When using WillMaker, if you change your state, the program does not return you directly to the review menu. Instead, it takes you back through your previous answers and asks you to verify them. It also erases any provisions you have made to provide management for property left to minors or young adults, and asks you to reconsider this issue. The reason for this is that different states provide different options for property management.

6. If Any of Your Beneficiaries Die

If a beneficiary you have named to receive a significant amount of property either as a specific or residuary beneficiary dies before you, you should make a new will. It is especially important to do this if you named only one beneficiary for the bequest and did not name an alternate—or if the alternate you named is no longer your first choice to get the property.

7. If the Guardian or Property Manager Cannot Serve

The first choice or alternate named to serve as a personal guardian for your minor children or manager for their property may move away, become disabled, or simply turn out to be someone you consider unsuitable for the job. If so, you will probably want to make a new will naming somebody else.

8. If the Personal Representative Cannot Serve

The personal representative or executor of your estate is responsible for making sure your will provisions are carried out. If you decide that the personal representative you named originally is no longer suitable, you may want to name another.

9. If Your Witnesses Become Unavailable

The witnesses who sign your will are responsible for testifying that the signature on your will is valid and that you appeared capable of making a will when you did so. If two or more of your witnesses become unable to fulfill this function, you may want to make a new will with new witnesses—especially if you have some inkling that anyone is likely to contest your will after you die. But a new will is probably not necessary if you have made your will self-proving. (See Chapter 9, Section B2.)

B. How to Make a New Will

If you want to make a new will, a subsequent swoop through the WillMaker program will proceed even more quickly than the first time through, since you will know what to expect and will likely be familiar with many of the legal concepts you had to learn the first time through.

If you make a new will, even if it only involves a few changes, you must follow the legal requirements for having it signed and witnessed just as if you were starting from scratch. If you choose to make your will self-proving, you must also complete a new affidavit.

> ### In with the New, Out with the Old
> As soon as you print, sign and have your new will witnessed, it will automatically replace all wills you have made before it. But to avoid possible confusion, you should physically destroy all other original wills and any copies of them. ▲

11 Explanatory Letters

In addition to the tasks that you can accomplish by using WillMaker, you may also wish to:

- explain why bequests are being given to certain beneficiaries and not to others

- explain disparities in bequests

- express positive or negative sentiments about a beneficiary

- explain why you are nominating a certain person as personal guardian for your minor children, or

- name someone to care for your pet after your death.

   WillMaker does not allow you to do these things in your will for one important reason: The program has been written, tested and re-tested with painstaking attention to allowing you to make your own legal and unambiguous will.

WillMaker does not allow you to enter general information, personal statements, or reasons for making or not making a bequest. That would risk the possibility that a person making the will might unwittingly produce a document with conflicting, confusing or possibly even illegal provisions.

Fortunately, there is a way you can have your final say about personal matters without risking your will's legal integrity. You can write a letter to accompany your will expressing your thoughts to those who survive you.

Since what you put in the letter will not have legal effect as part of your will, there is no danger that your expressions will tread upon the time-tested legal language of the will or cause other problems later. Nevertheless, writing a letter to your loved ones to explain why you wrote your will as you did— and knowing they will read your reasoning at your death—can give you a great deal of peace of mind during life.

A. An Introduction for Your Letters

Here is a formal introduction that makes it clear that the letter you write to attach to your will is an expression of your sentiments and not intended as a will, an addition to or an interpretation of your will.

To My Personal Representative:

This letter expresses my feelings and reasons for certain decisions made in my will. It is not my will, nor do I intend it to be an interpretation of my will. My will, which was signed by me, dated and witnessed on _____ is the sole expression of my intentions concerning all my property, and other matters covered in it.

Should anything I say in this letter conflict with, or seem to conflict with, any provision of my will, the will shall be followed.

I request that my personal representative give a copy of this letter to each person named in my will to take property, or act as a guardian or custodian, and to anyone else my personal representative determines should receive a copy.

After this introduction, you are free to express your sentiments, keeping in mind that your estate may be held liable for any false, derogatory statements you make about an individual or organization.

B. Expressing Sentiments and Explaining Choices

There is little that a manual such as this can say to guide highly personal expressions of the heart. What follows are some suggestions about things you might wish to cover.

1. Explaining Why Gifts Were Made

The WillMaker requirement that you must keep descriptions of property and beneficiaries short and succinct may leave you unsatisfied. You have thought hard and long about why you want a particular person to get particular property—and are constrained in your will to listing your wishes in a few bloodless words. You can remedy that by explaining the whys and wherefores of your will directives in a letter.

Example

[Introduction]

The gift of my fishing boat to my friend Hank is in remembrance of the many companionable days we enjoyed fishing together on the lake. Hank, I hope you're out there for many more years.

or

Julie, the reason I have given you the farm is that you love it as much as I do and I know you'll do your best to make sure it stays in the family. But please, if the time comes when personal or family concerns mean that it makes sense to sell it, do so with a light heart—and knowing that it's just what I would have done.

2. Explaining Disparities in Gifts

You may also wish to explain your reasons for leaving more property to one person than another. While it is certainly your prerogative to make unequal bequests, you can also guess that in a number of family situations, unbalanced shares may cause hurt feelings or hostility after your death.

Ideally, you could call those involved together during your life, explaining to them why you plan to leave your property as you do. However, if you wish to keep your property plans private until after you die—or would find such a lifetime meeting too painful or otherwise impossible—you can cure the uncomfortability by attaching a letter of explanation to your will.

Example

[Introduction]

I love all my children equally. The reason I gave a smaller percentage of my residuary estate to Tim than to my other children is that Tim received family funds to purchase a house, so it is fair that my other two children receive more of my property now.

or

I am giving the bulk of my property to my son John for one reason: because of his health problems, he needs it more.

Ted and Ellen, I love you just as much, and I am extremely proud of the life choices you have made. But the truth is that you two can manage fine without a boost from me, and John can't.

3. Expressing Positive or Negative Sentiments

Whatever your plans for leaving your property, you may wish to attach a letter to your will in which you clear your mind of some sentiments you formed during life. These may be positive—thanking a loved one for kind acts—or negative—explaining why you are leaving a person out of your will.

Example

[Introduction]

The reason I left $10,000 to my physician Dr. Buski is not only that she treated me competently over the years but that she was unfailingly gentle and attentive. I always appreciated that she made herself available—day or night—and took the time to explain my ailments and treatments to me.

or

I am leaving nothing to my brother Malcolm. I wish him no ill will. But over the years, he has decided to isolate himself from me and the rest of the family and I don't feel I owe him anything.

4. Explaining Your Choice for Personal Guardian

Having children is the biggest impetus for people to write their wills—and their prime concern is usually making sure that someone loving and competent will care for their children if the parents die while their children are still young. (See Chapter 6, Section C, for a discussion of naming a personal guardian for minor children.) As noted, the person you name in your will as personal guardian does not automatically take over the job: a court must sanction the choice. However, your choice will likely be accepted unless the court deems that the best interests of the child would better be served in another arrangement—or you have bypassed the other parent who normally takes legal precedence.

If you do name someone as personal guardian who might not be the first logical choice—the other surviving parent or a close relative—it is a good idea to attach a letter to your will pointing up your reasons. This will give you an opportunity to explain to the court why naming the person you have selected as guardian is in the best interests of your children.

Example

[Introduction]

I have nominated my companion, Peter Nickol, to be the guardian of my daughter Melissa, because I know he would be the best guardian for her. For the past six years, Peter has functioned as Melissa's parent, living with me and her, helping to provide care for her and loving her. She loves him and regards him as her father. She hardly knows her natural father, Tom Damm. She has not seen him for four years. He has not contributed to her support or taken any interest in her. If he were granted custody, Melissa would be taken from familiar surroundings and necessarily undergo emotional torment.

5. Providing Care for Your Pet

Legally, pets are property. Many pet owners, of course, disagree. They feel a true bond with their animals and want to make sure that when they die, their pets will get good care and a good home. The best way to do this is to make a formal arrangement. You cannot leave money or other property to your pet, either through a will or trust. Instead, the best legal approach is to use your will to leave your pet—and perhaps some money for the expenses of its care and feeding—to someone you trust to look out for it.

Make the bequest of pet and money in a specific bequest screen in your WillMaker will. Then attach a letter to your will explaining your wishes to the new owner, and include special instructions for the pet's care. Of course, make sure you get the new owner's welcome approval before making such a bequest.

Example

[Introduction]

I have left my dog Spot to my neighbor Belinda Mason, because she has been a willing and loving friend to him— grooming him willingly and well and taking him for walks when I was on vacation or unwell. I know that Belinda and her three children will provide a loving and happy home for Spot when I no longer can.

I request that Belinda continue to take Spot for his tri-annual check-ups with the veterinarian in town, Dr. Schuler, and have left her $2,000 to help cover the cost of that care. ▲

12 Estate Planning

Preparing a basic will such as the one produced by WillMaker is the essential first step in planning any estate. Especially for larger estates, however, many more options are available. This chapter provides a brief overview of what you might want to consider.

Estate Planning Resources from Nolo Press

Nolo Press publishes many resources that can help you with estate planning. You may conclude that this makes our recommendation a little prejudiced, but we believe these are the best book and software products available, and offer a money-back guarantee if you do not agree. See the catalog at the back of this manual for more information.

- *Nolo's Living Trust.* A software package that shows users how to create their own living trust documents.

- *Plan Your Estate.* Shows how to prepare an estate plan without the expensive services of a lawyer. It includes all the tear-out forms and step-by-step instructions needed to prepare living trusts and other estate planning devices. Considerable detail on federal estate taxes and simple strategies to avoid them.

- *5 Ways To Avoid Probate.* A 60-minute audio cassette tape covering the five principal probate avoidance techniques—joint tenancy, savings account trusts, insurance, living trusts and naming a beneficiary for IRAs, Keoghs and 401K Plans.

- *Make Your Own Living Trust.* Provides a thorough explanation of living trusts—a popular probate avoidance device. Includes information on how a living trust works, how to transfer property to a trust and what happens when the person who sets one up dies.

- *Who Will Handle Your Finances If You Can't?* Contains tear-out, fill-in-the-blank forms and complete instructions for how to make a durable power of attorney for finances—the document that can give a person legal authority to handle financial matters for someone who is not able to do so.

- *Nolo's Law Form Kit: Power of Attorney.* Line-by-line instructions for preparing powers of attorney for finances.

- *Nolo's Simple Will Book.* All instructions and forms needed to create a legally valid will, with examples of clauses to use to tailor your will to your needs.

- *Write Your Will.* A 50-minute audio cassette tape covering what provisions a will should contain, how to provide for children and grandchildren, how to assign an executor, how to have a will signed and witnessed.

- *Nolo's Law Form Kit: Wills.* Line-by-line instructions for preparing a simple will.

- *Beating the Nursing Home Trap: A Consumer's Guide to Choosing and Financing Long-Term Care.* A compendium of alternatives for those concerned about finding and financing long-term care. It discusses planning so that an elder's financial resources can supplement money available from public sources.

- *How To Probate an Estate* (California only). A simple explanation of how to read a will, handle probate paperwork, collect life insurance and other benefits, pay bills and taxes and distribute property left through trusts.

- *The Conservatorship Book* (California only). Guidance for determining when a conservatorship is necessary for a person incapacitated due to illness or age and whether there are suitable alternatives.

- *A Legal Guide for Lesbian and Gay Couples.* A complete guide to understanding the specialized interpretations and laws that affect gay and lesbian couples, this book includes a chapter on estate planning concerns.

- *The Living Together Kit.* A legal and estate planning guide geared to the needs of unmarried heterosexual couples.

- *Nolo's Personal RecordKeeper.* A software program that provides structure for a complete inventory of all your important legal, financial, personal and family records. Having accurate and complete records gets you organized, makes tax preparation easier and helps loved ones manage your affairs if you become incapacitated or die.

A. When You May Need More Than a Will

After using WillMaker to prepare a simple will, you may want to do additional estate planning to:

- avoid probate

- reduce or limit death taxes, or

- control how property left to one or more beneficiaries, such as a surviving spouse or a child, can be used.

Not surprisingly, these estate planning objectives are of interest primarily to people who own substantial property. Tax planning, especially, is the province of larger estates, because there are no federal estate taxes on the first $600,000 passed to one's inheritors. This assumes that the deceased person has not made substantial gifts of valuable property during life. (See Section C below for more on federal estate and gift taxes.)

Planning to avoid probate or place controls on the future use of property can make sense for smaller estates, but people who have little to leave their survivors will find there is little incentive to engage in sophisticated estate planning.

Even people with larger estates should face a blunt truth: Estate planning benefits your inheritors, not you. And your survivors will not benefit from your time and trouble until you die, which may be many years from now. In the meantime, healthy people who expect to live for many more years often waste time, effort and money planning and replanning their estates every couple of years.

Although you will rarely find a high-priced lawyer or financial planner who will admit it, it makes sense for many relatively healthy people with moderate-sized estates to rely primarily on a simple will and maybe several other fairly easy-to-use probate avoidance devices, but to postpone other types of estate planning until they reach late middle age or face a life-threatening illness.

Deciding whether or not to plan to avoid probate involves at least three considerations:

- **Your age** If you're under 60 or so and healthy, it probably makes sense to prepare a will, adopt the easier types of probate avoidance devices such as joint tenancy or pay-on-death bank accounts and leave the more complicated estate planning until later.

- **The size of your estate** The bigger your estate, the bigger the potential probate cost and tax liability. And the more reason to take steps to keep both at a minimum. Often with a large estate, it makes good sense to concentrate energy on seeing that major assets, such as real estate or business assets, are owned in a way that will avoid probate.

- **The type of property you own and how active you are in business** Some kinds of property are relatively easy to transfer directly to inheritors without a year's detour through probate—such as the bank balance in a pay-on-death account. Others are workier. For example, if you prepare a revocable living trust, you must keep it up-to-date, which can involve considerable time and trouble if you buy and sell a lot of property.

- **How much effort you are willing to expend** Planning to avoid probate typically saves your inheritors 5% to 7% of the value of your estate and allows them to get the property you leave them more quickly. You must decide how much time, trouble and expense you are willing to undergo to achieve these benefits.

B. Planning to Avoid Probate

This section summarizes the principal ways to avoid probate. But first, here is a brief discussion of probate and why you may want to avoid it.

1. What Is Probate?

Probate is the legal process that includes filing a deceased person's will with a court, locating and gathering his or her assets, paying debts and death taxes and eventually distributing what is left as the will directs. With the exceptions noted below, property left by will must, by law, go through probate. If there is no will and no probate avoidance devices were used, property is distributed according to state law—and it still must go through probate. Fortunately, property left using other legal devices, including joint tenancy and revocable living trusts, is not required to go through probate. It can be transferred directly to the inheritors.

▶ **Small Estates May Be Exempt from Probate**
▶
▶ Most states allow very small estates, usually in the $5,000 to $60,000 range, to pass
▶ to inheritors either free of probate or subject to a streamlined, do-it-yourself
▶ probate process. This is true even if you make a will and do not adopt any
▶ probate avoidance devices. Some states also simplify or eliminate the normal
▶ probate process for property left by one spouse to the other.

2. Why Avoid Probate

Probate has many drawbacks and few advantages. It typically takes from nine to 18 months, and is usually costly, involving fees for attorneys, appraisers, accountants and the probate court. All these costs are paid from estate property—reducing the amount left for inheritors. Fees which are set by state law or local custom vary somewhat, but often consume from 5% to 7% of an estate.

Not surprisingly, the major money bite goes for lawyers. Either by custom or law, a probate lawyer's fees are typically a percentage of the estate's value, even if the work involves no more than transferring the property to a surviving spouse or dividing it among several children. Even worse, in a few states, the lawyer's fees are based on the value of the property that goes through probate, without subtracting what the deceased person owed on the property.

Example

If Harry, a resident of California, dies with a gross estate—that's the total value of everything he owns, without subtracting debts owed on the property—of $500,000, the standard attorney's fees under that state's probate fee statute would be $11,500. The fee is based on the $500,000 figure, even if Harry's house has a $200,000 mortgage on it. Harry's relatives would be free to try to negotiate a lower fee with a lawyer—but no lawyer is likely to mention that when quoting a fee. Court filing fees, property appraisals and other costs would typically add thousands more to the cost of settling the estate. And if the probate involves anything beyond preparing routine paperwork, it may cost even more.

The fundamental problem with probate is that most consumers receive little value for their money. In most situations, an executor of the will, or close relative if there is no will, could pay debts and taxes and transfer property to inheritors quickly and safely without probate court supervision—for much less than the typical probate lawyer's fee. Unless relatives are fighting, or there are big claims against the estate, it is usually unnecessary for a court to step in and supervise.

There is one advantage of probate. It sets a deadline by which creditors who have been properly notified of the probate proceeding must file formal claims against the estate. People worried about big claims—a person with a lot of debts or a professional who might face malpractice suits—sometimes find it soothing to know that this cut-off date would be imposed.

3. Ways to Avoid Probate

There are six major ways to transfer property so that it avoids probate at your death:

- Pay-on-death accounts
- Gifts made during your life
- Life insurance
- Retirement accounts
- Joint tenancy
- Revocable living trusts

Pay-on-Death Bank Accounts (Informal Trusts)

Banks and savings and loans allow you to name someone to receive, at your death, any money remaining in your account. No probate is required. To set up such an account, anyone with a checking, savings, or bank money market account or a certificate of deposit need only add a designation that the money be held in trust for a named beneficiary. Depending on local custom and state law, these accounts are called pay-on-death, savings bank or informal trust accounts.

A particularly attractive feature of these pay-on-death accounts is that the person who establishes the account retains complete control over the money until his or her death. The named beneficiary has no right to the money until the person who established the account dies. The depositor can withdraw all the money or change the beneficiary any time before death.

Because it is so easy to accomplish, it makes sense for almost everyone with a substantial amount of money in the bank to use this technique—no matter their age or the size of their estate.

▶
▶   **U.S. Government Securities**
▶
▶   Pay-on-death designations can also be used with United States government bonds,
▶   treasury bills and treasury notes. As with bank accounts, the pay-on-death
▶   designation allows the securities to go directly to the beneficiary, without probate.
▶

Gifts Made During Your Life

Another simple way to keep property out of probate is to give property away during your life—even shortly before death. Anything you give away while you are alive is not part of your estate when you die, so it is not subject to probate. To make a legal gift, you must surrender ownership and control over the property. It is not enough to claim to give property away if for the rest of your life you hold onto it and continue to control it as if no gift had been made. (See Section D1 for a discussion of the impact of gifts on federal estate and gift taxation.)

Life Insurance

Americans have a tendency to over-insure their lives. Still, some life insurance can be useful, even essential, when a person wants to provide for children or disadvantaged dependents. The proceeds of a life insurance policy pass to its beneficiaries free of probate as long as a specific beneficiary is named. Normally, all that is needed to collect the proceeds is a certified copy of the death certificate. However, if you designate your own estate as the policy beneficiary, as is occasionally done when the estate will need immediate cash to pay debts or taxes, the proceeds will be subject to probate.

Retirement Accounts (IRAs, Keoghs and 401K Plans)

While retirement accounts were not designed as estate planning devices, they can be used that way. Funds in a person's retirement account at death pass to the beneficiary designated in the account documents and are not subject to probate. Although the retiree must withdraw a minimum amount—the sum varies each year, based on the person's life expectancy—beginning at age 70 1/2, the rest can stay in the account.

Community Property Note   In community property states (see Chapter 4, Section C, for a list), one-half of the money put in a retirement account while a couple is married belongs to the surviving spouse.

Joint Tenancy with Right of Survivorship

Joint tenancy (explained in Chapter 4, Section B), is an excellent probate avoidance technique for couples and co-owners of personal and real property who want the surviving owner to inherit their share. Couples who buy a house or other valuable property often take title in joint tenancy, so that when one of them dies, the other can get the property quickly and easily—and keep a significant portion of the estate out of probate.

Unfortunately, using joint tenancy as a probate avoidance technique for individually-owned property is often not a wise idea, for the following reasons.

- Property transferred into joint tenancy with someone else cannot be called back if you change your mind. With a will, pay-on-death bank account, insurance policy or living trust, you are free to change your mind and give or leave the property to someone else.

- Property transferred to a joint tenant belongs to the new joint tenant as soon as the transfer is made. The new owner can sell or give away the property, or it can be taken by his or her creditors or by the government to pay unpaid taxes. In short, your efforts to transfer property to avoid probate fees later can cause you serious problems now.

- If the original property owner is elderly and transfers the property into joint tenancy with a younger person, there is always the possibility that the younger person will die first and full ownership of the property will revert to the older one. If, in the meantime, the older individual is no longer competent to make business decisions, the property is likely to pass under the residuary clause of a will and end up in probate after all.

▶ **Joint Tenancy in Community Property States**
▶ **(Arizona, California, Idaho, Nevada, New Mexico, Texas,**
▶ **Washington and Wisconsin)**
▶
▶ Most married couples who live in states with community property laws prefer to
▶ take title to jointly-owned property as community property or as community
▶ property held in joint tenancy. The reason for this is that under federal estate tax
▶ rules, both shares of community property are automatically entitled to a stepped-
▶ up tax basis upon the death of either spouse. This can be a significant tax break.
▶ By contrast, only the deceased spouse's half of jointly-owned property that is not
▶ community property qualifies for a stepped-up tax basis.
▶   Property held in the name of one spouse or in joint tenancy may legally be
▶ community property. If so, it will still qualify for a stepped-up tax basis. The
▶ problem is that when one spouse dies, the IRS presumes that property held in
▶ joint tenancy is not community property, and it is up to the surviving spouse to
▶ prove that it is.
▶   In California and some other community property states, if the deceased
▶ person's share of community property is left to the surviving spouse, it qualifies
▶ for a quick and easy summary probate procedure that can be processed without a
▶ lawyer. Nevertheless, because some paperwork and delay is still involved, some
▶ estate planning experts recommend holding property in joint tenancy to avoid
▶ probate, while carefully documenting that it was purchased with community
▶ property funds or otherwise transferred to community property ownership, to
▶ qualify for the stepped-up tax basis.

Revocable Living Trusts

A revocable living trust is a legal entity you create by preparing and signing a
document that looks fairly similar to a will. In the trust document, you specify
who you want to receive certain property at your death. Unlike property left in
a will, however, property subject to a living trust avoids the cost and delay of
probate.

Revocable living trusts are extremely flexible. You can leave all of your
property by living trust. Or, as commonly occurs, you can use a living trust to
leave only some assets—leaving the remainder by will or one or more of the

other probate avoidance techniques discussed in this chapter. Unlike wills, living trusts are not made public at your death.

These trusts are called living or sometimes inter vivos (Latin for "among the living") because they are created while you are alive. They are called revocable because you can revoke or change them at any time, for any reason, before you die. During your lifetime, you still have control over all property transferred to your living trust and can do what you want with it—sell it, spend it, or give it away.

▶ **Living Trust Technicalities**

Living trusts are simple in concept. The person who establishes the trust—called either the settlor, grantor or creator—signs a trust document that contains these elements:

1. A list of the property that is subject to the trust—for example, the house at 12 Marden Road, Purchase, New York and brokerage account 1278 at Racafrax Co.

2. The name of a trustee, who has power to manage the trust property. Normally, the person who establishes the trust names himself or herself as trustee.

3. The names of the beneficiary or beneficiaries. These are the people who will receive the trust property at the creator's death.

4. The name of the successor trustee who will take over when the person who set up the trust dies and turn the trust property over to the beneficiaries. In most living trusts, the successor trustee is also given the power to manage the property if the creator becomes disabled. The successor trustee is often one of the trust's principal beneficiaries.

5. The terms of the trust. These always give the creator power to amend or revoke it at any time.

A living trust can transfer property to inheritors only if ownership of the property is transferred to the trust's name. Ownership documents—the title to your house, your securities, and your motor vehicle title slip—must be officially changed to the trust's name or the trust will not control the property.

One drawback of a living trust is the relatively small hassle of transferring ownership of property to the trust and conducting future personal business in the name of the trust. There may also be transfer taxes when you transfer property to the trust's name. Fortunately, there is no need to file a separate tax return for the trust. All transactions made by your living trust, such as the sale of property at a profit, are reported on your personal income tax return.

▶
▶   **Self-Help for Living Trusts**
▶
▶   You may be able to create a living trust without a lawyer's assistance by using
▶   *Plan Your Estate* or *Nolo's Living Trust*, both by Nolo Press. Order information is at
▶   the back of the manual.
▶
▶

Who Should Have a Living Trust?

Despite its probate avoidance advantages compared with a will, a living trust is not the best choice for everyone. As noted earlier, the amount of energy you should expend on avoiding probate probably depends on your age, health, the amount of property involved and the workiness of a particular probate avoidance device. Here's a thumbnail outline of how to approach the problem sensibly.

Age 70 or Over   Use a living trust for all or most valuable assets not covered by other probate avoidance devices.

   Exception   Married couples in community property states such as California, whose property is all community property and who want the survivor to inherit everything, may conclude it is unnecessary to go through hoops to avoid probate. Community property left to a surviving spouse can already pass through simplified probate.

Age 60–70   The older you get, the more sense it makes to plan to avoid probate on all or most of your estate. A revocable living trust is often the most comprehensive way to accomplish this.

Age 60 or under, in good health   Many people in this group conclude that they can get along fine for a while by using a will, coupled with some of the easier probate avoidance techniques, such as owning their house in joint tenancy or placing a pay-on-death designation on bank and retirement accounts. In this age group, with a normal life expectancy of at least 25 years, the time and trouble necessary to maintain a living trust for many years may be considerable.

Exception   People with estates worth more than $500,000 may conclude that placing a few of their most valuable assets in a living trust makes sense. For example, a business or real property not already held in joint tenancy could be transferred to a living trust while other assets are disposed of by a will.

Can a Living Trust Replace a Will?

Even if you use a living trust to pass all of your identifiable property, there are several reasons why you need a will, too:

- You can't nominate a personal guardian for minor children in a living trust—you need a will. (See Chapter 6, Section C.)

- A living trust works to pass only property you transfer to the trust's name. Property you may receive in the future, but do not have title to now, cannot be transferred by living trust. For example, if you have inherited property that is still tied up in probate, or you expect to receive money from the settlement of a lawsuit, you need a will. And because you cannot accurately predict what property you might receive shortly before death, it is advisable to back up a living trust with a will.

C. Federal Estate Taxes

The first $600,000 worth of property you leave at your death or give away while you are alive is exempt from federal estate tax. This means that if your estate is worth less than $600,000, and you haven't already given away large amounts, you need not worry about federal estate taxes. However, if you have an estate larger than $600,000, or if you are married and plan to leave your property to your spouse, who will then have an estate exceeding $600,000, read on.

This section helps you estimate your federal estate tax liability. Section D discusses what you can do to keep your tax bill to a minimum. Be aware that if an estate is large enough to be taxed, federal estate taxes are hefty. They begin at 37% for property valued between $600,000 to $750,000 and increase gradually for larger estates—topping out at 55% for estates larger than $3,000,000.

1. Estimate the Value of Your Net Estate

Your net worth is all you own less all you owe—assets minus liabilities. If you are married or co-own property with another person, be careful to distinguish between your property and your spouse's or other owner's when computing your net worth. For example, if you and your spouse own a house in joint tenancy, include only half of your combined equity when computing your net worth.

Example

If you own a house worth $350,000 with a $100,000 mortgage, it is worth $250,000 for estate tax purposes. If you and your spouse or any other co-owner own the house in equal shares, your share is only $125,000.

▶ **Marital Property: Who Owns What?**

Here is a brief outline of marital property ownership laws.

(A more thorough explanation is contained in Chapter 4, Section C.)

Community Property States

Arizona	Nevada	Washington
California	New Mexico	Wisconsin
Idaho	Texas	

All property either spouse earns or acquires during marriage is community property, jointly owned by both, with several exceptions. The most important is that the gifts or inheritances of one spouse are that person's separately-owned property. All property acquired by one spouse before marriage is also separate property.

Other States

In all other states, the person whose name is on the title or other ownership document for a particular piece of property owns it for estate tax purposes. If both names are on the document, ownership is joint. Property with no title document belongs to the spouse who used his or her money to purchase it, unless it was a gift to the other.

2. Deduct Allowable Estate Tax Exemptions

Federal law exempts certain property from estate tax, including:

- up to $600,000 left to any beneficiaries
- all property left to your spouse
- all property left to tax-exempt charitable organizations, and
- amounts paid for last illness, burial and probate costs.

The $600,000 Exemption

Property you own at your death worth up to $600,000 is exempt from federal estate tax. This is true no matter what type of property is involved, to whom you leave it and the legal device used to transfer it—will, living trust or joint tenancy.

Example

Bruce leaves his estate of $700,000 to his son. $100,000 is subject to federal estate tax. This is true whether he uses a will, a living trust or another transfer device.

There is an important qualification to this rule. Gifts made during life—if worth over $10,000 per year per person and not made to a tax-exempt charity—count toward the $600,000 exempt amount. The federal government feared that if large gifts were not taxed at the same rate as property left at death, people with estates large enough to be taxed would simply give the bulk of their property away shortly before death.

The result of this fear is a unified system of estate and gift taxes. If you make a taxable gift during your life, you must file a gift tax return, but you don't pay tax then. Instead, the amount of the gift that exceeds $10,000 per person is subtracted from your $600,000.

Example

Clint gives his son Larry and daughter-in-law Glenda $30,000 for the downpayment on a house. Since $10,000 can be given to an individual each year free of any gift tax consequences, only $10,000 is taxable. But no gift tax is due. The $10,000 is subtracted from the $600,000 lifetime estate and gift tax exemption. Had John wanted to avoid tax altogether, he could have given Larry and Glenda $20,000 in one calendar year and $10,000 the next year.

Property Left to Your Spouse

All property left to a surviving spouse, whether it's worth $10 or $10 million, is exempt from federal estate tax. In tax lingo, this exemption is called the marital deduction. Note, however, that this exemption does not apply if the surviving spouse is not a U.S. citizen.

Example

Sue has an estate valued at $6,600,000. She leaves $600,000 to her children and $6,000,000 to her husband. All of Sue's property is estate tax-exempt. The $6,000,000 is exempt as a result of the marital deduction, and the remaining $600,000 is exempt under the standard $600,000 exemption discussed above.

Often, however, you won't want to simply pile up all the money in the surviving spouse's estate. Alternatives are discussed in Section D3, below.

Unmarried Couples Note   There are no estate tax exemptions similar to the marital deduction for lovers or roommates.[1] However, the marital deduction is available for couples who entered into a common law marriage in one of the states that recognize this type of marriage. (See Chapter 3, Section B.) It is also available to people who marry very shortly before dying.

---

[1] Perhaps there is a certain perverse fairness in this, as unmarried couples normally receive significant income tax benefits if both have income. For a thorough discussion of the legal rights and responsibilities of unmarried couples, see *The Living Together Kit,* Warner and Ihara and *A Legal Guide for Lesbian and Gay Couples,* Curry, Clifford and Leonard, both published by Nolo Press.

Charitable Gift Exemption

All bequests made to tax-exempt charitable organizations are exempt from federal estate taxes; they don't need to be subtracted from the $600,000 exemption. If you plan to make large charitable bequests to an organization, doublecheck its tax-exemption status. The normal way an organization becomes a tax-exempt charity is by a favorable ruling from the IRS, under Internal Revenue Code Section 501(c)(3). Organizations that are active politically—a term not consistently defined by the IRS—are often not tax-exempt.

Other Estate Tax Exemptions and Credits

The other principal exemptions from federal estate tax and estate tax credits are:

- expenses of last illness, burial costs and probate costs, and

- a tax credit for money paid for state estate and inheritance taxes, and taxes imposed by foreign countries on property owned there. A few states have no estate or inheritance taxes. A second, larger group levies a small pick-up tax calculated to equal the maximum amount that can be credited against federal estate taxes. Other states, especially in the northeast, levy substantial death taxes on large estates. If your estate pays these, it will receive a small credit on your federal estate tax. (See Section D, below.)

3. Estimate Your Estate Tax

You are now ready to broadly estimate your tax liability. Do so by consulting the rates shown in the table below. The example that follows will help you understand how to estimate your tax.

► **Unified Federal Estate and Gift Tax Rates**

Column A	Column B	Column C	Column D
Net taxable estate over A	Net taxable estate not over	Tax on amount in column A	Rate of tax on excess over amount in column
$0	$10,000	$0	18 %
10,000	20,000	1,800	20
20,000	40,000	3,800	22
40,000	60,000	8,200	24
60,000	80,000	13,000	26
80,000	100,000	18,200	28
100,000	150,000	23,800	30
150,000	250,000	38,800	32
250,000	500,000	70,800	34
500,000	750,000	155,800	37
750,000	1,000,000	248,300	39
1,000,000	1,250,000	345,800	41
1,250,000	1,500,000	448,300	43
1,500,000	2,000,000	555,800	45
2,000,000	2,500,000	780,800	49
2,500,000	3,000,000	1,025,800	53
3,000,000	infinity		55

Example 1

Bernie, a resident of California, anticipates that after subtracting liabilities from assets and then subtracting exempt amounts, including charitable gifts and funeral costs, his estate's value is about $1.5 million. Bernie plans to leave $500,000 to his spouse and $1 million to his children and other beneficiaries. All property Bernie leaves to his spouse is exempt from federal estate tax because of the marital deduction. This means his net estate subject to tax is $1 million. Column C on the Estate Tax Chart reveals that the tax assessed on a $1 million estate is $345,800. Because $600,000 of that amount is not taxed, he subtracts $192,800—the tax assessed against a $600,000 estate. Bernie's estate will have to pay federal taxes of $153,000.

Bernie's estate would also be liable to pay state inheritance taxes. California takes some of the tax assessed by the federal government; it does not impose any extra tax.

Incidentally, Bernie is an excellent candidate to give money to his kids while he is still alive. By doing this, he can reduce the size of his estate and therefore the tax. (See Section D1.)

D. Reducing Federal Estate Taxes

Unfortunately, aside from leaving more money to your spouse or to charity, there are only a few major ways to lower estate taxes.

1. Give Away Property While You're Alive

An excellent way to reduce your estate tax liability is to reduce the size of your estate by giving property to the same people or organizations you want to get it at your death. But, if you make large gifts—more than $10,000 per person or organization per year—you accomplish nothing, because the amount of the gift over $10,000 is subtracted from your total $600,000 exemption. The key is to make a number of smaller gifts.

- Annually, you can give away property worth $10,000 or less per person or organization, tax-free.

- A couple can give $20,000 a year tax-free to one person and $40,000 to another couple.

- All gifts to tax-exempt nonprofits are exempt from gift and estate tax.

- This strategy can be repeated year after year.

Gift-giving to reduce estate tax liability works well for people who have enough property that they can afford to be generous. It is particularly advantageous for reasonably affluent people who have several children, grandchildren or other objects of their affection.

▶ **Gifts of Appreciated Property Shortly Before Death**

Someone who inherits property gets a stepped-up tax basis in the property to its then-current market value. Because the tax basis is the number used to figure capital gains and losses, this means an inheritor who promptly sells property for its fair market value pays no capital gains tax. However, property given away keeps the giver's tax basis—purchase price plus any capital improvements. In the case of greatly appreciated property, a person who receives it by gift faces a much larger tax bill when it's sold than does someone who inherits it.

Example

Ellen gives a 100-acre parcel of undeveloped land to her son John shortly before she dies. Since Ellen's tax basis in the land at the time of transfer was $100,000, this is now John's tax basis. If John sells the land for $500,000, he owes capital gains tax on $400,000. By contrast, had Ellen left John the property at death, his tax basis would have been stepped-up to $500,000, fair market value, and no tax would have been due had he sold it for that amount.

► Gifts of Life Insurance

Life insurance policies you own on your own life and give away at least three years before your death make good gifts from an estate planning vantage. Potential tax liability is assessed on the present value of the insurance policy, which is far less than the amount the policy will pay off at death. Indeed, in many instances, it will be less than the $10,000 annual tax exclusion for gifts.

To give away a life insurance policy, you must carefully follow fairly technical IRS rules, which should be available from your insurance company. Basically, you must make an irrevocable gift of the policy. If you keep the right to revoke the gift—that is, get the policy back—it will be taxed as part of your estate. If you prepay the entire policy with a single premium, giving it away creates no future payment problems. However, if you purchase a policy that requires annual premiums, the person you give it to must make future payments, which may mean you'll want to make annual gifts large enough to cover the payments.

Example

Bert has an estate worth $1 million. He purchases three single-premium life insurance policies for $50,000 each and immediately transfers ownership of the policies to his three children. Tax will be assessed on $120,000—the $150,000 value of the policies minus the $10,000 annual tax exemption for each gift. No gift tax need be paid at the time of transfer—the $120,000 is subtracted from the unified $600,000 estate and gift tax exemption, leaving $480,000 for use at death.

The policies pay off $200,000 each at Bert's death ten years later. Bert has transferred $600,000 to his children, but only $120,000 will be part of his taxable estate. Had he kept the policy because he wanted to borrow against it, or for some other reason, his estate would owe tax on the entire $600,000 of proceeds.

2. Generation-Skipping Trusts

Creating a generation-skipping trust for the benefit of your grandchildren will not reduce your own estate tax liability; it can, however, exempt up to $1 million from tax in the next generation. A generation-skipping trust, as the name indicates, leaves property in trust for beneficiaries two generations removed from the trust creator—normally, your grandchildren. For example, if you leave $1 million in trust for your grandchildren, with the income from the trust available to your children, that $1 million is excluded from your children's taxable estate when they die.

3. Create a Marital Life Estate Trust

Spouses who have a combined estate of more than $600,000 and who are both elderly should usually avoid leaving large sums to one another. This is because the survivor's estate will have to pay a much larger estate tax than if the other spouse had left the property directly to the children or other beneficiaries.

One way to avoid this problem, and also provide some income for the surviving spouse, is for each spouse to leave the other property in a marital life estate trust—sometimes called a spousal trust or A-B trust. With this kind of trust, the income goes to the survivor during his or her life, and the principal goes to named beneficiaries—often the children—when the second spouse dies. It allows you to avoid increasing the size of your spouse's estate.

The main drawback of a marital life estate trust is that the surviving spouse's rights in it are limited. While the surviving spouse can, at the option of the trust creator, be given the right to spend trust principal for medical needs and other basic necessities, in most cases he or she receives only the income from the money or property placed in trust—or the use of the property if it is tangible, such as a house. He or she does not own it.

For a spouse who already has more than enough property, this is not a problem. However, marital life estate trusts are generally not desirable for younger couples because should one die, the other spouse, who will likely live for many years, will want to own the property outright.

Example

Calvin and Phylo, husband and wife, are each in their mid-70s, and each has an estate worth $450,000. Calvin dies, leaving all his property to Phylo. Because of the marital deduction, no estate tax is assessed. Phylo dies the next year. Her estate consists of the entire $900,000 (plus appreciation), which she leaves to the children. Because $600,000 can be left to anyone free of estate tax, $300,000 of the money left to the children is subject to tax. Unfortunately, however, it is taxed at the hefty marginal rate of 39%.

If Calvin and Phylo had each established a marital life estate trust, with the income to go to the survivor for life and the principal to the children at the survivor's death, there would be no estate tax liability.

E. State Death Taxes

About half the states impose death taxes on:

• all real estate owned in the state, no matter where the deceased lived, and

• all other property of state residents, no matter where it's located.

If you live in a state that does not impose death taxes—and do not own any real property in one that does—skip to Section F.

▶ **States without Death Taxes**

Note that many of the states below charge a small pick-up tax equal to the amount of the federal tax credit for state inheritance taxes, but the result is no net tax.

Alabama	Hawaii	Oregon
Alaska	Illinois	Texas
Arizona	Maine	Utah
Arkansas	Minnesota	Vermont
California	Missouri	Virginia
Colorado	Nevada	Washington
District of Columbia	New Mexico	West Virginia
Florida	North Dakota	Wyoming
Georgia		

1. What State Will Tax You?

State death taxes are imposed on all those who reside in the state permanently. If you divide your time between states, you'll probably want to establish your residence in the one with the lower tax rate. (See Chapter 3, Section B, for a discussion of legal residence.)

Example

James and Vivian, a retired couple, divide the year between Florida and their native New York. Florida effectively has no death taxes. New York imposes comparatively stiff taxes—with rates ranging from 2% for $50,000 or less to 21% for $100,000 or more. Other things being equal, it makes sense for them to officially reside in Florida. To establish this, they should scrupulously maintain all their major business contacts in Florida, including registering all vehicles in that state and maintaining bank accounts there. In addition, they should vote there. And because real property is taxed in the state where it's located (regardless of its owner's residence), they might consider selling any New York real property and renting there instead.

Adjusting Your Tax State

Establishing residence in a no-tax state can sometimes be tricky if you also live in a high-tax one part of the year, because the high-tax state has an interest in concluding that you really reside there. If you find yourself in this situation and have a large estate, check your plan with a knowledgeable tax lawyer or accountant.

2. Estate Planning for State Death Taxes

In many instances, the bite taken out of estates by state death taxes is annoying, but relatively minor—especially when property is left to a spouse or children. But tax liability can be significant for property given to non-relatives. For example, Nebraska imposes a 15% death tax rate if $25,000 is given to a friend, but only 1% if it is given to a spouse. It is probably rare that someone would change the amount of property left to a beneficiary because of the impact of state death taxes, but you should at least be aware of them.[2]

F. Estate Planning to Control Property

Most people are content to leave their property to their inheritors outright, and not try to control what they do with it. However, there are times, especially for people with larger estates, when it can make sense to impose controls on what inheritors can do with property. The most common situations are discussed here.

---

[2]Death tax rules for all states that impose them are summarized in *Plan Your Estate with a Living Trust,* by Clifford (Nolo Press). More detailed information is available from your state tax officials.

1. Money Left to Minor Children and Young Adults

As discussed in Chapter 6, many people who leave property to minor children, either as first choice or alternate beneficiaries, want to delay the age at which the beneficiaries will receive the property.

2. Property Left to Children of Previous Marriages

People in second or subsequent marriages who have children from a previous marriage often want some or all of their estate to be left for the benefit of their current spouse, but want the property to pass eventually to the children. To take care of this concern—and for estates larger than $600,000, to simultaneously save on federal estate taxes—each spouse should leave his or her property in a marital trust.. (See Section D3, above.)

3. Money Left in Managerial Trusts

If a beneficiary will need long-term help with property management, you may want to establish a managerial trust that is carefully tailored to meet the complicated needs of the beneficiary.

Consult an Expert
See a lawyer with experience in this area in your state for help in drafting a managerial trust.

Trusts for People Who Can't Manage Money

If you want to leave property to a financially improvident adult in a way that prevents him or her from spending it all at once, a spendthrift trust, in which a trusted person or institution is empowered to dole out the money little by little, is a good idea.

Trusts for Disadvantaged People

A person with a physical or mental disability may not be able to handle property, no matter what age. The solution is often to establish a trust with a reliable adult as trustee to manage the disabled person's trust property. This is similar in concept to a spendthrift trust, but a trust for a disadvantaged person should be constructed to take full advantage of funds available from public sources.

Trusts for a Group of Beneficiaries

For a variety of reasons, someone may choose that the specific plan for how his or her estate is distributed should be determined after he or she dies instead of during life. The usual way to accomplish this is to create what is called a sprinkling trust, in legal parlance. Normally, the trust creator names the beneficiaries of the trust during life, but does not divide the property among them. That is done by the trustee, after the creator dies, under whatever general criteria the trust sets forth. ▲

13 Healthcare Directives

A. When and Why to Direct Your Medical Care

Nearly 80% of all Americans die in a hospital or other care facility. And doctors who work there are generally charged with preserving a patient's life through whatever means are available. When a patient can no longer communicate and has little chance of recovering or leading a meaningful life, this guiding proposition flies in the face of cost-efficiency, common sense—and most importantly, often contradicts what the patient would have wished had he or she been able to express wishes.

Doctors' egos are often at play, too. For many of them, keeping a patient alive with tubes, machines and chemicals is preferable to "losing" him or her through a natural death.

Of course, the reverse may also be true: A person may be provided with less extensive care than he or she would like. For example, a doctor may be unwilling to try experimental treatments or maintain long-term treatments on a patient he or she feels has slim chances of recovery. And a doctor may have far different views of what is "proper" treatment than the patient slated to receive it.

The only way for patients to override a doctor's general duty, and the religious, philosophical and economic underpinnings of the healthcare institution, is to leave written instructions for the medical care they prefer in case they become unconscious or otherwise incapable of expressing those wishes.

B. Legal History

Many assume that an individual's right to direct his or her own healthcare is a long-cherished legal principle. In fact, the first legal battles over patients' rights were fought during the last couple of decades. Not coincidentally, those battles coincided with dramatic advances in medical technology and equipment.

The first legal wranglings over healthcare were couched in terms of the Right To Die—cases that tested the bounds of what medical treatment can be administered in the face of a patient's desire to die naturally, free from artificial, life-prolonging machinery. Over time, the Right To Die took on a broader meaning, recognizing that patients' rights are paramount, and that some patients prefer that all possible treatment and procedures be used to treat them, even when that flies in the face of their doctor's asserted best medical judgment.

1. Court Decisions

The first time the public became aware of the right to direct medical care as a social issue was during the hard-fought legal battles over the life and death of Karen Ann Quinlan. The 22-year-old Quinlan was admitted to a New Jersey hospital after experiencing severe breathing difficulties. She lost and never regained consciousness. Severely brain damaged, she remained unresponsive, emaciated and in a fetal position—kept technically alive by round-the-clock nursing care, antibiotics, a respirator, catheter and feeding tube.

Doctors pronounced that there was no hope of Quinlan's recovery, but balked at her parents' repeated requests to remove the equipment attached to her, claiming that would clash with "medical practices, standards and traditions." After several expensive, time-consuming and personally wrenching appeals, the New Jersey Supreme Court held that Quinlan's right to privacy mandated that her family could enforce her right to refuse treatment. (*Matter of Quinlan*, 355 A.2d 647 (1976).)

The 1976 *Quinlan* decision galvanized family members who previously felt completely powerless up against the medical establishment. From 1976 through 1988, over 60 cases were filed nationwide, claiming that doctors should be legally bound to follow their patients' wishes for their own medical treatment.

In 1990, the U.S. Supreme Court was asked to decide the thorny issue of whether the Constitution grants individuals the right to have life-sustaining treatment withheld or withdrawn. The case arose when Nancy Cruzan, 30, was admitted to a Missouri hospital after suffering severe injuries in a car accident. Cruzan was diagnosed as permanently brain damaged and in a coma or persistent vegetative state, from which she would not recover. Her parents unsuccessfully pled with hospital officials to discontinue Cruzan's artificial food and water, which would eventually cause her death.

In later court challenges, the parents pointed to evidence of Cruzan's own wishes—conversations in which she told friends that if she were sick or injured, she "would not wish to continue her life unless she could live at least halfway normally." The Supreme Court held that everyone retains a constitutional right to control his or her own medical care. It held that "clear and convincing" evidence of an individual's wishes about his or her own medical care should be followed—even if they conflict directly with the wishes of close family members. (*Cruzan v. Director, Missouri Dept. of Health,* 497 U.S. 261 (1990).)

2. State Legislation

In the wake of court decisions carving out individuals' rights to direct their own healthcare, the first Living Wills were penned—usually simply-worded requests that a person "be allowed to die with dignity." These missives met with a mixed reaction in the medical community. Some doctors welcomed the Living Wills as legal permission to honor their patients' preferences for specific kinds of medical care, free from the threat of lawsuits charging them with negligence or even as criminal accomplices in a patient's suicide. Other doctors, unsure about whether to enforce the directives—most of which directed that life support be withheld or withdrawn—sought advice from lawyers. Most of the lawyers worked on the hospital staffs—and most cautiously advised that the documents could be ignored if the doctor thought that was "in the patient's best interest."

Waves of activism in the late 60s and early 70s led to catalytic consumer lobbying efforts for individual rights to direct healthcare. In 1976, California became the first state to pass a law allowing individuals to write healthcare directives—documents informing doctors of the specific kind of medical care they want provided, withheld or withdrawn. By the end of the 1980s, most states had followed suit. And today, every state has a law allowing some sort of directive.

3. Federal Law

Finally, a recent federal law, the Patient Self-Determination Act, has done much to increase the use and awareness of healthcare directives. The law, which became effective in December 1991, mandates that all facilities that receive Medicare or Medicaid must discuss healthcare directives with newly-admitted patients. When admitted to nearly any hospital, you should be given a written explanation of your state's law on healthcare directives, and an explanation of the hospital's policies in enforcing them. The law also directs healthcare facilities to record patients' healthcare directives as part of their medical records.

C. Putting Your Wishes in Writing

You will have the most thorough assurance that your wishes for your final healthcare will be followed if you leave specific written instructions setting out:

- what kind of medical care you want if you can no longer express your wishes, and

- the name of another person to whom you give the legal authority to supervise your wishes.

Using the WillMaker program, you can arrange for this full protection of your wishes.

1. Living Wills or Healthcare Directives

A healthcare directive, whether known as a Living Will, a Directive to Physicians or a Declaration, sets out a person's wishes about what life-prolonging treatment should be withheld or provided if a person becomes unable to communicate those wishes. In essence, the healthcare directive creates a contract with the attending doctor. Once the doctor receives a properly signed and witnessed directive, he or she is under the duty either to honor its instructions, or to make sure the patient is transferred to the care of another doctor who will honor them.

In the early confusion about healthcare directives, people were concerned that doctors who followed them would risk being prosecuted for aiding in a suicide. Every law on healthcare directives now exempts from prosecution doctors who follow their dictates. In fact, many laws now impose penalties on doctors who refuse to follow them.

Also, because healthcare directives sprung from the Right To Die movement, people tend to think of them as documents appropriate only for directing that life-prolonging procedures should be withdrawn or withheld. However, it is more correct to think of these documents as a way to direct doctors to provide you with whatever type of medical care you want. Some people want to reinforce that they would like to receive all medical treatment that is available—and a healthcare directive is the proper place to specify that.

2. Who Can Make a Healthcare Directive

In most states, you must be 18 years old to make a valid document directing your healthcare; a few states allow parents to make healthcare directives for their minor children.

Every state law requires that the person making a healthcare directive must be legally competent—that is, able to understand what the document means, what it contains and how it works. Mentally disabled people who cannot understand the contents of a healthcare document cannot make one that will be valid. Physically disabled people may make valid healthcare documents; they can direct another to sign for them if they are unable to do so.

3. Naming Someone to Supervise Your Wishes

In most states, it is possible to give another person authority to make healthcare decisions on your behalf in a document called a Durable Power of Attorney for Healthcare. In some states, this document is termed a healthcare proxy.

Using WillMaker, you can make a Durable Power of Attorney for Healthcare to give the representative you name the limited power to supervise the wishes you set out in your healthcare directive.

If you do not know anyone you trust to name as your healthcare proxy or agent, it is still important to complete and finalize a healthcare directive recording your wishes. That way, your doctors will still be bound to follow your wishes.

If you do name a proxy, in most states, two documents will print out when you are finished using the WillMaker program. It is essential that you attach these two documents and keep them in the same place after you have signed and finalized them. Together, they represent your complete wishes for your medical care.

In a few states, including Minnesota and South Carolina, only one document will be produced; any proxy you name to supervise your wishes will be included in that document. If you do not name a proxy in one of those states, the program will read in the words "Not applicable" in the blanks provided for the proxy.

Less Restricted Documents Are Possible

A Durable Power of Attorney for Healthcare can be used to delegate healthcare decisions in a number of additional situations. (See Section H, below.) If you wish to arrange for such a document, consult with an experienced attorney.

4. What Happens If You Have No Documents

If you have not completed either a formal document such as a healthcare directive to express your wishes, or a durable power of attorney to appoint someone to make healthcare decisions on your behalf, the doctors who attend you will use their own discretion in deciding what kind of medical care you will receive.

If there is a question about whether surgery or some other serious procedure is authorized, doctors may turn for consent to a close relative—spouse, parent, child. Friends and unmarried partners, although they may be most familiar with your wishes for your medical treatment, are rarely consulted, or are purposefully left out of the decision-making process.

Problems arise where partners and family members disagree about what treatment is proper. In the most complicated case scenarios, these battles over medical care wind up in court, where a judge, who usually has little medical knowledge and no familiarity with you, is called upon to decide the future of your treatment. Such legal battles—which are costly, time-consuming and usually painful to those involved—are unnecessary if you have the care and foresight to use a formal document to express your wishes for your healthcare.

5. The Documents You Produce Using WillMaker

State legislatures often jealously covet their power to control the specifics of what makes a document legal in their own state. And nowhere is this more evident than in the area of healthcare directives, where each state may impose its own requirements regarding the form of the document, whether it must be notarized, what can be included and even on the definitions of terminal illness and permanent coma.

The document you produce using WillMaker enables you to set out clear and effective directions for your medical care. If your state law requires you to use a specific form, your document will be in that format. However, in some instances, the directions that WillMaker produces as a result of your choices may go beyond what is addressed by your state law. For example, your state's law may be silent on whether individuals can direct their own healthcare if they become permanently comatose, or your state's law may specifically restrict you from having comfort care withheld, even though such care would prolong the dying process.

However, these state strictures contradict what the U.S. Supreme Court held in the *Cruzan* case: that the Constitution guarantees every individual the right to direct his or her own healthcare. The Court also ruled that if an individual has left "clear and convincing evidence" of his or her wishes for medical care, those wishes should be followed. While the Court intimated that evidence of conversations about healthcare wishes might pass legal muster as an indication of a person's wishes, detailed written instructions are even better.

The document you print using WillMaker produces clear and explicit instructions about the kind of medical care you would like to receive if you become unable to communicate your wishes to medical personnel. If these wishes go beyond your state's law, you will enhance your chances of receiving the specific medical care you want if you leave specific written directions about it.

You have nothing to lose from a legal standpoint by stating your preferences for your own medical care without regard to any restrictions imposed by your state. Your WillMaker healthcare directive will call special attention to the fact that the specific directions in the document you produce should be respected and followed, even if they go beyond what is allowed by your state law.

On the off-chance that anyone later challenges your healthcare directive in a court because it goes beyond your state law, there is an additional failsafe. Your document contains a paragraph that says that if any one of the directions you leave is found to be legally invalid, the rest of the document can still be enforced as written.

D. The Basics of Your Healthcare Documents

The initial screens in this portion of WillMaker ask you to provide some basic identifying information.

1. Your Name

Enter your name in the same form that you use on other formal documents, such as your driver's license or bank accounts. This may or may not be the name that appears on your birth certificate. If you customarily use more than one name for business purposes, list all of them in your WillMaker answer, separated by "aka," which stands for "also known as."

There is room for you to list several names. But use your common sense. For purposes of your healthcare directive, your name is needed to identify you and to match you with your medical records. Be sure to include the name you have used on other medical documents such as prior hospital or doctor records.

2. Your Address

Type the address of your residence—the place you live most of the year. Your address is just one additional piece of information that will help ensure that you are properly matched with your written directions for healthcare.

In most states, the healthcare documents produced will include the address of the person making the document; the WillMaker program will automatically read in the address that you type in to help produce a completed form.

3. Your State

You are asked to specify the state of your legal residence, sometimes called a domicile. This is the state where you make your home now and for the indefinite future. This information is important because it cues the WillMaker program to assemble and produce a healthcare directive that is specifically geared to the laws of your state.

If you divide up the year living in two or more states, you may not be sure which state is your legal residence. To decide, choose the state where you are the most "rooted"—that is, the state in which you:

• are registered to vote

- register your motor vehicles

- own valuable property—especially property with a title document, such as a house or car

- have checking, savings and other investment accounts, and

- maintain a business.

One legal fact that may help ease the difficulty of choosing your state is that many laws provide that a state will hold a healthcare directive from another state enforceable as long as the out-of-state document was written and finalized in accord with the out-of-state law. A number of states, however, specifically refuse to enforce a directive drawn up in another state. Such restrictions may be particularly important to you if you regularly visit out-of-state friends or relatives or customarily live in other states for part of the year.

The laws in several states—Arizona, Hawaii, Maryland, South Dakota, Texas and Utah—provide that if you have completed and formalized a written healthcare directive in more than one state, only the most recent directive will be given effect.

▶ **State Laws on Transferring Healthcare Directives**

The following states will recognize healthcare directives that are written and signed in accord with laws of another state: Alaska, Arkansas, Colorado, Hawaii, Indiana, Kansas, Massachusetts, New York, Rhode Island, South Dakota and Vermont.

Laws in the following states provide that they will recognize healthcare directives that are written and signed in accord with laws of another state to the extent they are consistent: Iowa, Maryland, Minnesota, Montana, New Hampshire, Oklahoma and Washington.

Laws in the following states specifically provide that they will recognize healthcare directives that are written and signed in accord with either laws of their own state or the other state: Arizona, California, Florida, Illinois, Maine, Nebraska, Nevada, New Jersey, North Dakota, Ohio, Tennessee, Virginia and West Virginia.

Laws in the following states are silent on the issue: Alabama, Connecticut, Delaware, District of Columbia, Georgia, Idaho, Kentucky, Michigan, Mississippi, Missouri, New Mexico, North Carolina, Oregon, Pennsylvania, South Carolina, Texas, Utah, Wisconsin and Wyoming.

E. Types of Medical Care

This section of the manual briefly discusses medical procedures that are most often deemed "life-prolonging"—and which you will encounter while using the WillMaker program. Bear in mind that the types of medical procedures that are available will change over time. Technological advances mean that currently unfathomable procedures and treatments will become available and treatments that are now common will become obsolete. Also, the treatments that are available vary drastically with region, depending on the sophistication and funding levels of local medical facilities.

While putting together your healthcare directive, the best that you can do is to become familiar with the kinds of medical procedures that are most commonly administered to patients who are terminally ill or permanently comatose. The best that the WillMaker program can do is to provide you with clear definitions. Both of these feats will help you to produce the healthcare document that most accurately reflects your wishes.

But the choice is yours. Be cautiously leery of those who try to convince you about the type of healthcare you should receive. Your ultimate decisions are likely to be influenced by many complicating factors: your medical history, your knowledge of other peoples' experiences with life-prolonging medical procedures, your religious beliefs. If you are having great difficulty in deciding about your preferences for medical care, take a few moments to figure out what's getting in your way. If you are unsure about the meaning or specifics of a particular medical treatment, turn to a doctor you trust for a more complete explanation. If the impediment is fear of sickness or death, talk over your feelings with family members and friends.

If you have definite ideas about some medical treatments that you do or do not want provided, but are confused or steadfastly undecided about others, do not let that stop you from completing what you can in your healthcare directive. While using the WillMaker program, you can skip the answers to many of the specific questions asked; your document will print out with the response "no preference" where you have opted not to make a decision. You can always rewrite your documents later—and sign them and have them witnessed or notarized—if you change your mind.

1. Blood and Blood Products

Blood is composed of a pale yellow fluid called plasma. Within the plasma, red blood cells (erythrocytes), white blood cells (leukocytes), platelets and a variety of chemicals including hormones, proteins, carbohydrates and fats are suspended.

Partial or full blood transfusions may be recommended to combat diseases that impair the blood system, to foster healing after a blood loss or to replenish blood lost through surgery, disease or injury.

2. Cardio-Pulmonary Resuscitation (CPR)

Cardio-pulmonary resuscitation (CPR) is used when a person's heart or breathing has stopped. CPR includes applying physical pressure and using mouth-to-mouth resuscitation. Electrical shocks are also used if available. CPR is often accompanied by intravenous drugs used to normalize body systems. A final step in CPR is often attaching the patient to a respirator.

3. Diagnostic Tests

Diagnostic tests are commonly used to evaluate urine, blood and other body fluids and to check on all bodily functions. Diagnostic tests can include X-rays and more sophisticated tests of brainwaves or other internal body systems. Some diagnostic tests, including surgery, can be expensive and invasive, producing pain and other side effects.

4. Dialysis

A dialysis machine is used to clean and add essential substances to the blood —through tubes placed in blood vessels or into the abdomen—when kidneys do not function properly. The entire cleansing process takes three or more hours and is performed on most dialysis patients from two to three times a week. With the portability of dialysis machines, it is often possible to have the procedure performed at home rather than in a hospital or other advanced care facility.

5. Drugs

The most common and most controversial drugs given to seriously ill or comatose patients are antibiotics—administered by mouth, through a feeding tube or by injection. Antibiotics are used to arrest and squelch infectious diseases. Patients in very weakened conditions may not respond even to massive doses of antibiotics.

Many healthcare providers argue that infectious diseases can actually be a benefit to those in advanced stages of an illness, since they may render a patient unconscious, and presumably not in pain, or help to speed up the dying process. Others contend that if an antibiotic can eliminate symptoms of an illness, it is almost always the proper medical treatment.

Drugs may also be used to eliminate or alleviate pain. Because high doses of pain control drugs can impair respiration, such drugs sometimes hasten death in a seriously ill patient. Also, medical experts disagree on whether a comatose patient can feel pain, so they also debate whether a comatose patient benefits from pain control medications.

6. Respirator

A mechanical respirator or a ventilator assists or takes over breathing for a patient by pumping air in and out of the lungs. These machines dispense a regulated amount of air into the lungs at a set rate—and periodically purge the lungs. Patients are connected to respirators either by a tube that goes through the mouth and throat into the lung or attaches directly through the lung surgically.

Respirators are often used to stabilize patients who are suffering from an acute trauma or breathing crisis. Once a patient has been attached to a respirator, most doctors will buck against removing the machinery unless there is clear written direction that this is what the patient would want.

7. Surgery

Surgical procedures such as amputation or a brain shunt are often used to stem the spread of life-threatening infections or to keep vital organs functioning. Major surgery such as a hysterectomy or a heart bypass are also typically performed on patients who are terminally ill or comatose. The cost, time spent recovering from the invasive surgery and the ultimate prognosis should all be factors in deciding whether surgery should be included in your final medical treatment.

8. Comfort Care

The laws of most states assume that people want relief from pain and discomfort and specifically exclude pain-relieving procedures from definitions of life-prolonging treatments that may be withheld. If that was all there was to it, most people would agree with this approach and welcome the relief. However, there is a medical controversy over how much pain or discomfort people can feel when they are close to death from a terminal illness or in a permanent coma—and whether providing food and water or drugs to make a person comfortable or alleviate pain will also have the effect of prolonging the person's life.

Some people are so adamant about not having their lives prolonged when they are comatose or likely to die soon that they choose to direct that all comfort care and pain relief be withheld in those circumstances even if the doctor thinks those procedures are necessary. Other people are willing to have their lives prolonged rather than face the possibility that discomfort or pain would go untreated. Obviously, this is a very personal choice.

9. Artificially-Administered Food and Water

If you are close to death from a terminal condition or in a permanent coma and cannot communicate to others your preferences for your own healthcare, it is also likely that you will not be able to voluntarily take in water or food through your mouth. The medical solution to this is to provide you with food and water—as a mix of nutrients and fluids—through tubes inserted in a vein, into your stomach through your nose, or directly into your stomach through a surgical incision, depending on your condition.

Intravenous feeding, where fluids are introduced through a vein in an arm or a leg, is a short-term procedure. Tube feeding through the nose (nasogastric tube), through the stomach (gastrostomy tube), intestines (jejunostomy tube) or largest vein, the vena cava (total parenteral nutrition) can be carried on indefinitely.

Controversies over artificially-administered food and water still rage because medical experts disagree about whether its purpose is to sustain life or to cure an illness. The state laws governing healthcare directives reflect this controversy. A few states specify that artificial feeding—also called nutrition and hydration—cannot be rejected; some states allow people to specify the circumstances under which they would want feeding; other state laws are silent on the topic.

WillMaker allows you to state whether you want artificially-administered food and water withheld or provided. If your state's law doesn't permit food and water to be withheld, but that is your wish, your healthcare directive will assert your right to have it withheld under the U.S. Constitution.

F. Directing Healthcare for Different Situations

Despite drastic technological advances in medicine, much about physical symptoms and effects remains uncharted. For example, medical experts disagree over whether comatose patients can feel pain, and over whether some treatments are reliable enough to be considered medically therapeutic.

People who have strong feelings about what kind of final medical care they want to receive are usually guided by personal experience rather than a greater knowledge of current medical capabilities or future advances. For example, if you have watched a grandparent suffer a prolonged death while attached to a respirator, you may opt not to have a respirator as part of your medical care. If a friend who was diagnosed as terminally ill was much improved by a newly-developed antibiotic, you may be adamant about demanding that drugs be administered to you, no matter what the medical prognosis.

WillMaker allows you to direct your final healthcare differently for when you are in a permanent coma and when you are diagnosed to be close to death from a terminal condition. This flexibility is built in to accommodate healthcare wishes stemming from personal preference and experience, while balancing the unknowns of medicine.

For example, the best educated guesses of medical personnel usually give those diagnosed to be terminally ill a short time to live—less than six months or so. Some people feel that the best medical care under such a prognosis would be to have as much pain and suffering alleviated as possible through drugs and IVs, without any heroic medical maneuvers, such as invasive surgery or additional painful diagnostic tests.

However, patients often prove doctors wrong. Those estimated to die of a terminal illness within a few months sometimes stabilize or improve and live on for many years. If you opt to direct that no life-prolonging treatments be provided, you gamble that your condition will not improve—a gamble you must weigh against your own definitions of life.

Comatose patients face even less certain futures. Many comatose patients are kept alive for many years with some mechanical assistance to keep their breathing, circulation and other vital bodily functions operating. While most long-term coma patients never recover, there are, of course, instances of miraculous awakenings.

There is no general rule, no strict legal guidance, to offer on this topic. People fashioning documents to direct their healthcare in the case of a coma will likely be guided by their own very personal definitions of quality of life. Some hold out hope for the possibility of some medical cure for their condition—and direct that all possible medical treatments be administered to them if they become comatose. Others feel strongly that life in a coma would completely lack meaning for them—and direct that all medical procedures, including food and water, be discontinued. And others walk the middle ground, opting to direct that only the minimum—food and water and pain-alleviating drugs—be administered to them if they become comatose.

If you are having a difficult time making this choice, you may get good guidance by discussing the matter with a doctor you trust, or with another experienced healthcare worker.

1. If You Are Close to Death from a Terminal Condition

Generally, a terminal condition is any disease or injury from which doctors believe there is no chance of recovery and from which death is likely to occur within a short time—such as the final stages of cancer or AIDS.

State laws on healthcare directives define terminal condition slightly differently, but commonly refer to it as "incurable," "hopeless" or "irreversible." Many state laws explain in addition that a patient who is terminally ill will die unless artificially supported through life-sustaining procedures.

Most states require that one or two physicians verify that the patient has a terminal condition before the documents directing healthcare will go into effect. In some states, this verification must be in writing.

2. If You Become in a Permanent Coma

A coma is a state of unconsciousness caused by various medical conditions, head traumas or other body injuries.

While comatose people appear to go through sleep cycles and to respond to some noises and physical stimulation, medical experts disagree over whether a person in a coma is capable of experiencing pain or discomfort. Most comatose people do not require mechanical assistance with breathing or circulation, but must be provided food and water through artificial means—usually through tubes inserted in the veins or stomach—if the condition persists.

Generally, people who become comatose either regain consciousness within a short time or enter a permanent coma or a persistent vegetative state in which it is uncertain whether consciousness will ever be regained. They may be kept alive for many months or even years. A person who remains in a persistent vegetative state for many months without change is often deemed to have passed into a terminal condition.

G. Choosing a Healthcare Proxy

By taking the time and making the effort to draw up documents to direct your healthcare if you become unable to do so, you have already done much to assure that your wishes will be followed. In most cases, doctors and relatives faced with difficult decisions about continuing or discontinuing another's medical care are relieved and delighted to take direction from the person by following the healthcare documents.

Occasionally, however, if your wishes for your healthcare are different than what your doctors or close relatives want for you, problems can arise in getting the documents enforced. For this reason, it is best to name a person—called a representative, an attorney-in-fact or a healthcare proxy—to reinforce that the wishes you have expressed are followed to the letter. That way, there will be someone to lobby on your behalf to get your wishes enforced, to make sure medical personnel know of your wishes, to argue with them if need be, to enforce your healthcare directives in court if necessary.

1. Guidance in Choosing a Proxy

The person you name as your healthcare proxy should be someone you trust—and someone with whom you feel confident discussing your wishes. While your proxy need not agree with your wishes for your medical care, you should believe that he or she respects your right to get the kind of medical care you want.

The person you appoint to oversee your healthcare wishes could be a spouse or partner, relative or close friend. Keep in mind your proxy may have to fight to assert your wishes in the face of a medical establishment hard to budge from its position—and against the wishes of family members who may be driven by their own beliefs and interests, rather than yours. If you foresee the possibility of a conflict in enforcing your wishes, be sure to choose a proxy who is strong-willed and assertive.

While you need not name someone who lives in the same state as you do, proximity should be one factor you consider. The reality is that the person you name may be called upon to spend weeks or months near your bedside, making sure medical personnel abide by your wishes for your healthcare.

You should not choose your doctor, or an employee of a hospital or nursing home where you are receiving treatment. In fact, the laws in many states prevent you from naming such a person. In a few instances, this legal constraint may frustrate your wishes. For example, you may wish to name your spouse or partner as your representative, but if he or she also works as a hospital employee, that alone may bar you from naming that person in some states. If the laws in your state ban your first choice, you may have to name another person to serve instead. (See the chart in Section 2, below, for more on your state's law on healthcare proxy restrictions.)

2. State Requirements for Proxies

A number of states have strict bans against allowing some people to serve as your healthcare proxy. Close relatives, attending physicians and other healthcare providers are those commonly banned from serving. Some states presume that the motivations of such people may be clouded by self-interest.

For example, an attending physician may be motivated to provide every medical procedure available—to try every heroic or experimental treatment—even if that flies in the face of a patient's wishes.

Consult the listing below for the specifics of your state's law on proxy requirements and restrictions before you select a proxy.

State Proxy Requirements

ALABAMA
No requirements

ARIZONA
Your healthcare representative may not be under the age of 18.

ARKANSAS
Your healthcare representative may not be under the age of 18.

CALIFORNIA
Your healthcare representative may not be:
- a witness to your durable power of attorney for healthcare
- your treating healthcare provider
- an employee of the treating healthcare provider, unless the employee is related to you
- an operator of a community care facility
- an employee of the operator of the community care facility, unless the employee is related to you
- an operator of a residential care facility for the elderly
- an employee of the operator of the residential care facility for the elderly, unless the employee is related to you, or
- your conservator.

COLORADO
No requirements

CONNECTICUT
If, when you appoint your healthcare representative, you are a patient or a resident of, or have applied for admission to, a hospital, home for the aged, rest home with nursing supervision or chronic and convalescent nursing home, your healthcare representative may not be:
- an operator
- an administrator, or
- an employee.

In any case, your healthcare representative may not be:

- a witness to the document appointing him or her as your healthcare representative
- your attending physician, or
- an employee of a government agency which is financially responsible for your medical care—unless that person is related to you by blood, marriage or adoption.

DELAWARE
No requirements

DISTRICT OF COLUMBIA
Your healthcare representative may not be your healthcare provider.

FLORIDA
Your healthcare representative may not be a witness to the document naming your healthcare representative.

GEORGIA

Your healthcare representative may not be your healthcare provider if your healthcare provider is directly or indirectly involved in the medical treatment given to you under your durable power of attorney for healthcare.

HAWAII

Your healthcare representative may not be your treating physician.

IDAHO

Your healthcare representative may not be:
- under the age of 18
- a witness to your durable power of attorney for healthcare
- your treating healthcare provider
- an employee of your healthcare provider, unless the employee is related to you
- an operator of a community care facility, or
- an employee of an operator of a community care facility, unless the employee is related to you.

ILLINOIS

Your healthcare representative may not be any healthcare provider.
Indiana
No requirements

IOWA

Your healthcare representative may not be:
- your healthcare provider

- an employee of your healthcare provider, unless these individuals are related to you by blood, marriage, or adoption—including parents, children, siblings, gendchildren, grandparents, uncles, aunts, nephews, nieces and great-grandchildren, or
- a witness to your durable power of attorney for healthcare.

KANSAS

Your healthcare representative may not be:
- your treating healthcare provider
- a witness to your durable power of attorney for healthcare.
- an employee of your treating healthcare provider, or
- an employee, owner, director or officer of a healthcare facility unless:
  — they are related to you by blood, marriage or adoption or
  — you and the agent are members of the same community of persons who have vowed to lead a religious life and who conduct or assist in conducting religious services and actually and regularly engage in religious, charitable or educational activities or the performance of healthcare services.

KENTUCKY

Your healthcare representative may not be:
- an employee, owner, director or officer of a healthcare facility where you are a resident or patient, unless they are related to you more closely than first cousins, once removed, or
- a witness or notary to the document in which you name your healthcare representative.

MAINE

No requirements

MARYLAND

No requirements

MASSACHUSETTS

Your healthcare representative may not be:
- a witness to your healthcare proxy document
- an operator, administrator or employee of a facility where you are a patient or resident or have applied for admission, unless the operator, administrator or employee is related to you by blood, marriage or adoption.

MICHIGAN

No requirements

MINNESOTA

Your healthcare representative may not be a witness to your healthcare declaration.

MISSISSIPPI

Your healthcare representative may not be:
- a witness to your durable power of attorney for healthcare
- a treating healthcare provider, or
- an employee of a treating healthcare provider.

MISSOURI

Your healthcare representative may not be:
- your attending physician, or
- an employee of the healthcare facility where you live unless
  — you and your healthcare representative are related as parents, children, siblings, grandparents, or grandchildren, or
  — you and your healthcare representative are members of the same community of people who have vowed to lead a religious life and who conduct or assist in conducting religious services and actually and regularly engage in religious, charitable or educational activities or the performance of healthcare services.

MONTANA

No requirements

NEBRASKA

Your healthcare representative may not be:
- under the age of 19, unless he or she is married
- a witness to your durable power of attorney for healthcare
- your attending physician
- an employee of your attending physician, unless the employee is related to you by blood, marriage, or adoption
- a person unrelated to you by blood, marriage or adoption who is an owner, operator, or employee of a healthcare provider of which you are a patient or resident, or
- a person unrelated to you by blood, marriage, or adoption who is presently serving as an healthcare representative for ten or more people.

NEVADA

Your healthcare representative may not be a witness to your durable power of attorney for healthcare.
Additionally, your healthcare representative may not be:
- your healthcare provider
- an employee of your provider of healthcare
- an operator of a healthcare facility, or
- an employee of a healthcare facility unless they are your spouse, legal guardian or next of kin.

NEW HAMPSHIRE

Your healthcare representative may not be:
- your healthcare provider
- an employee of your healthcare provider, unless the employee is related to you

- your residential care provider, or
- an employee of your residential care provider, unless the employee is related to you.

NEW JERSEY

Your healthcare representative may not be:
- under the age of 18
- a witness to your advance directive, or
- an operator, administrator or employee of a healthcare institution in which you are a patient or resident, unless the operator, administrator or employee is related to you by blood, marriage or adoption, or, in the case of a physician, is not your attending physician.

NEW MEXICO

No requirements

NEW YORK

Your healthcare representative must be an adult. "Adult" means any person who is 18 years of age or older, or is the parent of a child, or has married.
Your healthcare representative may not be:
- a witness to the execution of your healthcare proxy
- your attending physician
- a person who is presently appointed healthcare representative for ten other persons, unless this person is your spouse, child, parent, brother, sister or grandparent
- an operator, administrator or employee of a hospital if, at the time of the appointment, you are a patient or resident of, or have applied for admission to, such hospital. This restriction shall not apply to:
  — an operator, administrator, or employee of a hospital who is related to you by blood, marriage or adoption, or
  — a physician, who is not your attending physician, except that no physician affiliated with a mental hygiene facility or a psychiatric unit of a general hospital may serve as agent for you if you are living in or being treated by such facility or unit unless the physician is related to you by blood, marriage or adoption.

NORTH CAROLINA

Your healthcare agent may not be:
- under the age of 18, or
- providing healthcare to your for compensation.

NORTH DAKOTA

Your healthcare representative may not be:
- a witness to your durable power of attorney for healthcare
- your healthcare provider
- an employee of your healthcare provider, unless the employee is related to you
- your long-term care services provider, or

- an employee of your long-term care services provider, unless the employee is related to you.

OHIO

Your healthcare representative may not be:
- under the age of 18
- a witness to your durable power of attorney for healthcare
- your attending physician
- an administrator of any nursing home in which you are receiving care
- an employee or agent of your attending physician, or
- an employee or agent of any healthcare facility in which you are being treated, except that you may appoint any of the above employees or agents if they are 18 years of age or older and are members of the same religious order as you.

OKLAHOMA

Your healthcare representative must be at least 18 years old.

OREGON

Your healthcare representative may not be:
- under the age of 18
- a witness to your durable power of attorney for healthcare
- your attending physician or an employee of your attending physician who is unrelated to you by blood, marriage or adoption
- a person unrelated to you by blood, marriage or adoption who is an owner, operator or employee of a healthcare facility in which you are patient or resident.

PENNSYLVANIA

No requirements

RHODE ISLAND

Your healthcare representative may not be:
- a witness to your durable power of attorney for healthcare
- your treating healthcare provider
- an employee of your treating healthcare provider, unless the employee is related to you
- an operator of a community care facility, or
- an employee of an operator of a community care facility, unless the employee is related to you.

SOUTH CAROLINA

Your healthcare representative must not be:
- under the age of 18
- a witness to your healthcare power of attorney
- your healthcare provider at the time you execute your healthcare power of attorney
- an employee of your healthcare provider

- an employee of the nursing care facility where you live, or
- a spouse of your healthcare provider or employee, unless your healthcare provider, your healthcare provider's employee or spouse is related to you.

SOUTH DAKOTA

No requirements

TENNESSEE

Your healthcare representative may not be:
- a witness to your durable power of attorney for healthcare
- your treating healthcare provider
- an employee of your treating healthcare provider
- an operator of a healthcare institution
- an employee of an operator of a healthcare institution, or
- your conservator.

You may choose an employee of your treating healthcare provider or an employer of an operator of a healthcare institution as your healthcare representative if:
- the employee is related to you by blood, marriage or adoption, and
- the other requirements set out above are satisfied.

TEXAS

Your healthcare representative may not be:
- a witness to your durable power of attorney for healthcare
- your healthcare provider
- an employee of your healthcare provider, unless the employee is related to you
- your residential care provider, or
- an employee of your residential care provider, unless the employee is related to you.

UTAH

Your healthcare representative must be at least 18 years old.

VERMONT

Your healthcare representative may not be:
- under the age of 18
- a witness to your durable power of attorney for healthcare
- your healthcare provider
- an employee of your healthcare provider, unless the employee is related to you
- your residential care provider, or
- an employee of your residential care provider, unless the employee is related to you.

VIRGINIA

Your healthcare representative must be at least 18 years old.

WASHINGTON

Your healthcare representative must not be:
- any of your physicians
- your physicians' employees
- owners, administrators or employees of the healthcare facility where you live or receive care.

WEST VIRGINIA

Your healthcare representative may not be:
- a witness to your medical power of attorney
- your treating healthcare provider
- an employee of your treating healthcare provider, unless the employee is related to you
- an operator of a healthcare facility serving you or
- an employee of an operator of a healthcare facility, unless the employee is related to you.

WISCONSIN

Your healthcare representative may not be:
- a witness to your durable power of attorney for healthcare
- your healthcare provider
- an employee of your healthcare provider, or
- an employee of the healthcare facility in which you are a patient or a spouse of any of these persons, unless he or she is related to you.

WYOMING

Your healthcare representative may not be:
- a witness to your durable power of attorney for healthcare
- your treating healthcare provider
- an employee of your treating healthcare provider, or
- an operator of a community care facility or residential care facility

You may choose an employee of your treating healthcare provider, an employee of an operator of a community care facility or an employee of a residential care facility as your healthcare representative if:
- the employee is related to you by blood, marriage or adoption, and
- the other requirements set out above are satisfied.

3. Choosing an Alternate

Do not choose as an alternate someone who may be disqualified by state law from serving in your state because he or she is related to you or involved in caring for you. (See Section 2, above.)

> ► **A Bad Idea: Naming More Than One Representative**
> ►
> ► Name only one person as your representative, even if you know of two or more
> ► people who are suitable candidates and who say that they will undertake the job
> ► together. There may be problems, brought on by passing time and human nature,
> ► with naming two or more to share the job. In the critical time during which your
> ► representatives will be overseeing your wishes, they could disagree or suffer a
> ► change of heart, rendering them ineffective as lobbyists on your behalf.
> ►   If you know of two people you would like to name as your representatives, it
> ► is better to name only one person for the job—and name the other as an alternate
> ► to take over in case your first choice is unable to act when needed.

4. If You Choose Not to Name a Representative

Naming a representative is an optional part of making out your directives for
your healthcare. If you don't know of anyone you trust to oversee your
medical care, skip this part of the program. It is better not to name anyone
than to name someone who is not comfortable with the directions you leave—
or who is not likely to assert your wishes strongly.

Medical personnel are still technically bound to follow your written wishes
for your healthcare—or to find someone who will care for you in the way you
have directed. It is far better to put your wishes for final healthcare in writing
than to let the lack of a representative stand in the way.

H. Broader Durable Powers of Attorney

As mentioned, the durable power of attorney you produce with WillMaker
gives the person you name the limited authority to supervise and enforce your
written wishes for the type of medical care you wish to receive.

The power of attorney that prints out specifically gives the person you
name as your healthcare proxy the authority to:

- review your medical records
- grant releases to medical personnel

- take any legal action necessary to ensure your wishes are followed
- hire and fire medical personnel, and
- visit you in a hospital or other healthcare facility.

This should allow your proxy to do everything needed to make sure your healthcare wishes are carried out as written—and if they are not, to get you transferred to another facility or to the care of another doctor who will enforce them.

1. Additional Powers

Be aware that most states allow you to prepare Durable Powers of Attorney for Healthcare that delegate much broader authority than the one produced for you by the WillMaker program. Such powers of attorney may authorize your proxy to make healthcare decisions for you if you are not terminally ill or permanently comatose, for example, but you have an ongoing medical condition such as Alzheimer's disease. Because that type of durable power of attorney must be closely tailored to your needs and the abilities of your proxy—and must often be revised to meet changing medical conditions—you need the help of an experienced attorney or other estate planning expert to fashion one. (See Chapter 15, Section B.)

2. Durable Powers of Attorney for Finances

Another type of durable power of attorney—called a Durable Power of Attorney for Finances—can be used to give a person you trust the legal authority to handle many of your financial matters if you become unable to do so.[1] People who are facing illness, injury or old age are particularly good candidates for this type of document.

---

[1] For more information about durable powers of attorney for finances and all the forms and instructions needed to establish one, see *Who Will Handle Your Finances If You Can't?* by Clifford and Randolph (Nolo Press).

The person you name in a Durable Power of Attorney for Finances, who is usually called an attorney-in-fact, can be given broad authority to handle your finances and investments. Powers commonly given an attorney-in-fact include the authority to:

- use your assets to pay for expenses for you and your family, including food, mortgage, education, cars and medical expenses
- buy, sell and maintain real estate and other property
- collect benefits from Social Security, Medicare or military service
- invest your money in stocks, bonds and mutual funds
- handle transactions with banks and other financial institutions
- handle insurance policies
- file and pay your taxes, and
- operate your small business.

3. Why Separate Documents Are Required

Some state laws allow people to draw up a single durable power of attorney in which one person is named to oversee both healthcare and financial matters. While this sounds like a logical and simple solution to planning for possible incapacity, it is usually not a good idea, for a number of reasons.

- Most forms for durable powers of attorney that combine medical and financial matters do not allow you to include many specific details about how you would like to direct your medical care.
- Each of these types of durable power of attorney will be used for a very different purpose and must be presented to different people and organizations—often at different times.
- If you use two separate documents, you do not have to show your medical wishes to people who are concerned only with your finances—and vice versa.
- It is essential for the documents delegating authority for your healthcare and finances to be kept current to reflect your changing wishes, adjustments in your money matters—even advances in medical technology.

Having a single document that controls both finances and healthcare makes it unwieldy to update any of your wishes.

I. When Your Documents Take Effect

Your healthcare directive takes effect when three things happen:

- You are diagnosed to be close to death from a terminal condition or to be permanently comatose.
- You cannot communicate your own wishes for your medical care—orally, in writing or through gestures, and
- The medical personnel attending you are notified of your written directions for your medical care.

In most instances, you can ensure that your directive becomes part of your medical record when you are admitted to a hospital or other care facility. But to ensure that your wishes will be followed if your need for care arises unexpectedly or while you are out of your home state or country, it is best to give copies of your completed documents to several people. (See Section L, below.)

1. You Control Your Healthcare If You Are Able

Most people know it is a good idea to complete a healthcare directive. But some run smack into a psychological roadblock. They are worried that they may experience a change of heart or mind later—and that they will receive more or less medical care than they would want in a particular situation.

There are two soothing axioms for such people to keep in mind.

First, the directions set out in your written healthcare directive will only be followed if you later become unable to communicate your wishes about the treatment. If, for example, you indicate in a healthcare directive that you do not wish to have water provided, healthcare providers will not deny you a glass of water as long as you are able to communicate your wishes for one.

Second, you can change or revoke your written healthcare wishes at any time in the future. If you find that your document no longer accurately expresses your wishes for your medical care, you can easily draw up and finalize a new document which does reflect your wishes. (See Section N, below.)

2. How Pregnancy May Affect Your Directions

One target zone to watch—in which a patient's specific directions about healthcare might be ignored—is when the patient is a pregnant woman. Many state laws have specific limitations that say that a healthcare document directing the withdrawal or removal of life support will not be honored if a woman is pregnant.

These state restrictions have rankled many feminists and have become legally suspect since the U.S. Supreme Court set out and reaffirmed that women have a constitutionally-protected right to choose whether or not to bear children. In 1973, the Court in the case of Roe *v. Wade* (401 U.S. 113 (1973)), overturned a restrictive Texas anti-abortion law, with a tersely delineated holding. The Court held that:

- during the first trimester of pregnancy, states may not intervene to regulate pregnancy.

- during the second trimester, states may set up restrictions only to protect a woman's health.

- during the third trimester, or at the point of viability, when a fetus "presumably has the capability of meaningful life outside the mother's womb," states can intervene to protect it.

Several states fashioning or refining their healthcare directives took a cue from this holding, writing into their legislation the condition that a healthcare directive will not take effect "if your doctors believe the fetus can be brought to term while you are receiving life-sustaining procedures."

Other state attempts to control your choices about healthcare before a fetus is viable would most certainly be held unconstitutional. However, it is good to be aware of the restrictions that may exist in your state for pregnant women's healthcare directives. (See the chart below.)

In addition, if you are pregnant and have strong feelings about overcoming your state's strictures—that is, you live in a state that renders your directive completely ineffective if you are pregnant, but you wish to have it enforced—it is especially important for you to name a proxy to lobby on your behalf. Discuss your wishes and alert your proxy to any differences between your wishes and your state law. It would also be wise to write a brief explanation of your thoughts and understanding on this specific issue and attach it to your healthcare directive.

State Laws on Pregnancy and Healthcare Directives

"No Effect" means that the law in your state does not allow your document directing healthcare to take effect when you are pregnant.

"To Term" means that the law in your state will not allow your document directing healthcare to take effect if you are pregnant and your doctors believe the fetus could be brought to term while you are receiving life-sustaining treatment.

"Other" signifies that your state has specific qualifications on directing medical care during pregnancy.

"No Statute" means that your state does not have any law about pregnancy and your healthcare document.

STATE	NO EFFECT	TO TERM	NO STATUTE
Alabama	X		
Alaska		X	
Arizona			X
Arkansas		X	
California	X		
Colorado		X	
Connecticut			X
Delaware	X		
Dist. of Columbia		X	
Florida			X
Georgia	X		
Hawaii	X		
Idaho	X		
Illinois		X	
Indiana	X		
Iowa		X	
Kansas	X		
Kentucky	X		
Maine			X
Maryland	X		
Massachusetts			X
Michigan	Your healthcare representative cannot make any medical decision to withhold or withdraw treatment that would result in your death if you are pregnant.		
Minnesota		X	
Mississippi	X		

STATE	NO EFFECT	TO TERM	NO STATUTE
Missouri	X		
Montana		X	
Nebraska			X
Nevada			X
New Hampshire	X		
New Jersey	If you are pregnant when diagnosed to be terminally ill and near death or permanently comatose, your express wishes as to your care during pregnancy, if written in your Advance Directive, will be carried out.		
New Mexico			X
New York			X
North Carolina			X
North Dakota	If you are pregnant, life-sustaining procedures will be provided unless the fetus could not develop to the point of live birth with continued application of those life-sustaining procedures, or your doctors conclude that prolonging your life would cause you unreasonable pain or prolong severe pain that cannot be alleviated by medication.		
Ohio			X
Oklahoma	X		
Oregon			X
Pennsylvania	If you are pregnant, life-sustaining procedures will be provided unless the fetus could not develop to the point of live birth with continued application of those life-sustaining procedures, or your doctors conclude that prolonging your life would cause you unreasonable pain or prolong severe pain that cannot be alleviated by medication.		
Rhode Island			X
South Carolina	X		
South Dakota	If you are pregnant, life-sustaining procedures will be provided unless the fetus could not develop to the point of live birth with continued application of those life-sustaining procedures, or your doctors conclude that prolonging your life would cause you unreasonable pain or prolong severe pain that cannot be alleviated by medication.		
Tennessee			X
Texas	X		
Utah	X		
Vermont			X
Virginia			X
Washington			X
West Virginia			X
Wisconsin	X		
Wyoming	X		

J. Where to Go for More Help

Awareness of healthcare directives has skyrocketed in the past few years. This rapid-fire education was aided substantially by the 1991 Patient Self-Determination Act, which requires admitting room personnel in most health-care facilities to discuss medical directives with patients and note whether they have one in effect. This familiarity has meant not only that many more people have healthcare directives, but that doctors are more likely to recognize and enforce them.

But because hospital admission time may not be the best time to learn about your options in directing healthcare or to reflect on your wishes, it is a better idea to become informed and complete your documents in a less stressful time and place.

A side benefit of healthcare directives' increased popularity is that there are a growing number of places you can turn if you need more assistance in completing your healthcare directive or have specific questions about them.

1. Local Resources

Local senior centers may be good resources for help. Many of them have trained healthcare staff on hand who will be willing to discuss your healthcare options.

The patient representative at a local hospital may also be a good person to contact for help. If you have a regular physician, by all means discuss your concerns with him or her.

Local special interest groups and clinics may provide help in filling out healthcare directives—particularly organizations set up to meet the needs of the severely ill such as AIDS groups or cancer organizations. Check your telephone book for a local listing—or call one of the group's hotlines for more information or a possible referral.

There are also a number of seminars offered. Beware of groups that offer such seminars for a hefty fee, however. Hospitals and senior centers often provide them free of charge.

2. Nolo Resources

For information on why and how to set up a Durable Power of Attorney for Finances—including forms and step-by-step instructions on how to complete them, see *Who Will Handle Your Finances If You Can't?* by Clifford and Randolph, also published by Nolo Press.

K. Making It Legal: Final Steps

By proceeding through this portion of the WillMaker program and answering all the questions you can about your future healthcare, you have put the hard parts are behind you. You have overcome the twin evils of procrastination and death-avoidance to assert your right to keep control over your own healthcare.

However, there are still a few technical requirements with which you must comply before the documents that print out will be considered legally valid and binding. First, review the documents that print out and make sure they are accurate.

1. Signing Your Documents

Every state law requires that you sign your documents—or direct another person to sign them for you—as a way of verifying that you understand them and that they contain your true wishes.

But do not sign them immediately. Every state law also has a requirement that you sign your documents in the presence of witnesses or a notary public—sometimes both. The purpose of this additional formality is so that there is at least one other person who can attest that you were of sound mind and of legal age when you made the documents. (See Section C2, above.)

2. Having Your Documents Witnessed and Notarized

In some states, you may have your documents notarized instead of witnessed. In others, you will be required to have both witnesses and a notary sign your document. The instructions that accompany your healthcare directive will specify who can and cannot be a witness for your documents. And a few vexatious states have different requirements for your document directing your healthcare and your document naming a proxy. (See the chart below.)

Witnessing   Many states require that two witnesses see you sign your healthcare documents and that they verify in writing that you appeared to be of sound mind and signed the documents without anyone else influencing your decision.

Each state's qualifications for these witnesses are slightly different. In many states, for example, a spouse, other close relative or any person who would inherit property from you, is not allowed to act as a witness for the document directing healthcare. And many states prohibit your attending physician from being a witness.

The purpose of the laws restricting who can witness your documents is to avoid any appearance or possibility that another person was acting against your wishes in encouraging specific medical care. States that prevent close relatives or potential inheritors from being witnesses, for example, justify their restrictions by noting that these people may be specially influenced by another person's healthcare. Some people, anxious to hold on to any sign of life, may urge that all possible medical treatments be administered, no matter what little hope they offer for a cure. Others, driven by fears of bankruptcy or dreams of riches, may encourage that no additional treatment be administered. Either course may not be what an individual patient would want.

If your state has restrictions on who may serve as witnesses to your healthcare documents, those restrictions will be noted on your documents, just before the witness signature lines.

Notarizing A Notary Public is an individual who is certified to verify signatures on documents. You can locate one by looking in the telephone book; most banks, insurance and title companies also have a Notary on staff. Most will charge a small fee for notarizing your documents.

In addition to the requirement that witnesses sign the healthcare document, some states also require that you and the witnesses appear before a Notary Public and swear that the circumstances of your signing, as described on the documents, are true. In some states, you have the option of having a Notary sign your document instead of having it witnessed.

The instructions accompanying your documents will tell you if your state requires that your documents be notarized.

If you do go to a Notary, bring with you some identification that will help prove that you are who you say you are.

State Witnessing and Notarizing Requirements

"Witnesses" means witnesses are required to finalize your healthcare document; the number of required witnesses is noted.

"Notarization" means that your document will need to be notarized.

State Witnessing and Notarizing Requirements

"Witnesses" means witnesses are required to finalize your healthcare document; the number of required witnesses is noted.

"Notarization" means that your document will need to be notarized.

"Witnesses or Notarization" means that you may either have your document witnessed or notarized and that you are not required to have both procedures performed.

"Witnesses and Notarizaton" means that you must have your document witnessed and notarized.

"Witnesses/Optional Notarization" means that you must have your document witnessed, but you need not have it notarized.

STATE	DOCUMENT APPOINTING HEALTHCARE REPRESENTATIVE	HEALTHCARE DIRECTIVE
Alabama	2 Witnesses or Notarization	2 Witnesses
Alaska	Notarization	2 Witnesses or Notarization
Arizona	1 Witness or Notarization	1 Witness or Notarization
Arkansas	2 Witnesses or Notarization	2 Witnesses
California	2 Witnesses	2 Witnesses
Colorado	Notarization	2 Witnesses/Optional Notarization
Connecticut	2 Witnesses/Optional Notarization	2 Witnesses
Delaware	2 Witnesses or Notarization	2 Witnesses
D.C.	2 Witnesses	2 Witnesses
Florida	2 Witnesses	2 Witnesses
Georgia	2 Witnesses	2 Witnesses
Hawaii	2 Witnesses and Notarization	2 Witnesses and Notarization
Idaho	2 Witnesses or Notarization	2 Witnesses
Illinois	1 Witness	2 Witnesses
Indiana	Notarization	2 Witnesses
Iowa	2 Witnesses or Notarization	2 Witnesses or Notarization
Kansas	2 Witnesses or Notarization	2 Witnesses
Kentucky	2 Witnesses or Notarization	2 Witnesses and Notarization
Maine	2 Witnesses	2 Witnesses
Maryland	2 Witnesses or Notarization	2 Witnesses
Massachusetts	2 Witnesses	2 Witnesses
Michigan	2 Witnesses	2 Witnesses

STATE	DOCUMENT APPOINTING HEALTHCARE REPRESENTATIVE	HEALTHCARE DIRECTIVE
Minnesota	None	2 Witnesses or Notarization
Mississippi	2 Witnesses or Notarization	2 Witnesses
Missouri	Notarization	2 Witnesses
Montana	Notarization	2 Witnesses
Nebraska	Notarization	2 Witnesses or Notarization
Nevada	2 Witnesses or Notarization	2 Witnesses
New Hampshire	2 Witnesses/Optional Notarization	2 Witnesses and Notarization
New Jersey	2 Witnesses or Notarization	2 Witnesses or Notarization
New Mexico	Notarization	2 Witnesses
New York	2 Witnesses	2 Witnesses
North Carolina	2 Witnesses and Notarization	2 Witnesses and Notarization
North Dakota	2 Witnesses	2 Witnesses
Ohio	2 Witnesses or Notarization	2 Witnesses
Oklahoma	2 Witnesses and Notarization	2 Witnesses
Oregon	2 Witnesses	2 Witnesses
Pennsylvania	2 Witnesses or Notarization	2 Witnesses
Rhode Island	2 Witnesses and Notarization	2 Witnesses
South Carolina	2 Witnesses	2 Witnesses and Notarization
South Dakota	2 Witnesses or Notarization	2 Witnesses/Optional Notarization
Tennessee	2 Witnesses and Notarization	2 Witnesses/Optional Notarization
Texas	2 Witnesses	2 Witnesses
Utah	Notarization	2 Witnesses
Vermont	2 Witnesses	2 Witnesses
Virginia	2 Witnesses	2 Witnesses
Washington	2 Witnesses or Notarization	2 Witnesses
West Virginia	2 Witnesses and Notarization	2 Witnesses and Notarization
Wisconsin	2 Witnesses	2 Witnesses
Wyoming	2 Witnesses or Notarization	2 Witnesses

3. Glossary of Witnessing Terms

Most states that require healthcare documents to be witnessed prohibit certain people from serving as witnesses. As a general rule, a witness may not be anyone who is likely to have a claim against some or all of your property when you die. This usually includes anyone:

- you have named in a will or living trust to inherit your property

- who would inherit your property if there were no will, or

- to whom you owe money because of a debt or an injury for which you are liable.

The qualifications for witnesses in your state are set out in your healthcare documents just above where the witnesses sign. In many instances, these qualifications are written in legalese—by your state's legislature—and may be hard to interpret.

Below, for your convenience, are brief definitions of the terms that most commonly occur.

Beneficiary   Any person who is entitled to receive property belonging to a deceased person.

Beneficiary of a will   Any person or organization named in a will to receive property, either as a first choice or if the first choice as beneficiary does not survive the person making the will.

Claim against the estate   Any right that a person has to receive property from a person's estate. This may arise under a will or living trust, from a contract, or because of a legal liability that the deceased owes to the person.

Codicil   An amendment to a will, prepared with the same formality as is required for the will.

Devisee   A person who has been named to receive property in a will.

Domicile   The state where the person makes his or her home.

Heir at law   Any person who qualifies to inherit property from a person on the basis of his or her relationship with that person. Usually, heirs at law are spouses, children, parents, brothers and sisters. However, if none of these people exist, an heir at law might be a niece, nephew or even a distant cousin.

Inchoate claim   A claim against a person's estate that does not yet exist but might if certain conditions occur. For instance, a person named as an alternate beneficiary in a will has an inchoate claim against the estate— conditional upon the first choice beneficiary not surviving the willmaker.

Inherit by operation of law When a person dies owning property that has not been distributed in a will or by some other legal device, such as a living trust, the property will be distributed according to the laws of the state where the person died—that is, by operation of law. These laws—commonly referred to as the "laws of intestate succession"—usually cause the property to be distributed first to a spouse and children and then to parents, brothers and sisters.

Lawful heirs Anyone who is entitled to inherit property from a deceased person under the state's laws of intestate succession.

Laws of intestate succession Rules that a state uses to decide what should happen to the property of a deceased individual if the property has not be left in a will or other legal device—such as a living trust. While the rules are slightly different for every state, the property will go first to a spouse and children, and if none survive, then to brothers and sisters and parents.

Legatee A person who has been named to receive property in a will.

Presumptive heir or known devisee Any person who either is entitled to inherit property from a person under the state's law or who has been named to inherit the property in a will or living trust.

Rules of descent and distribution Rules that a state uses to decide what should happen to the property of a deceased individual if the property has not been left in a will or other legal device—such as a living trust. While the rules are slightly different for every state, the property will go first to a spouse or children, and if there are not any, then to brothers and sisters and parents.

Testamentary instrument A document that describes who is to receive property upon the death of the person making the document and that goes into effect when the document maker dies.

L. Making and Distributing Copies

Ideally, you should make an effort to make your wishes for your future healthcare widely known. Keep a copy of your healthcare directive, and give other copies to:

* any physician with whom you now consult regularly

- the proxy you named in your directive
- the office of the hospital or other care facility in which you are likely to receive treatment
- the patient representative of your HMO or insurance plan
- close relatives, particularly immediate family members—a spouse, children, siblings, and
- trusted friends.

Some people are hesitant to discuss the particulars of their medical care with other people, feeling that it is an intensely private issue. However, in the case of healthcare directives, you must weigh this yen for privacy against the need for the documents to be effective. Quite simply, your carefully-reasoned medical directive will simply be wasted words unless you make sure it gets into the hands of the people who need to know about it.

At a minimum, give copies of your signed and completed healthcare directive to the doctors or medical facility most likely to be treating you and to any proxy you have named.

Keep Your Documents Together

If you have named a healthcare representative or proxy, he or she will need to have a copy of your healthcare directive to learn the specific details of your medical care directions. And hospital personnel will need to see a copy of the Durable Power of Attorney for Healthcare that authorizes your agent to supervise your wishes, to get copies of your medical records and to hire and fire medical personnel.

M. Keeping Your Documents Up-to-Date

Review your healthcare documents occasionally—at least once a year—to make sure they still accurately reflect your wishes for your medical care. Advances in technology and changes in health are two changes in course that prompt many people to change their minds about the kind of healthcare they want.

In addition, you should consider making new documents if:

- you move to another state (see Section D3 for more information on this point)

- you made and finalized a healthcare directive many years ago (because your state's law controlling them have probably changed substantially), and

- the proxy or representative you named to supervise your wishes becomes unable to do so.

N. How to Revoke Your Documents

If you have a change of mind and wish to revoke or cancel your healthcare directive, you can do so at any time. The safest, most direct and most common sense way to cancel your document is to destroy it physically—by burning it up or tearing it into pieces. Be sure to contact all those who have copies of your document and ask that they be returned so you can destroy them, too. ▲

14 Final Arrangements

A. Making Final Arrangements in Advance

Most people avoid the subject of death—and are especially uncomfortable thinking about their own mortality. You, too, may be tempted to leave the details of your final arrangements for what happens to your body after death to those who survive you.

But there are two good reasons not to do this: care and cost.

Anyone who has lost a loved one knows how agonizing it can be to decide what he or she would have wanted as a commemoration. And most people have attended funerals or other after-death services that seem uniquely unsuited to the person who has died.

Letting your survivors know what kind of disposition and ceremonies you envision saves them the pain of making such decisions at what is likely to be a difficult time for them.

And many family members and friends have found discussing preferences for final arrangements openly to be a relief—especially if a person is elderly or in poor health and death is likely to occur soon.

Planning some of these details in advance can also help save money. For many people, after-death goods and services are the third most costly expense—just after homes and cars. Advance planning, with some wise comparison shopping, can help ensure that costs will be controlled or kept to a minimum.

Without some direction, your survivors are most likely to choose the most expensive goods and services available, to assuage their own feelings of guilt or grief or due to coercion by funeral industry providers. The best way to prevent this from happening is to leave a written instruction of your preferences with as much detail as you are able to give.

► **A Will Is Not the Way**

Many people think of a will as the proper document in which to specify final instructions for whether they want to be buried or cremated and whether they wish to have any ceremonies held after they die.

In fact, a will should be reserved only for directions on how to divide and distribute your property, and, if you wish, may include your preferences for who should get care and custody of your minor children after you die.

But a will is a singularly poor place to express your death and burial preferences for one simple reason: Your will probably won't be located and read until several weeks after you die—long after the time such final arrangements must occur.

1. The Legal Effect of Your Document

In most cases, your arrangements will be carried out as written.

However, if a dispute arises among your loved ones—for example, between your mate or spouse and other relatives—the funeral industry personnel involved are usually bound to follow any written instructions the deceased person has left.

Court battles over body-disposal preferences or funeral ceremonies almost never arise, primarily because of the lack of time and the prohibitive cost of litigation.

► **Attaching a Letter of Explanation**

The document you produce using WillMaker will set out the details of what you want to occur after your death. Depending on your responses while using the WillMaker program, your instructions may be as sparse or as detailed as you wish.

In addition to the specifics of body disposition and ceremonies, some people may want to explain their choices or leave some final message to their survivors. An excellent way to do this is to write a letter and attach it to the Final Arrangements document that WillMaker produces.

2. What Happens If There Is No Document

If you die without leaving written instructions about your preferences, the person who has the right to control how your remains will be disposed of are determined by state law. In most states, the right—and the liability for paying for the reasonable costs of a disposition—is with the following people, in order:

- surviving spouse

- surviving child or children

- surviving parent or parents

- the next of kin, and

- the public administrator, who is appointed by a court.

Most disputes arise where there is more than one person—three children, for example—who disagree over a fundamental decision, such as whether the body of a parent should be buried or cremated. As mentioned, such disputes can be avoided if you are willing to do some planning—and put your wishes in writing.

▶ If You Have Already Made Some Final Arrangements

Those who have already made arrangements for burial or cremation may wonder whether it is necessary to use this portion of the WillMaker program. It would be wise to do so. It will only take a few minutes—and the program may direct your attention to one or more issues that you have not already addressed in your previous arrangements.

In addition, WillMaker produces a document that allows you to organize your thoughts and directions for your final disposition in one place. This may be essential for your survivors who want to see that your wishes are carried out as written. Also, the program prompts you to describe two very common types of arrangements that you may have made:

- donation of one or more organs, and

- donation of your body to a medical institution.

Setting out these arrangements in writing will help assure that the donations are carried out.

B. The Basics of Your Final Arrangements

This portion of the WillMaker program allows you to state your preferences on the following specific issues:

- the name of the mortuary or other institution that will handle your burial or cremation

- whether you wish to be embalmed

- the type of casket or container in which you will be buried or cremated, including whether you want it present at any after-death ceremony

- the details of any ceremony you want before the burial or cremation, including specific clothing and jewelry in which you want your body to be attired

- who your pallbearers will be

- how you will be transported to the cemetery and gravesite

- where your remains will be buried, stored, or scattered

- the details of any ceremony you want to accompany your burial, interment or scattering

- the details of any marker you want to show where your remains are buried or interred

- any epitaph you wish placed on your burial marker, and

- the details of any ceremony you want held after you are buried or cremated.

> ### Attend to as Many Details as Possible
> This portion of WillMaker covers a wide variety of after-death details—from specifics of body disposition to the type and tenor of ceremonies you wish to be held. The questions posed to you while using this portion of the WillMaker program are intended as a structure so that you can leave the most complete instructions possible.

For people who have very simple plans, many of the WillMaker questions will not be relevant. And a number of other people may simply be stumped or undecided about some aspects of the instructions they wish to leave.

In the Final Arrangements portion of WillMaker, you need only respond to those questions you wish to answer. While it behooves you and your survivors for you to be as specific as you can in your instructions, the document produced can be as sketchy or complete as you wish. If there is an issue you do not wish to address, simply skip the questions that pertain to it.

C. Help with Your Final Arrangements

1.   Mortuaries

Most mortuaries or funeral homes are equipped to handle many of the details related to disposing of a person's remains. These include:

- collecting the body from the place of death
- storing the body until it is buried or cremated
- making burial arrangements with a cemetery
- conducting ceremonies related to the burial

- preparing the body for burial, and
- arranging to have the body transported for burial.

2. Memorial or Funeral Societies

Choosing the institution to handle your burial is probably the most important final arrangement that you can make, from an economic standpoint. For this reason, many people join memorial or funeral societies, which help them find local mortuaries that will deal honestly with their heirs and charge prices that accurately reflect the value of their services.

Society members are free to choose whatever final arrangement they wish. Most societies, however, emphasize simple, dignified arrangements over the costly, elaborate services often promoted by the funeral industry.

While the services offered by each society differ, most societies distribute literature and information on options and legal controls on final arrangements.

Members receive a prearrangement form upon joining, which allows them to plan for the goods and services they want—and to get them for a predetermined cost. The society also serves as a watchdog—making sure that individuals get and pay for only the services they have specified.

The cost for joining and getting these organizations is low—usually from $20 to $40 for a lifetime membership, although some societies charge a small renewal fee periodically.

To find a funeral or memorial society nearest you, look in the yellow pages of your telephone book under Funeral Information & Advisory Services, or contact the Continental Association of Funeral and Memorial Societies, 800-458-5563, for additional information.

3. Finding a Mortuary on Your Own

If you are not a member of a funeral or memorial society, then it is important that you find the institution that best needs your needs in terms of style, proximity and cost.

This has become somewhat easier than it used to be, since the Federal Trade Commission (FTC) passed regulations to stem the tide of abuses by the funeral industry. Under the FTC Funeral rule, those who provide death goods and services must give price lists to consumers who visit a funeral home—and must disclose prices and other information to those who ask for it over the phone.

The law also enables consumers to select and purchase only the goods and services they want, and clamps down on untoward practices such as false or unclear advertising.

▶ Beware of Prepayment Plans

Shopping around for the most suitable and affordable funeral goods and services is a wise consumer idea. However, be extremely cautious about paying in advance—or prepaying—for them.

While there are a number of legal controls on how the funeral industry can handle and invest funds earmarked for future services, there are many reported abuses of mismanaged and stolen funds. A great many other abuses go unreported by family members too embarrassed or too grief-stricken to complain.

There are additional pitfalls. When mortuaries go out of business, the consumer who has prepaid is often left without funds and without recourse. Also, many individuals who move to a new locale during their lifetimes are dismayed to find that their prepayment funds are nonrefundable—or that there is a substantial financial penalty for withdrawing or transferring them. In addition, money paid now may not cover inflated costs of the future—meaning that survivors will be left to cover the substantially inflated costs.

If you are interested in setting aside a fund of money to pay for your final arrangements, a more prudent approach for most people is to set up a Totten Trust—a trust or savings plan earmarked to pay for your final arrangements—with a bank or savings institution. Most will do so for a very slight charge, the trust funds are easily transferred or withdrawn if need be and you have complete control over the money during your life.

4. Survivors Caring for the Dead

There is a growing trend in America for people to revert to caring for their own dead, from preparing to burying the deceased person—doing an end-run around all funeral industry personnel.

Despite a monied funeral industry lobby, most states do allow individuals to act completely on their own. But those who do so must be armed with information on what is and what is not allowed. For example, most states do have laws that regulate the depth of a site for a body burial.

In addition, the laws in several states—including Louisiana, Massachusetts, Michigan, Nebraska, New Hampshire, New Jersey and New York—specifically require that a funeral director must handle the disposition of a deceased person.

If you are considering directing that a family member or friend handle your disposition independently, consult a local funeral or memorial society for information on what restrictions may apply. In addition, a book entitled *Caring for Your Own Dead* by Lisa Carlson (Upper Access Publishers, Vermont) includes a state-by-state synopsis of relevant statutes and a discussion of other concerns for those who wish to bury their own dead.

D. Body and Organ Donations

1. Whole Body Donations

Most medical schools need donations of whole bodies for medical research and instruction—and shortages may be especially acute at osteopathic and chiropractic schools. The reason they are called whole body donations is that the donation will be rejected if any of the organs have been removed.

After using a donated body for study or instruction, a medical institution will usually cremate it—and bury or scatter the cremains in a specified plot. However, the remains or cremains can be returned to family members for burial—usually within a year or two. Those who want the body or cremains returned to a friend or family members for the final disposition should specify this when the donation is arranged.

No medical institution is allowed to buy a body, but there is usually little or no expense to the survivors when a body is donated. When a death occurs, most medical schools will pay to transport the body, as well as pay for any final disposition. Ask the nearest medical institution that accepts body donations whether it has specific arrangements for transporting and disposing of bodies to avoid any unexpected charges.

Body donations are usually arranged with a particular institution while the donor is living, but some institutions will accept the donation at death with the written permission of the next of kin.

There are currently medical schools in every state except for Alaska, Delaware, Idaho, Montana and Wyoming. The medical schools in Arizona, Nebraska, Nevada, South Carolina and Wisconsin have the strictest rules about enrolling in body donation programs before death.

If you live in a state with no medical school or one that has very strict requirements for whole body donations, you may wish to find out more about your body donation options from the National Anatomical Service, which operates 24-hour phone services out of New York (718-948-2401) and St. Louis (314-726-9079).

▶ Your Donation May Be Rejected

Even if you have arranged in advance to donate your body to a medical institution, the institution may reject the donation if:

- you have also donated one or more of your organs and these are taken at your death
- the institution's current supply exceeds its demand and there are no facilities for storage
- you die during surgery, or
- your body is unsuitable for study because it is extremely obese, or you have died of a number of diseases that render it unacceptable according to the institution.

2. How to Make Whole Body Donations

Whole body donations must usually be made while you are alive, although some medical schools will accept a cadaver through arrangements made after death.

The best place to contact to arrange a whole body donation is the nearest medical school. Or call the National Anatomical Service at 800-727-0700 for additional information on how to arrange for body donation.

3. Organ Donations

As medical technology has made successful organ and tissue transplants cheaper, easier and safer, organs and tissues are in great demand.

Among the organs and tissues now commonly being transplanted are:

- corneas
- hearts
- livers
- kidneys
- bone and bone marrow
- tendons, ligaments, connective tissue
- skin
- pancreas, and
- lungs.

Tissues and corneas can be taken from almost anyone—and are often used for research and study. However, there are far greater problems with donating major organs such as hearts and livers. For example, while there are tens of thousands of people now on waiting lists to receive kidneys alone, only about 1% of all people who die are suitable kidney donors.

▸ When Organs Are Removed

Major organs for transplantation must be taken from a donor who is in reasonably good health—and must be removed while the donor's heart is still beating, but he or she is brain-dead. In reality, nearly all suitable donors of major organs are short-term patients who have been hospitalized and who have received artificial respiration.

Some people fear that agreeing to donate an organ will mean that they run the risk of being declared dead prematurely while eager doctors rush to remove their organs.

There is a strong safeguard against this possibility. Before any organ is removed from a donor, two doctors who are not involved in the transplantation must declare that the patient is "irretrievably deceased"—with an ultimate diagnosis of being brain-dead. From that time on, the cadaver must be maintained on a respirator to keep blood flowing through the organ.

4. How to Arrange for Organ Donations

The principal method for donating organs is by indicating your intent to do so on a uniform donor card. Once signed, this card identifies you to medical personnel as a potential organ donor.

You can get a donor card or form from most hospitals, the county or state office of the National Kidney Foundation or a community eye bank.

In most states, you can also obtain an organ donation card from the local Department of Motor Vehicles. Depending on where you live, you can check a box, affix a stamp or seal, or attach a separate card to your license, indicating your wish to donate one or more organs.

If you fill out an organ donor card, make sure you tell family members you have done so.

Even if you have not signed a card or other document indicating your intent to donate your organs, your next of kin can approve a donation at the time of your death. And conversely, even if you have indicated an intent to donate your organs, an objection by your next of kin will often defeat your intention; medical personnel will usually not proceed in the face of an objection from relatives. The best safeguard is to discuss your wishes with close friends and relatives, emphasizing your strong feelings about donating your body for research or teaching.

▶ **Tell Other People About Your Wishes**
For organ donations to be successful, several people must know about the arrangement before you die. These people are your doctors, personnel at the hospital or other healthcare facility where you die, and the people who your doctors or the institution are likely to contact if there are any questions about the donation. These might be your spouse, other close relatives or the people you have named to supervise your healthcare in a durable power of attorney or other document. At a minimum, it is essential that you notify your spouse and closest relatives about your wishes for organ donation.

5. Laws on Organ Donations

In most states, if a deceased person has not left explicit instructions about donating an organ, a coroner must make a reasonable search for a deceased's person's next of kin or get the express consent of the next of kin before an organ may be removed for donation.

Nearly half the states have recently passed laws that specify that a coroner may authorize that certain organs, body parts or tissues may be removed from a body as long as certain conditions are met.

Under these laws, you become an automatic organ donor when you die and need not take any action while you are alive. However, a number of conditions must be satisfied first:

- There must be a request for the organ by a qualified recipient.
- There must not be a pending investigation or autopsy of the body.

• The deceased's facial appearance must not be altered in the process of becoming a donor.

• The coroner must not be aware of any objections from the next of kin.

The following are states that have some such form of presumed consent to organ donation.

STATE	ORGAN
Arkansas	pituitary gland
California	pituitary gland, corneas
Colorado	pituitary gland
Connecticut	pituitary gland, corneas
Delaware	corneas
Florida	corneas
Georgia	eyes, corneas
Kentucky	corneas
Maryland	corneas
Michigan	corneas
Missouri	pituitary gland
Nebraska	eyes, pituitary gland
North Carolina	corneas
Ohio	corneas
Oklahoma	pituitary gland
Tennessee	corneas
Texas	corneas
West Virginia	corneas

E. Burial or Cremation

When using WillMaker, you are asked to decide whether:

• your whole body, minus any organs you have donated, is to be buried in the ground or other place, or

• your body is to be cremated and whether the remains, called cremains, should be buried, stored or scattered.

This choice must be made even if you have arranged to have some organs or your entire body donated to a medical institution. Even if one or more of your organs is accepted for donation, the rest of your body must be disposed of or buried.

Whether you choose cremation or burial, your choice will likely be guided by a number of personal preferences—which may include religion, community custom, family tradition and cost.

Even if you have arranged to have your entire body donated, there is the possibility that donation may be rejected because of the condition of your body or simply because it is not needed. Also, after the medical institution has finished using the body for teaching or research, it must be disposed of or buried—usually, between one to two years after it is accepted for donation.

1. Body Burial

While cremation is gaining popularity as an option, most bodies in the U.S. are buried. Contrary to popular misconception, embalming prior to burial is not usually required by law. However, a number of other substantial charges may be added for:

- getting and processing the death certificate
- transporting the body
- opening and closing a grave
- burial vaults, required by most cemeteries
- the cost of a casket, and
- additional handling and service charges paid to funeral industry personnel.

2. Cremation

When a body is cremated, it is heated intensely—1,800 degrees Fahrenheit or higher—in an ovenlike device called a retort, until it is reduced to several pounds of ash and some fragments of bones, called cremains. The entire process takes from two to three hours.

Larger bone fragments within the cremains are usually pulverized before being gathered. They can then be placed in an urn or other container to be buried, stored or scattered. The cost of cremation varies widely, but usually runs from $200 to $500—substantially less than embalming and full body burial. The costs differ depending on your locale.

However, a number of other substantial charges may be added for:

* getting and processing the death certificate
* a certificate releasing the body for cremation, issued by a medical examiner or coroner ion some locales
* transporting the body
* disposing of the cremains
* the cost of a casket or container, and
* additional handling and service charges paid to funeral industry personnel.

In addition, most cremation facilities require that a pacemaker be removed before a body is cremated, since the devices can explode and damage the cremation chamber—and there is usually a charge for the removal operation.

▶ **Cremation Witnesses**
▶
▶ In recent years, some mortuaries and crematoriums have been disciplined for
▶ mixing the remains of the bodies they cremate, in violation of state laws.
▶
▶ While this may not bother some people, others are horrified at the thought of
▶ having their remains mixed with those of other people or animals and want to do
▶ everything possible to prevent this. One way is to appoint someone to witness the
▶ cremation, which force the mortuary or crematorium to be scrupulous about not
▶ mixing cremains and bodies.
▶
▶ Not all mortuaries and crematoriums cooperate to allow this witnessing. If
▶ this concerns you, check with the mortuary or crematorium you have selected. If
▶ it does not allow witnesses—and that is what you want—select a different
▶ institution.

F. Embalming

1. About Embalming

Embalming is a process in which the blood is drained and replacement fluids
are pumped into the body to temporarily retard its disintegration.

The process has a rich history in the United States. Originally considered
barbaric and paganistic, embalming first gained popularity during the Civil
War, when bodies of the war dead were transported over long distances
through tough travel arrangements. When the war ended, embalming was
promoted, mostly by those who performed the service, as a hygienic means of
preserving the body.

While it has now become a common procedure, embalming is rarely
necessary; refrigeration serves the same purpose.

2. When Embalming Is Required

There is a popular misconception that embalming is always required by law after death. In fact, it is legally required only in some states and only in a few instances, such as:

- when a body will be transported by plane or train from one country or state to another

- where there is a relatively long time—usually a week or more—between the death and burial or cremation, and

- in some cases, where the death occurred because of a communicable disease.

3. What Happens If Your Body Is Not Embalmed

If you choose not to be embalmed, it should have no effect on your final arrangements. Your body will be refrigerated until the time of burial, and, if you choose, you can have a funeral or other service with an open casket.

The only effect of not being embalmed will be that if you opt to be buried, your body will decompose within days instead of weeks.

4. The Cost of Embalming

The cost of embalming ranges from about $100 to $500, depending on your location and on the individual setting the rate of the charges.

Refrigeration is usually less costly, involving a daily charge of about $10 to $30, depending on the facility.

G. Caskets

The container in which your body will be buried is called a casket or coffin. This item has been subject to more controversy in recent years than any other aspect of the funeral industry, because it traditionally carries the biggest mark-up of all funeral goods and services.

Anyone who has been asked to choose a casket for a deceased loved one knows the complex feelings that this choice engenders—often a mix of pride and guilt tempered by the reality of affordability. The sales personnel are well aware of their customers' vulnerabilities and some do their best to sell the most expensive models. Lower-priced caskets are often displayed in the dingy, out-of-the-way corners of a funeral home's showroom.

Most funeral establishments now also carry caskets that may be rented and lined with inexpensive liners during viewing of the body instead of purchased for use. However, these too, are generally relegated to far-off, poorly-lit corners—or the funeral director may fail to mention this option to grieving family members.

While they are rare, there are some independent casketmakers or artisans who specialize in making low-cost or uniquely-styled caskets. To locate an independent casketmaker, check the yellow pages of your telephone book under Funeral Information and Advisory Services, or a similar heading. Your local funeral or memorial society may also provide guidance on how to find a local independent casketmaker.

▶ The High Cost of Caskets

Those in the funeral industry mark up the cost of caskets substantially, pricing them from hundreds to many thousands of dollars. The price differentials are usually based on the type of material used for the lining and exterior of the container and the type of hardware used for the handles and clasps. They range from $200 for a simple wooden casket to $20,000 for an elaborate engraved container with goldleaf decorations.

Caskets for children should be priced considerably below adult models.

Most state laws require that caskets displayed in a showroom for potential purchase must be tagged with prices, a description of their composition and identifying model numbers. If an establishment uses a catalog to show the caskets it offers for sale or order, the same information must be included there. These laws allow individuals who have decided on a particular type or model of casket to comparison shop for the best price.

H. Ceremonies

Death often involves at least one ceremony and sometimes more. The most common is the funeral, which occurs just prior to burial—although smaller informal ceremonies, often called wakes or visitations, are also commonly held the night before burial occurs. The specific details of a funeral or wake can vary enormously, depending on community custom and the religious, cultural and personal backgrounds of the deceased and his or her survivors.

1. Pre-Burial Ceremonies

There are two good reasons to describe your wishes for a ceremony to be held before your body is buried. The first is that the ceremony is an indirect last way for your survivors—your friends and family members—to say goodbye to you, to comfort one another and to continue the grieving process.

The second is that the more details you arrange while you are alive, the fewer decisions will be left for your survivors at a time when decisions are likely to be hard for them to make.

Common Elements of Pre-Burial Ceremonies

Some concerns you may wish to address when planning a pre-burial ceremony are:

- where the ceremony should be held
- who should be invited
- whether clergy should be invited to participate, along with specific names of clergy you would like
- any specific music you would like played, along with the names of the musicians or singers you would like to perform it
- preferences for a eulogy, and the name of the person or people you would like to speak

- whether you want your body to be present in a casket at the ceremony, and if so, whether you would like the casket open or closed
- any specific clothing or jewelry in which you wish to be attired, and
- whether you want to direct survivors to send flowers or memorial donations.

▶ Making the Choice

Most people will want at least one ceremony held after they die but before they are buried, even if it is simple and informal. However, there may be reasons why a pre-burial ceremony is not appropriate. One may be that you live far from most of your friends and family members, and they would have to drop everything and attend a pre-burial ceremony at a great personal cost.

Since burial typically occurs within a few days of death, attending ceremonies held before burial can be very disruptive. For this reason, many people opt to not have a funeral, but instead prefer a memorial ceremony, usually held days or weeks after the burial, that is more accessible to more people.

2. Pre-Cremation Ceremonies

The most common of these ceremonies is the funeral, which occurs just prior to burial—although smaller informal ceremonies, often called wakes or visitations are also commonly held before cremation occurs.

The specific details of a funeral or wake can vary enormously, depending on community custom and the religious, cultural and personal backgrounds of the deceased and his or her survivors.

Common Elements of Pre-Cremation Ceremonies

While people who choose cremation over body burial are often predisposed to direct that any ceremonies held be low on frills, you are free to direct your pre-cremation ceremony to be as simple or as elaborate as you like.

Some concerns you may wish to address when planning a pre-cremation ceremony are:

- where the ceremony should be held

- who should be invited

- whether clergy should be invited to participate, along with specific names of clergy you would like

- any specific music you would like played, along with the names of the musicians or singers you would like to perform it

- preferences for a eulogy, and the name of the person or people you would like to speak

- whether you want your cremains present at the ceremony, either in a casket or other container, or whether you would like a picture displayed, instead, and

- whether you want to direct survivors to send flowers or memorial donations.

3. Informal Get-Togethers

Some people wish to direct that an unstructured gathering of friends and family be held before their bodies are buried or cremated, usually in an informal setting such as a home or perhaps a favorite restaurant or club. This is a common choice for people who have not adhered to a specific religion during their lifetimes—and for those who are not strongly tied to family or community traditions.

Common Elements of Informal Get-Togethers

There are few common elements to more informal after-death ceremonies, which range from the austere to the zany. These ceremonies are most dependent upon the whims and wishes of the deceased person. If you want some sort of informal ceremony held after your death, at a minimum, you may wish to consider:

- where the ceremony should be held
- who should be invited
- any specific music you would like played, along with the names of the musicians or singers you would like to perform it
- preferences for a eulogy, and the name of the person or people you would like to speak, and
- whether you want to direct survivors to send flowers or memorial donations.

There are a great number of additional details you can specify, of course. Some people have directed the survivors who attend to wear bright colored clothing, to bring their favorite pets, to read a favorite poem.

4. Funerals

A traditional funeral is a brief ceremony, most often held in a funeral home chapel or a church. The body is usually present—either in an open or a closed casket. Beyond that, there are no absolutes or requirements about what constitutes a funeral. If the deceased person adhered to a particular religion, funerals often include a brief mass, blessing or prayer service.

In some traditions, only family members attend the funeral, while friends and the general public are invited to attend other scheduled ceremonies. In other locales and traditions, this is reversed—and the funeral is the less private event.

Some concerns you may wish to address when planning a funeral are:

- where the ceremony should be held
- who should be invited
- whether clergy should be invited to participate, along with specific names of clergy you would like
- any specific music you would like played, along with the names of the musicians or singers you would like to perform it
- preferences for a eulogy, and the name of the person or people you would like to speak

- whether you want your body or cremains present at the ceremony, either in a casket or other container, or whether you would like a picture displayed, instead, and

- whether you want to direct survivors to send flowers or memorial donations.

Pallbearers

In some funeral ceremonies, the casket is carried to and from the place where the ceremony is held—and sometimes again carried from a transportation vehicle to a burial site. The people who carry the casket are termed pallbearers. If you envision a ceremony in which your casket will be carried, you can name here people you would wish to serve as pallbearers.

The number of pallbearers usually ranges from four to eight, but you can name as many or as few as you wish here.

Transportation to Grave

You may have a preference about the type of vehicle that will carry your body to the cemetery and gravesite from the place where the funeral ceremony is held. This might be a horse-drawn carriage, a favorite antique car or a stretch limousine.

If you have selected a mortuary to handle some of your arrangements, it may have only one type of vehicle available. If the vehicle customarily provided is not what you would want for yourself, check to be sure the mortuary is flexible about that—and be sure that it will not add its transportation charge to your costs. If this is an important issue for you, check with the mortuary you selected earlier and, if their arrangements about transportation are not satisfactory, shop for another mortuary.

5. Commitment Ceremonies

In addition to or instead of holding a ceremony prior to burial, it is common to hold a brief ceremony at the gravesite at which a religious leader or relative or family friend says a few prayers or words of farewell.

If this is something you want, and have an idea of who should be there, who should speak and what they should say, describe those details.

6. Memorial Ceremonies

A memorial ceremony is an informal ceremony held to commemorate someone who has died. It usually takes place some time after burial or cremation, so the body is not usually present. Memorial ceremonies may be held anywhere—a funeral home, religious building, a home, outside or even a restaurant.

Because memorial ceremonies are not structured or dominated by those in the funeral industry, there is more opportunity to tailor them to the deceased person's personality than a traditional funeral. Memorial ceremonies are more often the choice of those who wish to have an economic, simple after-death commemoration.

While traditional professionals—funeral directors, grief counselors, clergy —may be involved in memorial ceremonies, they are not the people to consult for objective advice. Many will advocate that traditional funerals—traditionally more costly and less personalized—are most effective in helping survivors through the mourning process. The truth is that most survivors are likely to take the greatest comfort in attending a ceremony that reflects the wishes and personality of the deceased person.

I. Final Disposition of Your Body

1. Body Burial

If you have a decided upon a cemetery in which you wish to be buried, describe it here. If you have purchased a gravesite in advance, describe it—and attach any pertinent documents to the Final Arrangements document that will print out when you are finished using this portion of WillMaker.

If you have not purchased a gravesite, but you have a preference as to the part of the cemetery you want to be buried in, state that preference here. There is no guarantee that it will be available to you when you die, but your survivors will know what you had in mind.

2. Scattering Cremains

Many people wish to have their cremated remains, or cremains, scattered over some area that has special significance for them—a garden, look-out point or the ocean.

California is the only state that has specific legal controls over the disposition of cremains. That law was passed after a commercial scattering firm was discovered to have mishandled cremains and consistently overcharged for its services. In California, cremains may be scattered at sea after being removed from their container; however, a verified statement must be filed nearest the point where the scattering occurred. Also in California, cremains may be buried, but may not be scattered on land.

Wisconsin law requires that cremains must be scattered or buried within 60 days after the body is cremated.

A Caveat on Scattering Services

Most people opt to have family members or friends conduct the scattering in private, in their own time and style.

However, there are some commercial firms that arrange to transport and scatter cremains over land or sea. Beware when dealing with such groups. While several masquerade as nonprofit groups by appending the term Society to their names and charging a membership fee, they are in the business for profit.

If you do decide to hire one of these services, make sure you understand their pricing structures in advance. Also, attach a copy of any written agreement you may enter to the Final Arrangements that print out when you are finished using this portion of the WillMaker program.

Contact your local funeral or memorial society—or contact the Continental Association of Funeral and Memorial Societies, 800-458-5563, for additional information.

3. Placing Cremains in a Container

Crematories will usually arrange to return cremains to a family member or friends in a small, inexpensive plastic or cardboard container. The cremains may then be shipped, buried or placed in a niche above ground in a columbarium.

Some people opt to purchase a special container, usually called an urn, in which to store or bury cremains. There are no legal controls on the size, shape or type of urn that may be used, although a number of columbariums and cemeteries impose restrictions due to space if the cremains will be interred or buried.

Urns may be purchased from funeral homes, usually at a substantial mark-up. A small number of artists now also craft low-cost or specialized urns for cremains. Look in the yellow pages of the telephone under Funeral Information and Services or a similar heading, or contact the local funeral or memorial society for more information on alternatives for containers for cremains.

4. Burying Cremains

Cremains can be buried in the ground. While there are some legal controls in some states on where the burial may take place—such as that they must be buried a specified distance from a residence—most of these controls are part of local zoning ordinances.

If you wish to have a family member or friend bury your cremains independently, it is a good idea to first check local zoning ordinances to see whether burial is permitted on the site you have chosen. Contact the local funeral or memorial society for more information on local rules about burying cremains.

Cremains can also be buried in a cemetery, either in a special urn garden or in a plot. It is not necessary to place the cremains in an urn before burial, although some places may require a plot liner to prevent the earth from sinking over time.

J. Markers and Headstones

1. Crypt Markers

If you have chosen to have your cremains placed in a crypt or drawer in a columbarium, you may wish to have a marker identifying where they are. Depending on the location, you may be restricted to a marker of a certain type or size.

For instance, if your cremains are placed interred in a columbarium, you may be limited to a plaque of specific dimensions and of a specific style.

2. Cemetery Markers

Many people want the place they are buried to be identified by a marker. Often this consists of an upright block of stone with words engraved on it. Some tend toward the elaborate—including sculptures and detailed etchings. However, many cemeteries require that all grave markers be flush with the ground to facilitate mowing—or may have other restrictions according to either aesthetic or land quality controls.

If you have identified a cemetery where you wish to be buried, check whether it has any restrictions on burial markers. Then, within those constraints, identify the marker you want for your grave.

K. Epitaphs

Perhaps the most entertaining aspect of making final arrangements is choosing the words that you wish to appear on your burial marker. These words are known as your epitaph. Your epitaph can be extremely simple, stating only the years you were born and died—or it can reflect your personality by including a witty saying, favorite phrase or poem.

L. Choosing Someone to Oversee Your Wishes

If you have definite ideas about who should carry out your wishes as you have stated them, name the person.

If you do not name anyone, it is likely that your closest relatives will become responsible.

If you name someone to handle this responsibility, make sure that he or she has a copy of the document that sets out your wishes and agrees to carry them out as you express them.

It is always a good idea to pick an alternate person to carry out your wishes, in case your first choice is unable or unwilling to perform this role when the time comes.

▶
▶
▶ ## The Importance of Attaching Other Documents
▶
▶ Many people make burial or cremation arrangements while they are still alive,
▶ through a local funeral or memorial society or directly with funeral industry
▶ providers. These arrangements may consist of:
▶
▶   • buying a burial plot
▶
▶   • contracting for a specific or similar type of casket, and
▶
▶   • indicating that cremation or burial is preferred.
▶
▶   If you have made any such arrangements, you should have documents that
▶ specify them. Attach copies of those documents to the Final Arrangements
▶ document you create using this part of WillMaker. ▲
▶

15 If You Need Expert Help

Experience has shown that most WillMaker users do not need a lawyer's help. The issues involved in making a basic will are normally straightforward and easy to understand.

The same goes for basic estate planning to avoid probate and save on estate taxes. If your estate is worth less than $1 million and you have a book such as Nolo's *Plan Your Estate*, you probably will not need more help.

Legal questions can arise, however, for which you will want to see an expert—especially if you have a very large estate, if you must plan for an incapacitated minor, or if you have to deal with the assets of a small business.

A. What Kind of Expert Do You Need?

The first question to decide if you want to consult an expert is what type you need.

Here are a few suggestions.

- A financial planner is probably your best bet if you want to integrate estate planning into the rest of your life, including your retirement. A planner can help advise you about a number of variables such as how much you are saving, the most suitable type of investments given your age and family structure, expected retirement income and insurance needs.

- A certified public accountant (CPA) is most appropriate if you are primarily concerned about determining federal and state death tax liability. If you conclude that you will need a trust or other legal document drafted, this may mean you will also need to consult an attorney. But it is usually best, and less expensive, to start with a CPA.

- A lawyer is most appropriate if you have questions about drafting a will, a probate-avoiding living trust or a more sophisticated trust designed to save on federal estate taxes or to provide extensive management for a beneficiary who cannot handle assets on his or her own.

B. Finding a Lawyer

If your estate is large—worth $1 million or more—and you want to plan to minimize estate taxes, or you need a trust to provide management for a mentally disadvantaged beneficiary or to provide a life estate for a surviving spouse, it would be wise to consult an experienced attorney. Also, even though they have no potential legal complications, some people are simply more comfortable having a lawyer check over their completed legal documents. Or you may just have a straightforward question about your will or estate planning options.

Finding a competent lawyer who charges a reasonable fee and respects your efforts to prepare your own will may not be easy. Especially when it comes to being involved in making your own untrained decisions and drafting your own will, many lawyers will instinctively react with barely-disguised hostility. But like all generalizations, this one has exceptions. Lawyers who will work willingly and well with people who want to be actively involved in their own legal lives do exist.

Here are some suggestions on how to find one.

1. Ask Friends and Business Associates

Almost anyone running a small business has a relationship with a lawyer. Ask around to find someone you know who has been satisfied with a lawyer's services. If that lawyer does not handle estate planning, he or she will likely know one who does. And because of the continuing relationship with your friend, the lawyer making the referral has an incentive to recommend someone who is competent. These days, most urban areas have a number of lawyers who specialize in estate planning, so if you want a specialist, you don't need to settle for a friend of a friend who does an occasional will.

Also ask people you know in any political or social organization in which you are involved. They may know of a competent lawyer whose attitudes are similar to yours. Senior citizen centers and other groups that advise and assist older people are particularly likely to have a list of local lawyers who specialize in wills and estate planning and who are generally regarded as competent and caring.

2. Look into a Group Legal Plan

Some unions, employers and consumer action organizations offer group legal plans to their members or employees, who can obtain comprehensive legal assistance free or for low rates. If you are a member of such a plan, check with it first. Your problem may be covered free of charge. But if the plan gives you only a slight reduction in a lawyer's fee, as many do, keep in mind that you may be referred to a lawyer whose main virtue is the willingness to reduce fees in exchange for a high volume of referrals.

3. Check Out a Prepaid Legal Plan

Prepaid legal plans are sold by companies such as Bank of America, Montgomery Ward and Amway, and are often offered to credit card holders or sold door-to-door. They typically offer the subscriber the right to have simple questions answered, letters written or a straightforward will drafted. Often, the will that comes with the plan is less sophisticated than WillMaker's, so there is little reason to consult one of these plans merely to draft a simple will. The basic fee in most plans will rarely cover more sophisticated estate planning, but of course, plan lawyers will usually be happy to sell you their time and expertise.

Unfortunately, there's no guarantee that the lawyers available through these plans are of the best caliber. In fact, competent, busy lawyers rarely join these plans because they already have enough business. As with any consumer transaction, if you do go the prepaid route, check out the plan and the lawyer to whom you are referred—before signing up.

Whenever you avail yourself of any service offered by these prepaid insurance plans, be forewarned: The lawyer you see receives at most $2 or $3 for dealing with you, and may have agreed to this minimal amount in the hope of finding clients who will pay for extra legal services not covered by the monthly premium. For example, some plans that offer a will for no charge beyond the original membership fee charge hundreds of dollars extra if you want to include a simple children's trust such as the one included in the WillMaker will. So, if the plan lawyer recommends an expensive legal procedure rather than a simple will or probate avoidance device such as a living trust, get a second opinion.

4. Consult a Law Clinic

Law clinics such as Hyatt Legal Services and Jacoby & Meyers loudly advertise their low initial consultation fees. This generally means that a basic consultation is cheap—often about $20. Anything beyond that is not so cheap. Generally, the rates are about the same as those charged by the average lawyer in general practice.

What is not advertised is that most clinics have extremely high lawyer turnover and, as a result, it is usually impossible to form a long-term relationship with a lawyer. This may be fine if you want a simple question answered. However, if you want a lawyer to help you draft a fairly complicated estate plan and then be available over the years to redraft it a number of times as your needs change, a legal clinic is probably a poor choice.

5. Call an Attorney Referral Service

Most county bar associations maintain referral services that will give you the name of an attorney who practices in your area. Usually you can get a referral to an attorney who claims to specialize in wills and estate planning and who will give you an initial consultation for a low fee. A problem with these services is that they usually provide minimal screening for the attorneys listed, which means those who participate may not be the most experienced or competent. It may be possible to find a skilled estate planning specialist following this approach, but be sure to take the time to check out the credentials and experience of the person to whom you're referred.

6. Read the Classified Ads

Check the classified ads under Attorneys. There are quite a few attorneys around who are no longer interested in handling court-contested matters but do provide consultations at relatively low rates. This could be just what you need—especially if yours is a fairly basic question.

C. Managing a Lawyer

Once you have concluded on the basis of a reliable referral that a particular lawyer is probably competent, your next job is to check his or her attitude. People who use self-help tools such as WillMaker typically expect professionals to help educate them to make their own informed decisions—not to treat them as a traditional, obedient client. Such a match may be difficult to find.

Most important, be sure you've settled your fee arrangement—in writing— at the start of your relationship. Depending on where you live, generally, fees of $100 to $150 per hour are reasonable for a general practice lawyer. Experienced specialists are likely to charge closer to $200 per hour. In addition to the hourly fee, get a clear, written commitment from the lawyer concerning how many hours it is likely to take to resolve your problem.

Finally, ask the lawyer several specific questions about your problem. Do you get clear, concise answers? If not, try someone else. If the lawyer acts wise but says little except to ask that the problem be placed in his or her hands— for a substantial fee, of course—watch out. You're either dealing with some- one who doesn't know the answer and won't admit it, a common complication, or someone who finds it impossible to let go of the "me expert, you plebeian" philosophy—even more common. ▲

Index to the Legal Guide

CATALOG

...more books from Nolo Press

Estate Planning & Probate

Plan Your Estate
Attorney Denis Clifford. National 2nd ed.
Covers every significant aspect of estate planning and gives detailed, specific instructions for preparing a living trust. Includes all the tear-out forms and step-by-step instructions to let you prepare an estate plan designed for your special needs. Good in all states except Louisiana.
$19.95/NEST

Make Your Own Living Trust
Attorney Denis Clifford. National 1st ed.
Find out how a living trust works, how to create one, and how to determine what kind of trust is right for you. Contains all the forms and instructions you need to prepare a basic living trust to avoid probate, a marital life estate trust (A-B trust) to avoid probate and estate taxes, and a back-up will.
$19.95/LITR

Nolo's Simple Will Book
Attorney Denis Clifford. National 2nd ed.
It's easy to write a legally valid will using this book. Includes all the instructions and sample forms you need to name a personal guardian for minor children, leave property to minor children or young adults and update a will when necessary. Good in all states except Louisiana.
$17.95/SWIL

Who Will Handle Your Finances If You Can't?
Attorneys Denis Clifford & Mary Randolph. National 1st ed.
Give a trusted person legal authority to handle your financial matters if illness or old age makes it impossible for you to handle them yourself. Create a durable power of attorney for finances with the step-by-step instructions and fill-in-the-blank forms included in this book.
$19.95/FINA

The Conservatorship Book
Lisa Goldoftas & Attorney Carolyn Farren. California 1st ed.
Provides forms and all instructions necessary to file conservatorship documents, appear in court, be appointed conservator and end a conservatorship.
$24.95/CNSV

How to Probate an Estate
Julia Nissley. California 7th ed.
Save costly attorneys' fees by handling the probate process yourself. This book shows you step-by-step how to settle an estate. It also explains the simple procedures you can use to transfer assets that don't require probate. Forms included.
$34.95/PAE

LAW FORM KITS

Nolo's Law Form Kit: Wills
Attorney Denis Clifford & Lisa Goldoftas. National 1st ed.
All the forms and instructions you need to create a legally valid will, quickly and easily.
$14.95/KWL

AUDIO CASSETTE TAPES

Write Your Will
Attorney Ralph Warner with Joanne Greene. National 1st ed. 60 minutes
If you're getting ready to write your will, this tape is a good place to start. It answers the most frequently asked questions about writing a will and covers all key issues.
$14.95/TWYW

WillMaker®
Version 5.0

Make your own legal will and living will (healthcare directive)—and thoroughly document your final arrangements—with WillMaker 5. WillMaker's easy-to-use interview format takes you through each document step-by-step. On-line legal help is available throughout the program. Name a guardian for your children, make up to 100 property bequests, direct your healthcare in the event of coma or terminal illness, and let your loved ones know your wishes around your own final arrangements.
WINDOWS $69.95/WIW5
DOS $69.95/WI5
MACINTOSH $69.95/WM5

Nolo's Personal RecordKeeper
Version 3.0

Finally, a safe, accessible place for your important records. Over 200 categories and subcategories to organize and store your important financial, legal and personal information, compute your net worth and create inventories for insurance records. Export your net worth and home inventory data to Quicken®.
DOS $49.95/FRI3
MACINTOSH $49.95/FRM3

Nolo's Living Trust
Version 1.0

Put your assets into a trust and save your heirs the headache, time and expense of probate with this easy-to-use software. Use it to set up an individual or shared marital trust, transfer property to the trust, and change or revoke the trust at any time. Its manual guides you through the process, and legal help screens and an on-line glossary explain key legal terms and concepts. Good in all states except Louisiana.
MACINTOSH $79.95/LTM1

Going to Court

Fight Your Ticket
Attorney David Brown. California 5th ed.
Shows you how to fight an unfair traffic ticket—when you're stopped, at arraignment, at trial and on appeal.
$18.95/FYT

Everybody's Guide to Small Claims Court
Attorney Ralph Warner
National 5th ed.. California 11th ed.
These books will help you decide if you should sue in Small Claims Court, show you how to file and serve papers, tell you what to bring to court and how to collect a judgment.
National $15.95/NSCC
California $16.95/CSCC

Everybody's Guide to Municipal Court
Judge Roderic Duncan. California 1st ed.
Sue and defend cases for up to $25,000 in California Municipal Court. Gives step-by-step instructions for preparing and filing forms, gathering evidence and appearing in court.
$29.95/MUNI

Collect Your Court Judgment
Gini Graham Scott, Attorney Stephen Elias & Lisa Goldoftas. California 2nd ed.
Contains step-by-step instructions and all the forms you need to collect a court judgment from the debtor's bank accounts, wages, business receipts, real estate or other assets.
$19.95/JUDG

How to Change Your Name
Attorneys David Loeb & David Brown. California 5th ed.
All the forms and instructions you need to change your name in California.
$19.95/NAME

The Criminal Records Book
Attorney Warren Siegel. California 3rd ed.
Shows you step-by-step how to seal criminal records, dismiss convictions, destroy marijuana records and reduce felony convictions.
$19.95/CRIM

AUDIO CASSETTE TAPES

Winning in Small Claims Court
Attorneys Ralph Warner with Joanne Greene. National 1st ed. 60 minutes
Guides you through all the major issues involved in preparing and winning a small claims court case—deciding if there is a good case, assessing whether you can collect if you win, preparing your evidence, and arguing before the judge.
$14.95/TWIN

The Legal Guide for Starting & Running a Small Business

Attorney Fred S. Steingold. National 1st ed.
An essential resource for every small business owner. Find out how to form a sole proprietorship, partnership or corporation, negotiate a favorable lease, hire and fire employees, write contracts and resolve disputes.
$19.95/RUNS

Sexual Harassment on the Job: What it is and How To Stop it.

Attorneys William Petrocelli & Barbara Kate Repa. National 1st ed.
An invaluable resource for both employees experiencing harassment and employers interested in creating a policy against sexual harassment and a procedure for handling complaints.
$14.95/HARS

Marketing Without Advertising

Michael Phillips & Salli Rasberry. National 1st ed.
Outlines practical steps for building and expanding a small business without spending a lot of money on advertising.
$14.00/MWAD

Your Rights in the Workplace

Dan Lacey. National 2nd ed.
The first comprehensive guide to workplace rights —from hiring to firing. Covers wages and overtime, parental leave, unemployment and disability insurance, worker's compensation, job safety, discrimination and illegal firings and layoffs.
$15.95/YRW

How to Write a Business Plan

Mike McKeever. National 4th ed.
This book will show you how to write the business plan and loan package necessary to finance your business and make it work.
$19.95/SBS

The Partnership Book

Attorneys Denis Clifford & Ralph Warner. National 4th ed.
Shows you step-by-step how to write a solid partnership agreement that meets your needs. It covers initial contributions to the business, wages, profit-sharing, buy-outs, death or retirement of a partner and disputes.
$24.95/PART

How to Form a Nonprofit Corporation

Attorney Anthony Mancuso. National 1st ed.
Explains the legal formalities involved and provides detailed information on the differences in the law among all 50 states. It also contains forms for the Articles, Bylaws and Minutes you need, along with complete instructions for obtaining federal 501(c)(3) tax exemptions and qualifying for public charity status.
$24.95/NNP

The California Nonprofit Corporation Handbook

Attorney Anthony Mancuso. California 6th ed.
Shows you step-by-step how to form and operate a nonprofit corporation in California. It includes the latest corporate and tax law changes, and the forms for the Articles, Bylaws and Minutes.
$29.95/NON

How to Form Your Own Corporation

Attorney Anthony Mancuso California 7th ed.. New York 2nd ed.. Texas 4th ed. Florida 3rd ed.
These books contain the forms, instructions and tax information you need to incorporate a small business yourself and save hundreds of dollars in lawyers' fees.
California $29.95/CCOR
New York $24.95/NYCO
Texas $29.95/TCOR
Florida $39.95/FLCO

The California Professional Corporation Handbook

Attorney Anthony Mancuso. California 4th ed.
Health care professionals, lawyers, accountants and members of certain other professions must fulfill special requirements when forming a corporation in California. Contains up-to-date tax information plus all the forms and instructions necessary.
$34.95/PROF

The Independent Paralegal's Handbook

Attorney Ralph Warner. National 2nd ed.
Provides legal and business guidelines for anyone who wants to go into business as an independent paralegal helping consumers with routine legal tasks.
$24.95 PARA

AUDIO CASSETTE TAPES

Getting Started as an Independent Paralegal

Attorney Ralph Warner. National 2nd ed.
Two tapes, approximately 2 hours
Practical and legal advice on going into business as an independent paralegal from the author of *The Independent Paralegal's Handbook.*
$44.95/GSIP

How to Start Your Own Business: Small Business Law
Attorney Ralph Warner with Joanne Greene.
National 1st ed. 60 minutes
This tape covers what every small business owner needs to know about organizing as a sole proprietorship, partnership or corporation, protecting the business name, renting space, hiring employees and paying taxes.
$14.95/TBUS

Nolo's Partnership Maker
Version 1.0

Attorney Tony Mancuso & Michael Radtke
Prepares a legal partnership agreement for doing business in any state. Select and assemble the standard partnership clauses provided or create your own customized agreement. Includes on-line legal help screens, glossary and tutorial, and a manual that takes you through the process step-by-step.
DOS $129.95/PAGI1

California Incorporator
Version 1.0 (good only in CA)
Attorney Tony Mancuso

Answer the questions on the screen and this software program will print out the 35-40 pages of documents you need to make your California corporation legal. A 200-page manual explains the incorporation process.
DOS $129.00/INCI

The California Nonprofit Corporation Handbook
Attorney Anthony Mancuso. Version 1.0
This book with disk package shows you step-by-step how to form and operate a nonprofit corporation in California. Included on disk are the forms for the Articles, Bylaws and Minutes.
DOS $69.95 NPI
MACINTOSH $69.95 NPM

How to Form Your Own Corporation
Attorney Anthony Mancuso
These book with disk packages contain the instructions and tax information and forms you need to incorporate a small business and save hundreds of dollars in lawyers' fees. All organizational forms are on disk. All come with a 250-page manual.
New York 1st Ed.
DOS $69.95 NYCI
MACINTOSH $69.95 NYCM

Texas 1st Ed.
DOS $69.95 TCI
MACINTOSH $69.95 TCM

Florida 3rd Ed.
DOS 3-1/2 $39.95/FLCO

Neighbor Law: Fences, Trees, Boundaries & Noise
Attorney Cora Jordan. National 1st ed.
Answers common questions about the subjects that most often trigger disputes between neighbors: fences, trees, boundaries and noise. It explains how to find the law and resolve disputes without a nasty lawsuit.
$14.95/NEI

Safe Homes, Safe Neighborhoods: Stopping Crime Where You Live
Stephanie Mann with M.C. Blakeman.
National 1st ed.
Learn how you and your neighbors can work together to protect yourselves, your families and property from crime. Explains how to form a neighborhood crime prevention group; avoid burglaries, car thefts, muggings and rapes; combat gangs and drug dealing; improve home security and make the neighborhood safer for children.
$14.95/SAFE

Dog Law
Attorney Mary Randolph. National 1st ed.
A practical guide to the laws that affect dog owners and their neighbors. Answers common questions about biting, barking, veterinarians and more.
$12.95/DOG

Stand Up to the IRS
Attorney Fred Daily. National 1st ed.
Gives detailed strategies on surviving an audit, appealing an audit decision, going to Tax Court and dealing with IRS collectors. It also discusses filing delinquent tax returns, tax crimes, concerns of small business people and getting help from the IRS ombudsman.
$19.95/SIRS

How to File for Bankruptcy
Attorneys Stephen Elias,
Albin Renauer & Robin Leonard.
National 4th ed.
Trying to decide whether or not filing for bankruptcy makes sense? This book contains an overview of the process and all the forms plus step-by-step instructions you need to file for Chapter 7 Bankruptcy.
$25.95/HFB

Money Troubles: Legal Strategies to Cope with Your Debts

Attorney Robin Leonard. National 1st ed.
Essential for anyone who has gotten behind on bills. It shows how to obtain a credit file, negotiate with persistent creditors, challenge wage attachments, contend with property repossessions and more.
$16.95/MT

Simple Contracts for Personal Use

Attorney Stephen Elias & Marcia Stewart. National 2nd ed.
Contains clearly written legal form contracts to buy and sell property, borrow and lend money, store and lend personal property, release others from personal liability, or pay a contractor to do home repairs. Includes agreements to arrange child care and other household help.
$16.95/CONT

LAW FORM KITS

Nolo's Law Form Kit: Personal Bankruptcy

Attorneys Steve Elias, Albin Renauer & Robin Leonard and Lisa Goldoftas. National 1st ed.
All the forms and instructions you need to file for Chapter 7 bankruptcy.
$14.95/KBNK

Nolo's Law Forms Kit: Rebuild Your Credit

Attorney Robin Leonard. National 1st ed.
Provides strategies for dealing with debts and rebuilding your credit. Shows you how to negotiate with creditors and collection agencies, clean up your credit file, devise a spending plan and get credit in your name.
$14.95/KCRD

Nolo's Law Form Kit: Power of Attorney

Attorneys Denis Clifford & Mary Randolph and Lisa Goldoftas. National 1st ed.
Create a conventional power of attorney to assign someone you trust to take of your finances, business, real estate or children when you are away or unavailable. Provides all the forms with step-by-step instructions.
$14.95/KPA

Nolo's Law Form Kit: Loan Agreements

Attorney Stephen Elias, Marcia Stewart & Lisa Goldoftas. National 1st ed.
Provides all the forms and instructions necessary to create a legal and effective promissory note. Shows how to decide on an interest rate, set a payment schedule and keep track of payments.
$14.95/KLOAN

Nolo's Law Form Kit: Buy and Sell Contracts

Attorney Stephen Elias, Marcia Stewart & Lisa Goldoftas. National 1st ed.
Step-by-step instructions and all the forms necessary for creating bills of sale for cars, boats, computers, electronic equipment, household appliances and other personal property.
$9.95/KCONT

Family Matters

Divorce & Money

Violet Woodhouse & Victoria Felton-Collins with M.C. Blakeman. National 1st ed.
Explains how to evaluate such major assets as family homes and businesses, investments, pensions, and how to arrive at a division of property that is fair to both sides.
$19.95/DIMO

The Living Together Kit

Attorneys Toni Ihara & Ralph Warner. National 6th ed.
A detailed guide designed to help the increasing number of unmarried couples living together understand the laws that affect them. Sample agreements and instructions are included.
$17.95/LTK

A Legal Guide for Lesbian and Gay Couples

Attorneys Hayden Curry, Denis Clifford & Robin Leonard. National 7th ed.
This book shows lesbian and gay couples how to write a living-together contract, plan for medical emergencies, understand the practical and legal aspects of having and raising children and plan their estates. Includes forms and sample agreements.
$21.95/LG

California Marriage & Divorce Law

Attorneys Ralph Warner, Toni Ihara & Stephen Elias. California 11th ed.
Explains community property, pre-nuptial contracts, foreign marriages, buying a house, getting a divorce, dividing property, and more. Pre-nuptial contracts included.
$19.95/MARR

Divorce: A New Yorker's Guide to Doing it Yourself

Bliss Alexandra. New York 1st ed.
Step-by-step instructions and all the forms you need to do your own divorce and save thousands of dollars in legal fees. Shows you how to divide property, arrange custody of the children, set child support and maintenance (alimony), draft a divorce agreement and fill out and file all forms.
$24.95/NYDIV

How to Raise or Lower Child Support in California

Judge Roderic Duncan & Attorney Warren Siegal. California 1st ed.
Appropriate for parents on either side of the support issue. All the forms and instructions necessary to raise or lower an existing child support order.
$16.95/CHLD

The Guardianship Book

Lisa Goldoftas & Attorney David Brown. California 1st ed.
Provides step-by-step instructions and the forms needed to obtain a legal guardianship of a minor without a lawyer.
$19.95/GB

How to Do Your Own Divorce

*Attorney Charles Sherman
(Texas ed. by Sherman & Simons)
California 18th ed. & Texas 4th ed.*
These books contain all the forms and instructions you need to do your own uncontested divorce without a lawyer.
California $18.95/CDIV
Texas $17.95/TDIV

Practical Divorce Solutions

*Attorney Charles Sherman.
California 2nd ed.*
Covers the emotional aspects of divorce and provides an overview of the legal and financial considerations.
$12.95/PDS

How to Adopt Your Stepchild in California

Frank Zagone & Attorney Mary Randolph. California 3rd ed.
Provides sample forms and step-by-step instructions for completing a simple uncontested stepparent adoption in California.
$19.95/ADOP

Family Law Dictionary

Attorneys Robin Leonard & Stephen Elias. National 2nd ed.
Here's help for anyone who has a question or problem involving family law—marriage, divorce, adoption or living together.
$13.95/FLD

Patent, Copyright & Trademark

Trademark: How to Name Your Business & Product

Attorneys Kate McGrath & Stephen Elias, With Trademark Attorney Sarah Shena. National 1st ed.
Learn how to choose a name or logo that others can't copy, conduct a trademark search, register a trademark with the U.S. Patent and Trademark Office and protect and maintain the trademark.
$29.95/TRD

Patent It Yourself

Attorney David Pressman. National 3rd ed.
From the patent search to the actual application, this book covers everything including the use and licensing of patents, successful marketing and how to deal with infringement.
$36.95/PAT

The Inventor's Notebook

Fred Grissom & Attorney David Pressman. National 1st ed.
Helps you document the process of successful independent inventing by providing forms, instructions, references to relevant areas of patent law, a bibliography of legal and non-legal aids and more.
$19.95/INOT

The Copyright Handbook

Attorney Stephen Fishman. National 1st ed.
Provides forms and step-by-step instructions for protecting all types of written expression under U.S. and international copyright law. Covers copyright infringement, fair use, works for hire and transfers of copyright ownership.
$24.95/COHA

Landlords & Tenants

The Landlord's Law Book, Vol. 1: Rights & Responsibilities

Attorneys David Brown & Ralph Warner. California 3rd ed.
Essential for every California landlord. Covers deposits, leases and rental agreements, inspections (tenants' privacy rights), habitability (rent withholding), ending a tenancy, liability and rent control. Forms included.
$29.95/LBRT

The Landlord's Law Book, Vol. 2: Evictions

Attorney David Brown. California 4th ed.
Show step-by-step how to go to court and evict a tenant. Contains all the tear-out forms and necessary instructions.
$32.95/LBEV

Tenants' Rights

Attorneys Myron Moskovitz & Ralph Warner. California 11th ed.
This practical guide to dealing with your landlord explains your rights under federal law, California law and rent control ordinances. Forms included.
$15.95/CTEN

Homeowners

How to Buy a House in California
Attorney Ralph Warner, Ira Serkes & George Devine. California 2nd ed.
Effective strategies for finding a house, working with a real estate agent, making an offer and negotiating intelligently. Includes information on all types of mortgages as well as private financing options.
$19.95/BHCA

For Sale By Owner
George Devine. California 2nd ed.
Everything you need to know to sell your own house, from pricing and marketing, to writing a contract and going through escrow. Disclosure and contract forms included.
$24.95/FSBO

Homestead Your House
Attorneys Ralph Warner, Charles Sherman & Toni Ihara. California 8th ed.
Shows you how to file a Declaration of Homestead and includes complete instructions and tear-out forms.
$9.95/HOME

The Deeds Book
Attorney Mary Randolph. California 2nd ed.
Shows you how to fill out and file the right kind of deed when transferring property. Outlines the legal requirements of real property transfer.
$15.95/DEED

Just For Fun

Devil's Advocates: The Unnatural History of Lawyers
by Andrew & Jonathan Roth. National 1st ed.
A hilarious look at the history of the legal profession.
$12.95/DA

29 Reasons Not to Go to Law School
Attorneys Ralph Warner & Toni Ihara. National 3rd ed.
Filled with humor, this book can save you three years, $70,000 and your sanity.
$9.95/29R

Poetic Justice: The Funniest, Meanest Things Ever Said About Lawyers
Edited by Jonathan & Andrew Roth. National 1st ed.
A great gift for anyone in the legal profession who has managed to maintain a sense of humor.
$8.95/PJ

Nolo's Favorite Lawyer Jokes on Disk
Over 200 jokes and hilariously nasty remarks about lawyers organized by categories (Lawyers as Vultures, Nobody Loves a Lawyer, Lawyers in Love...). 100% guaranteed to produce an evening of chuckles and drive every lawyer you know nuts.
DOS 3-1/2 $9.95/JODI
MACINTOSH $9.95/JODM

Older Americans

Beat the Nursing Home Trap: A Consumer's Guide to Choosing and Financing Long-Term Care
Joseph Matthews. National 2nd ed.
This practical guide provides all the information you need to help make the best arrangements for long-term care. It shows how to protect assets, arrange home health care, find nursing and non-nursing home residences, evaluate nursing home insurance and understand Medicare, Medicaid and other benefit programs.
$18.95/ELD

Social Security, Medicare & Pensions
Attorney Joseph Matthews with Dorothy Matthews Berman. National 5th ed.
Offers invaluable guidance through the current maze of rights and benefits for those 55 and over, including Medicare, Medicaid and Social Security retirement and disability benefits, and age discrimination protections.
$15.95/SOA

Research & Reference

Legal Research: How to Find and Understand the Law
Attorneys Stephen Elias & Susan Levinkind. National 3rd ed.
A valuable tool on its own or as a companion to just about every other Nolo book. Gives easy-to-use, step-by-step instructions on how to find legal information.
$19.95/LRES

Legal Research Made Easy: A Roadmap Through the Law Library Maze

2-1/2 hr. videotape and 40-page manual Nolo Press/Legal Star Communications. National 1st ed.
Professor Bob Berring explains how to use all the basic legal research tools in your local law library with an easy-to-follow six-step research plan and a sense of humor.
$89.95/LRME

Consumer

Nolo's Pocket Guide to California Law

Attorney Lisa Guerin & Nolo Press Editors. California 1st ed.
Get quick clear answers to questions about child support, custody, consumer rights, employee rights, government benefits, divorce, bankruptcy, adoption, wills and much more.
$10.95/CLAW

Barbara Kaufman's Consumer Action Guide

Barbara Kaufman. California 1st ed.
Practical advice on hundreds of consumer topics. Shows Californians how and where to complain about everything from accountants, misleading advertisements and lost baggage to vacation scams and dishonored warranties.
$14.95/CAG

Legal Breakdown: 40 Ways to Fix Our Legal System

Nolo Press Editors & Staff. National 1st ed.
Forty common-sense proposals to make our legal system fairer, faster, cheaper and more accessible.
$8.95/LEG

How to Win Your Personal Injury Claim

Attorney Joseph Matthews. National 1st ed.
Armed with the right information anyone can handle a personal injury claim. This step-by-step guide shows you how to avoid insurance company run-arounds, evaluate what your claim is worth, obtain a full and fair settlement and save for yourself what you would pay a lawyer.
$24.95/PICL

Immigration

How to Get a Green Card: Legal Ways to Stay in the U.S.A.

Attorney Loida Nicolas Lewis with Len T. Madlanscay. National 1st ed.
Written by a former INS attorney, this book clearly explains the steps involved in getting a green card. It covers who can qualify, what documents to present, and how to fill out all the forms and have them processed. Tear-out forms included.
$19.95/GRN

Visit Our Store in Berkeley

If you live in the Bay Area, be sure to visit the Nolo Press Bookstore on the corner of 9th & Parker Streets in west Berkeley. You'll find our complete line of books and software—new and "damaged"—all at a discount. We also have t-shirts, posters and a selection of business and legal self-help books from other publishers.

Call 1-510-549-1976 for hours.

order form

CODE	QUANTITY	ITEM	UNIT PRICE	TOTAL

	Subtotal	
	California residents add Sales Tax	
Shipping & Handling ($4 for 1 item; $5 for 2-3 items; +$.50 each additional item	
2nd day UPS (additional $5; $8 in Alaska & Hawaii)	
T O T A L	

Name

Address (UPS to street address; Priority Mail to P.O. boxes)

FOR FASTER SERVICE, USE YOUR CREDIT CARD AND OUR TOLL-FREE NUMBERS

Monday-Friday, 8am to 5pm Pacific Time
ORDER LINE   1-800-992-6656
CUSTOMER SERVICE   1-510-549-1976
FAX YOUR ORDER   1-800-645-0895

METHOD OF PAYMENT

☐ Check enclosed   ☐ VISA   ☐ Mastercard   ☐ Discover Card   ☐ American Express

Account #   Expiration Date

Authorizing Signature   Daytime Phone

SEND TO

Nolo Press, 950 Parker Street, Berkeley, CA 94710
Allow 2-3 weeks for delivery. PRICES SUBJECT TO CHANGE.